A Doctor in Galilee

A Doctor in Galilee

The Life and Struggle of a Palestinian in Israel

HATIM KANAANEH

with a Foreword by Jonathan Cook

Pluto Press

LONDON • ANN ARBOR, MI

First published 2008 by Pluto Press
345 Archway Road, London N6 5AA
and 839 Greene Street, Ann Arbor, MI 48106

www.plutobooks.com

Copyright © Hatim Kanaaneh 2008

The right of Hatim Kanaaneh to be identified as the author of this work has been
asserted by him in accordance with the Copyright, Designs and Patents Act 1988.

British Library Cataloguing in Publication Data
A catalogue record for this book is available from the British Library

ISBN   978 0 7453 2787 7 hardback
ISBN   978 0 7453 2786 0 paperback

Library of Congress Cataloging in Publication Data applied for

10   9   8   7   6   5   4   3   2   1

Designed and produced for Pluto Press by
Chase Publishing Services Ltd, Fortescue, Sidmouth, EX10 9QG, England
Typeset from disk by Stanford DTP Services, Northampton
Printed and bound in the United States of America

*To those who have suffered with me: my family, Didi, Rhoda and Ty,
my extended family, the Kanaanehs, my fellow villagers in Arrabeh,
and my people, the Palestinians, and to all suffering people in the
world with love.*

―――――

*The closing chapter in the book tells of an ancient olive tree that
I transplanted to my garden. The passage encapsulates, conceptually
and emotionally, the entire narrative of this book of memoirs.
This olive tree serves as a metaphor for my community's
struggle for survival and its sense of belonging.*

Contents

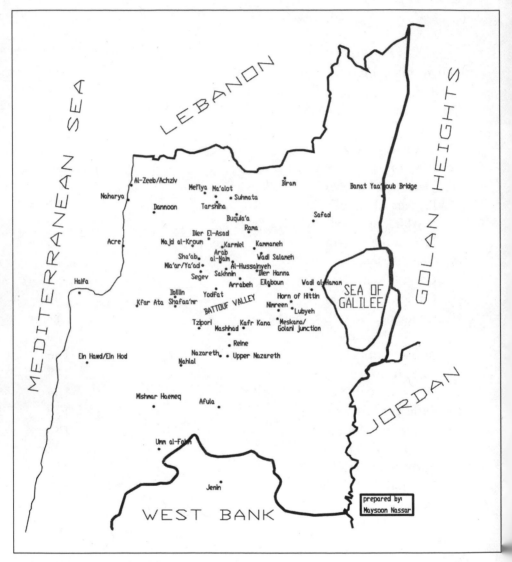

A schematic map of the Galilee with localities mentioned in the book.
(Prepared by Maysoon Nassar.)

Preface

A Doctor in Galilee: The Life and Struggle of a Palestinian in Israel is a memoir arising from my struggle as a physician to bring the benefits of public health and community development to my people, the Palestinian Arab minority citizens of Israel. The intimate personal narrative introduces readers to this little known and often misunderstood population that is nonetheless key to understanding the Arab-Israeli conflict.

I was born in 1937 in Arrabeh Village in the Galilee at the height of the Palestinian peasant uprising against the British Mandate for its sympathy with and accommodation of the designs of the Zionist Movement on their land. On my eleventh birthday, Israel was officially declared an independent state, marking the Palestinian Nakba or catastrophe. The vast majority of Palestinians from the area of the new state became refugees in neighboring Arab countries. Their towns and villages were systematically raised or their homes occupied by Jewish immigrants. We, the few Palestinians who remained on their land, found ourselves on the wrong side of the border, a leaderless and alienated minority in an enemy state. For 18 years we were placed under oppressive military rule.

As subsistence olive farmers my family sacrificed much to put me through the Nazareth Municipal High School. Two years later, in 1960, I struck out to study medicine in the USA. In 1970, having obtained Harvard degrees in medicine and public health and turning down several lucrative offers in America, I returned with my Hawaiian wife, a teacher, to Arrabeh and found employment with the Ministry of Health in my field of specialty. The dearth of physicians in my region forced me to double as solo village general practice doctor. I lasted for six years before I could take it no more. I found my public health work unproductive in light of state systems openly hostile to Arab citizens. This included policies of massive land confiscation that led to a mini uprising by my people, known thereafter as Land Day.

Frustrated and angry, in 1976 I moved with my wife and two children to Hawaii.

After two years of vacillating we returned home to the Galilee and to the same setting we had left. I started looking for a way around the discriminatory and antagonistic governmental system in which I worked. Within three years I and three other disgruntled local physicians established a non-governmental organization, the Galilee Society, dedicated to improving the health and welfare of the Palestinian minority within Israel. This NGO became the conduit for my professional endeavors actively challenging the system of which I was formally a part and to which, for pragmatic considerations, I continued to hold for another ten years. The Ministry of Health, under Ehud Olmert, eventually ejected me and I became persona non grata in my former professional home. For four additional years I continued to use the NGO service sector as a means of consciousness raising and community mobilization. I reached out to international circles and built alliances with like-minded minority rights activists abroad. This, together with a confrontation with the Israeli military-industrial complex over environmental protection of the Galilee, apparently was beyond the tolerance of all concerned. In 1995 I found myself out of a job at the Galilee Society, the institution I created and led for a decade and a half. On my way to retirement I then served briefly as a consultant to UNICEF's mission to the Palestinian National Authority before returning to my home village to establish a center for child rehabilitation.

The narrative follows a simple chronological pattern, but is replete with contemplative pauses, flashbacks, village scenes and foibles from rural Palestine and from my childhood days. In terms of its subject matter, the major theme of the book revolves around the politics of dispossession and the nature of Israel's majority-minority 'coexistence' as it plays out in the life of Arrabeh and similar communities and as experienced and recorded by me in real time. Straddling the socioeconomic and political divide between this disadvantaged minority amongst whom I lived and the dominant Jewish majority amongst whom I worked, my daily experience bordered on the schizophrenic. The book delves particularly deep into the struggle over land, which underlies all aspects of the conflict between the two groups that people my two realities.

On July 12, 2006, as I was working on these memoirs, war broke out between Israel and the Lebanese Hezbollah. My wife and I were beseeched by family and friends in the US to leave Israel right away. We had planned a lengthy vacation in Hawaii in late summer and we considered advancing the date of our departure. But that didn't seem right: we had a couple of weddings to attend; there were two scheduled functions at Elrazi Center for Child Rehabilitation, my last public service venture; and the fig, grape, passion fruit, and prickly pear season was at its peak in my orchard. True, in Arrabeh, our village in the Galilee, the deafening shriek of Israeli jet fighters alternated with the sirens from close-by Jewish communities and the thud of Katyusha rockets falling there. And at night we could see the fireworks in the northern skies. In Arrabeh, as in other Palestinian towns and villages in Israel, we lack such civil defense amenities as sirens or shelters, but we felt secure in the knowledge that we were not targeted; Hezbollah had maps and knew there were no military installations close by; their aim was fairly accurate. We decided to stick to our original schedule.

Two weeks into the war I sat in my garden sipping my morning coffee, reading the paper, and observing two dozen finches noisily feed at the thicket of decorative sunflowers around the ancient olive tree I had recently transplanted to my garden. The thud of Katyushas was rhythmically repetitive, almost hypnotic. With each beat of the drum the finches would interrupt their feeding, raise their heads, and look north. Then the conductor went berserk; the beat picked up; the explosions became continuous and moved closer; the finches flew southward in formation; I lost my nerve. Quickly, I entered my study, turned my computer on and wrote a lengthy email to my friends in the States. Within an hour I regained my equanimity; I put the war out of my mind; I was in control again.

Since high school this has been my way of dealing with crises and with the imponderables of the ebb and flow of life. Together with gardening, writing has been my psychotherapy. Whenever a major issue weighed heavily on my mind, whenever I wanted to maximize the pleasure from an experience I enjoyed, to savor the aftertaste of an achievement or to lick the wounds of a defeat, I would steal time from my busy schedule to sit in a quiet corner and write. I would read each piece I wrote after I had finished it and then I would put it away never to look at it again.

On occasion I would find what I wrote in a letter to a friend or relative meaningful enough to make a copy of it and to store it away as well. Soon I realized that the experience of putting my especially troubling and indigestible thoughts to paper was therapeutically more effective if I addressed them to a specific person, even when I had no intention of sending the material to her or him. When in the United States I would address my brother Ahmad or my childhood friend Toufiq. When in Israel I had a different set of imaginary confessors, recipients of my telepathic communications: my adopted Indonesian, Indian and Dutch brothers from college days. Especially to Bessel, my Dutch psychiatrist friend, I related as my "confidant in absentia" because of his professional competence, everlasting childlike innocence, open mindedness, and creative appreciation of much of what I say or do. Whenever I was in a tight spot where I felt particularly vulnerable, I would speak to him in my mind.

I have always enjoyed penning down my thoughts. But, alas, I became a physician; in 1970 I returned to practice my profession in Arrabeh, my home village in the Galilee. With the mounting demands on my time at the prime of my professional, family and public life, as my sleep deprivation turned every quiet period into naptime, and with the enticement of technical gadgetry, I found an easy-out; I shifted to recording my "compositions," my soul-searching diatribes, and my confessions, on audiotapes that I stored away never to hear again. The act of facing myself across the page or vocally, not the content itself, had the therapeutic effect I sought in my many hours of need.

In 2004, upon formally retiring, I found myself at a loss—and who wouldn't at such a time. The urge to further serve my community, my people and humanity at large, in that order and using the former as the conduit to the latter, was still the driving force of my life. But how could I serve? I could afford the time and effort for personal enjoyment, a luxury I had always been short on. But what pleasurable activity could I engage in that would be productive? I traveled and, between trips, I gardened, but both activities failed the criterion of significant benefit to others. And I felt tethered to my past; my future perspective was too limited to permit movement in new directions.

Why not, then, indulge myself in reminiscences? I had a vague premonition that something significant might lurk in the shipping box in my study full of old papers and shoeboxes stuffed with audiotapes.

Why not start to read my old "compositions" and to put them in order. I found much in those reams of handwritten papers, but even more, much more, in the audiotapes. After listening to a few, I set out to transcribe them. I had not realized how efficient the audio-storage system was; I must have had several thousand pages of material on tape. The transcribing proved to be a daunting exercise in self-rein-terpretation. Some of the sensitive recorded episodes of soul searching and self-questioning were emotionally devastating to listen to, too intimate for me to stay focused on the transcribing task. The audiotapes captured not only the words spoken, but also my mood and emotions. In retrospect, it is clear that much of the material would be highly charged, for it was when I had sought to relieve myself of mental anguish that I turned to this escape route. On occasion, the narrator on those tapes sounded so downcast, defeated and tormented that he would mumble under his breath; he would recoil, dim-out and hide behind his inaudible speech. I could hardly make out the words or guess at the content. Had it been on videotape, the body language would have been something to behold.

Some of what I wrote was in Arabic, my mother tongue, but of a quality and style that required little more than straightforward translation. I always "composed" my written pieces, never permitting spontaneity to take over or random thoughts to be jotted down uncontrolled. Taping was a different matter entirely: sometimes in Arabic, other times in English, but always done extemporaneously, more casually and sufficiently disordered to warrant redrafting in a consistent style and order. Additionally, I now assumed the role of interpreter in enunciating thoughts half-expressed in the original material. Quickly, the task evolved into a full blown writing exercise, pleasurable at times, painful at others, but always fulfilling in the utmost.

Putting the contents of each tape in final written form was a major achievement and I rewarded myself by sharing the final product with family and friends. Slowly, that narrow circle of reviewers receiving my weekly emails turned into a small fan club; they thought the material was publishable. By the time the process of transcribing ended, I had started speaking of "my book of memoirs." That raised the mother of all questions in publishing a book: Who would my target readership be?

That is when it all clicked; it all came together. A 1969 clipping from the *Christian Science Monitor* brought back memories of the time when I still thought I could change the world. In a letter to the editor I had advised the readers of the existence of an Arab minority in Israel and expounded its potential as a peace bridge in the Middle East. A photo I had kept shows me, much later, proselytizing from the same clipping to Ephraim Katzir, the president of Israel; the look of disenchantment on his face sums up the standard response my ideas have received in "my" country over the years. It suddenly dawned on me that that statement summed up my life mission. Throughout my professional years of service, whether in medicine, in public health or in development, and especially in my proactive role in the NGO movement, I had one overarching goal: to introduce my community to the world, to transcend the wall of seclusion and concealment behind which our state had isolated us. That had been my strategy for fighting the racial discrimination practiced against my community. And it all was right there, on audiotapes. Here was my chance for a last attempt at exposing our secret existence, suffering and promise to the world. Here was my chance finally to gain "permission to narrate," as Edward Said puts it.

Then a chance meeting with Jonathan Cook, a fellow Galilean, inspired me with a working scheme: I should focus on the power of the shock element in the strange and schizoid life I had led, and the fact that its events had unfolded in the shadow of one of the world's major ongoing conflicts, in an area of sacred fascination to much of the English-speaking world. With Jonathan Cook's guidance, the selections in this book concentrate on the socio-political struggle of my people as reflected in my own life in their midst.

Hatim Kanaaneh, MD, MPH
Arrabeh, Israel
January 13, 2008

Foreword

Jonathan Cook

In September 1976 the Israeli media published a lengthy and confidential memorandum that had been presented six months earlier to the prime minister of the day, Yitzhak Rabin. It was from a senior Interior Ministry official, Israel Koenig, Commissioner of the Northern District. His job was to oversee the Galilee, a region dominated by a non-Jewish population officially referred to as "Israel's Arabs,"[1] or "the minorities"—perhaps to conceal from the international community, and from successive generations of "Israel's Arabs" themselves, that they were the last remnants of the Palestinian population living on their own land inside Israel.

Palestine was "wiped off the map" in 1948 during a war that carved out the borders of a new Jewish state. The Jewish community called it their War of Independence; for the Palestinians, it was the *Nakba*, or Catastrophe. Israel emerged as the sovereign ruler of 78 percent of Palestine (with the remainder—the West Bank and Gaza—captured in 1967). During the war, Jewish forces expelled or terrorized into flight some 750,000 Palestinians—the overwhelming majority of the 900,000 Palestinians living inside Israel's new borders. The remaining 150,000 Palestinians were mostly in the Galilee, though smaller concentrations lived in the Little Triangle, a strip of land hugging the north-west corner of the West Bank, and in the Negev desert. There were also pockets of Palestinians in larger cities, such as Haifa, Jaffa, Acre, Lid and Ramle. Israel's early census figures, based on its citizens' religion, showed that of the non-Jewish population 70 percent were Muslims, 20 percent Christians and 10 percent Druze.

The Palestinian minority was unwelcome from the outset. Although the state moved quickly to erase any traces of the Palestinian refugees by demolishing their hundreds of villages, the Palestinians who were left behind, nearly a fifth of Israel's population, could not be so easily ignored. Their continuing presence threatened to expose as hollow

Israel's carefully crafted image as a state that was both Jewish and democratic, and served as a lingering reminder that the Jewish state stood on the ruins of Palestinian society. These Palestinians, supposedly equal citizens in the new state, were also the legal owners of large tracts of prime agricultural land, particularly in the Galilee, that the state coveted for the development of the Jewish economy and for housing the Jewish immigrants it hoped to attract. Dispossessing the Palestinian minority of what little was left of its homeland would be one of the state's first tasks.

Early Israeli governments hoped that, with the floodgates open to Jewish immigration, "Israel's Arabs" would soon be overwhelmed and the state's "Jewishness" guaranteed. But with the Palestinian minority's birth rate far higher than that of the Jewish community, the task proved more difficult than expected: Palestinians inside Israel remained at nearly 20 percent of the population. Officials agonized about the demographic danger this posed long-term to Israel's future as a Jewish state and worried that a substantial Palestinian minority might one day become a bridgehead for either the Arab nationalism of Nasser or the Palestinian nationalism of the PLO. Decades of quiescence by Israel's Palestinian citizens have done nothing to allay such concerns.

In Koenig's shadow

In early 1976, as Israel Koenig was completing the draft of his memorandum, Hatim Kanaaneh, the author of this important memoir, was resolving to leave Israel and his village of Arrabeh in the Galilee, outraged by the endemic discrimination faced by the Palestinian minority. He returned to the United States, where he had spent many years as a Harvard medical student. Two years later, however, he returned to the Galilee believing that, as one of the few trained Palestinian doctors in Israel, he could make a difference to his own village and his wider community. The shadow of the Koenig Memorandum hangs over his account of his frustrations as a physician struggling to raise the standard of health care and sanitation in his village, and of his experiences working for the bureaucracy of a Health Ministry that could barely conceal the superior value it placed on the lives of the country's Jews.

Koenig, an immigrant from Poland, was there to enforce the inferior status of the Palestinian minority, then numbering nearly half a million.

His main task was controlling local authority budgets, rewarding compliant Palestinian community leaders with small favors while ensuring that overall their towns and villages were starved of the funds available to Jewish communities.

Zionism's central tenet—the need to create a sanctuary in the form of a pure Jewish state—counted neither assimilation nor integration of the Palestinian minority into Israeli society as desirable. By ensuring that Palestinian citizens were separated from Jewish citizens, and forced to struggle to make ends meet and to compete with each other for the support of the authorities, they would have neither the opportunities nor incentive to make use of the democratic institutions available to Jews. Palestinians inside Israel faced "divide and rule," not from a colonial ruler like the Mandatory British authorities, but from their own, supposedly democratic, government. Koenig was the lynchpin of this policy.

The Israeli scholar Ian Lustick argued that the unexpected quiescence of the Palestinian minority, given its oppression, could only be explained by the state's development of a complex system of absolute control. Palestinians lived in isolated and fragmented communities, entirely dependent on the Jewish economy for their livelihoods, with leaders co-opted by denying them alternative avenues for advancement. The goal of this system was to crush the Palestinian minority's fledgling struggle for equality. By the 1970s, Lustick noted, the minority's leadership thought less of waiting for Palestine's liberation and more of making "Israel a liberal, secular democratic state with full equality of Arabs and Jews."[2] In other words, Palestinians were willing to accept an Israeli identity, as long as it involved genuine civic integration, not ethnic exclusion. Hatim Kanaaneh shared such hopes, though his experiences on returning to Israel soon taught him that coexistence was impossible in a state that defined itself in ethnic terms.

Faced with growing demands for equality, Koenig, the Jewish official in closest daily contact with Israel's Palestinian citizens, concluded that the system of control was in danger of breaking down. In his memorandum to Rabin, he noted the growing difficulty of controlling Israel's Palestinian citizens since the dismantling of the military government that once ruled over them. From 1948 until 1966 "Israel's Arabs" had been governed entirely separately from Jewish citizens, with military regions created to imprison them in their heartlands of the

Galilee, Triangle and Negev. Each military governor was responsible for cultivating loyal "notables," usually elderly clan leaders, whose support ensured the backing of their younger followers. Martial law, based on emergency regulations inherited from the British, severely limited the freedoms of Palestinian "citizens." Travel between their villages, or to places of work, required permits, invariably issued in return for favors or promises of collaboration; independent political parties, newspapers and organized protests were banned; and community activists who rejected Zionist orthodoxy were blacklisted and often put in detention without charge.

Meanwhile, state officials confiscated the lands on which their villages depended for agriculture by designating them as "closed military zones." These areas were later transferred to Jewish farming collectives like the *kibbutz* and *moshav*. Most Palestinian workers found themselves transformed from independent farmers and landholders into landless casual laborers, commuting to Jewish areas to service the construction, quarrying and agricultural industries of a Jewish economy.

The cruelties of this period have been well documented.[3] But Hatim Kanaaneh's account is the first in English of the Koenig era and its legacy for Israel's Palestinians, making it a key text for scholars, diplomats and journalists. But it is also a lively, insightful and troubling memoir, accessible to a much wider readership, of a period when Israel was being fêted as "the only democracy in the Middle East." While many analysts have publicly doubted the legitimacy of Israel's rule over the Palestinians in the occupied West Bank and Gaza, few have dared question Israel's democratic pretensions inside its recognized borders. Kanaaneh's account is unequivocal, revealing the striking parallels between Israel's treatment of Palestinians in the occupied territories and those officially classed as having citizenship in a Jewish state.

The Jewish "national interest" defined

In a sense, Koenig's task was to fill the void that followed the military regime. He was the civilian reincarnation of the military governor, less powerful but just as unaccountable. The end of military rule, Koenig observed, "enabled the younger generation [of Palestinian citizens] to feel the power that had come into its hands in a democratic society" and "exposed the state as a target for [its] struggle"—a struggle for equal rights Koenig regarded as entirely negative. The "Jewish national interest," he argued, required "a long-term plan for the creation of a loyal Arab citizen," who would accept his or her inferior status.[4]

Koenig, however, had a further, and deeper, concern. Palestinians were concentrated in the Galilee, a large and fertile region bordering Lebanon and Syria. With their rapid growth in numbers, and the reluctance of Jews to move to this area, Koenig saw the demographic arithmetic turning against the Jews. Such concerns were not new. David Ben Gurion, Israel's first prime minister, had declared shortly after the state's birth that the proportion of Palestinians in the population should never exceed 15 percent, though his successors raised the figure to 20 percent.[5] But in parts of the Galilee, Koenig noted, "Israel's Arabs" were already 67 percent of the population.

His fear was that over time the state might be unable to hold on to the Galilee, particularly if a "nationalistic momentum" were to build up among the Palestinians, a development made more likely by the 1967 war, following which Palestinians inside Israel could meet their kin in the occupied territories. Koenig perceived two separate threats: if the Palestinian minority organized and made its voice heard, Israel might be forced to give autonomy to the Galilee's Palestinians; or, if neighboring Arab states attacked as successfully as they had in the 1973 Yom Kippur War, they might be able to recruit Galilee's Palestinians to assist in an invasion. The minority's population growth "will create possibilities for military forces from the north to infiltrate into that area in proportion to the acceleration of the nationalistic process among Israeli Arabs."

Koenig proposed several policies, designed to rein in the aspirations of the Palestinian minority for equality and to reverse the "demographic problem" they posed. His racist premise was that Israeli Arabs, like other Arabs, were distinguished by a "superficial character" and an imagination that "tends to exceed rationality," implying that they could be controlled as if they were wayward children—with an iron hand. He was suggesting a set of policies to reinvent the military government without damaging Israel's democratic image.

Regarding leadership, Koenig observed that the minority's prole-tarianization had led to the breakdown of Arab society's traditional hierarchical structures. Clan leaders, previously favored by the regime, were rapidly losing status and authority, and the younger generation's rebellion against its elders was threatening to "become a struggle against the establishment and the state." Koenig particularly feared the rise of Rakah, the joint Jewish and Arab Communist party—the only non-Zionist party free to stand in national elections. The Communists, who opposed the ethnic privileges promoted by the state, were taking a growing share of the Palestinian minority's vote away from the Zionist parties, which ran separate "Arab lists" of loyal minority representatives. Koenig proposed that the government distance itself from the traditional Arab leadership by creating charismatic leaders loyal to the state, assist them in establishing an Arab party, and take undefined "steps" against "negative personalities" among the minority.

For the economy, Koenig pointed out that the Zionist principle of "Hebrew labor," which required Jewish businesses to hire only other Jews, was being eroded. Employers needed a large pool of cheap manual labor and, given the reluctance of most Jews to do such work, Palestinian citizens faced little threat of unemployment. This gave them a "feeling of power" and had allowed families to accumulate "large sums of cash." "This social and economic security that relieves the individual and family of economic worries and day-to-day pressures grants them, consciously and sub-consciously, leisure for 'social-nationalist' thought." Given the country's dependence on Arab labor, strikes could cause "serious damage to the economy and to the state." Koenig therefore suggested that: the number of Arab employees in any business not exceed 20 percent; the authorities "intensify" tax collection from Arab employees; Jewish businesses be promoted over Arab ones; and responsibility for welfare payments be transferred from the government to unaccountable Zionist organizations such as the Jewish Agency. The last policy had been recommended by Ben Gurion two decades earlier.[6]

Regarding education, Koenig ignored the role of schools in controlling the Palestinian minority, presumably because the state had already established a separate, deprived education system for Palestinian pupils. Also, the domestic security service, the Shin Bet, had infiltrated Israel's Arab schools to create a network of collaborators among both teaching staff and pupils. Instead, Koenig concentrated on higher education, noting that, despite discrimination, Palestinian students were gaining increasing access to universities. This "created a large population of frustrated 'intelligentsia'" whose resentment was "directed against the Israeli establishment of the state." Unless checked, members of this disillusioned elite might become leaders of the minority. Koenig proposed that: Arab students be steered towards the physical and natural sciences because such "studies leave less time for dabbling in nationalism and the dropout rate is higher"; emigration be encouraged by making study trips abroad easier "while making the return and employment more difficult"; college administrations crack down on any signs of protest by Palestinian students; and a small number of loyal students be cultivated as leaders.

Finally, Koenig considered the "demographic problem," particularly birth rates: the Palestinian population was growing at 5.9 percent a year, and the Jewish population by only 1.5 percent. Palestinian citizens were becoming more numerous, threatening to outnumber Jews in the Galilee and exhibiting an increasing political and ideological confidence. A push towards confrontation, argued Koenig, reflected "the wish of a clear majority of these people to demonstrate against the establishment and the Israeli authorities."

To counter these trends, Koenig proposed containing Palestinian communities to prevent them from merging and becoming more powerful. In particular, the Galilean towns of Nazareth and Acre, the only potential urban areas still available to Palestinian citizens, should be the subject of intensified government "Judaization" programs (to make them more Jewish). Nazareth, the effective capital of the Palestinians inside Israel, had been contained since 1957 by the creation of Jewish Upper Nazareth on its confiscated lands. Koenig, a resident of Upper Nazareth from 1962, was worried by "indications of organized activity" by Nazarenes who, unable to build in their own city because of the loss of land, were seeking to buy homes in the neighboring Jewish town. In general, Palestinian communities could be contained by a program to "expand and deepen Jewish settlement" in Palestinian areas and by "diluting existing Arab population concentrations." Koenig recommended further confiscation of Palestinian land, together with strict enforcement of planning laws criminalizing most Palestinian house-building.

Land Day and its aftermath

Koenig presented his memorandum on March 1, 1976. Within weeks, Israel faced the largest confrontation with its Palestinian citizens in its short history. The minority called its first general strike for one day, March 30, to protest against continuing expropriation of its land, particularly in the Galilee. The usual pretext was the need for a green belt or military training area, but invariably the land would be turned over to developers to build Jewish settlements.

In the 1970s, a new wave of confiscations began. In particular, three neighboring villages—Sakhnin, Dier Hanna and Arrabeh, the latter home to Hatim Kanaaneh's family—faced the loss of swaths of agricultural land, most of which had been declared a "closed military zone" decades ago. The villages were still reeling from an earlier loss of 750 acres of farmland to build the National Water Carrier.[7] In response to the strike, Prime Minister Rabin ordered the army to enforce a curfew in Palestinian areas, and sent the army into the three villages. Using the army, rather than the police, gave a clear signal that the authorities regarded the minority as an enemy rather than as citizens. In his memoir, Kanaaneh expresses shock and disgust at seeing tanks on the streets of his village. During the strike, the army fired on unarmed demonstrators, killing six. The day is commemorated annually by Palestinians around the world as Land Day.

For Koenig and other Zionists, land in Israel was a "national resource"—it should be exclusively owned by and for *Jews*—and any resistance by the Palestinian minority to its nationalization was a subversive attack on the state. In Koenig's assessment, Land Day was the first time "the Arab population has identified openly and cognizantly—contrary to the government's request—with an Arab extremist-nationalist demand." If the strike organizers won the backing of the PLO, they might in the long run "cause Israel to disintegrate from within and bring about the Palestinianization of the state."

Koenig's memorandum deviated significantly from the official discourse about encouraging democratic coexistence between Jews and Arabs inside Israel. There are, however, strong grounds for believing that his racist views were widely shared in the political and security establishments, and that they continue to shape policy towards the Palestinian minority. No action was taken against Koenig when, six months later, the memorandum's contents were leaked. The Interior Minister, Yosef Burg, declared his complete faith in Koenig, and one newspaper reported that Rabin's officials attached great importance to the memo.[8] One of Koenig's advisors, Tzvi Alderoty, mayor of Migdal

Haemek, was soon afterwards nominated by Rabin as director of the
Labor party's Arab department.[9] Koenig held the post of Commissioner
for 26 years, apparently never renouncing his views. In 2002 he said
that Israeli Arabs "only want to suck the best out of us."[10]

  Although there is evidence that some of Koenig's ideas were put into
practice, in truth his proposals were only a refashioning of the earlier
military government's approach. The most important, and related,
goals of that regime had been: containing Palestinian communities
through land nationalization, followed by "Judaization" as Jews settled
it. Today 93 percent of Israel's territory is nationalized for the benefit
of Jews, with the rest privately owned. About 3 percent of the total
land belongs to Palestinian communities or landowners.

  During the military government, Israel devised laws to make wholesale
confiscation of Palestinian land possible, including declaring areas
"closed military zones" or agricultural land "fallow." But the most
effective legislation was the 1950 Absentee Property Law, under which
refugees from the 1948 war were treated as having abandoned their
property and as having forfeited their ownership rights.[11] "Refugees"
included many internally displaced Palestinians who had remained
inside Israel and received citizenship. Under the law, anyone who had
left their property for as little as a day during the war could be classified
as a "present absentee"—present in Israel, but absent from his property.
The homes, lands and bank accounts of such citizens were seized by
the state with the same ruthlessness faced by refugees outside Israel.
There are no precise figures, but about one in four Palestinian citizens
is a present absentee or descended from one.

  A further justification for land confiscation was introduced in 1965
by the Planning and Building Law, which listed every location where
a community had been recognized by the newly established planning
authorities. The permitted development area of Palestinian communities
was tightly confined, making natural growth impossible and justifying a
harsh policy of enforcing house demolitions against Palestinian citizens.
Today, tens of thousands of Palestinian-owned homes and buildings
are subject to demolition orders.[12]

  The same law recognized just 124 Palestinian communities. Dozens
more, mainly Bedouin villages in the Negev and the Galilee that
predated Israel's creation, became "unrecognized." The inhabitants
of these villages were effectively criminalized: public companies were

banned from supplying their homes with water, sewerage systems and electricity; no schools or medical clinics were allowed, however large the village; and all homes were automatically subject to demolition orders. The goal was to make conditions unbearable for residents so that they would move off their land and into overcrowded but recognized Palestinian communities. The state could then expropriate their land and property. Around 80,000 Bedouin in the Negev have relocated to "planned townships," deprived communities at the bottom of every socio-economic index. A tenth of the Palestinian minority still live in appalling conditions in unrecognized villages, under the constant threat of house demolition.

Once land had been taken by the state, it needed to be "Judaized." One way was to pass it to the so-called "national institutions," international Zionist organizations such as the Jewish Agency and the Jewish National Fund. The JNF now owns 13 percent of Israel's territory, most of it acquired from the state in its early years. Both organizations have implemented many racist policies related to Jewish settlement. According to the JNF charter, only Jews are allowed to live on its land—much of the habitable land in Israel.[13] The organizations also oversee admission committees that vet candidates to the 700 or so rural communities that control most of the nationalized land in Israel, ensuring that applications from Palestinian citizens are blocked. In this way a form of apartheid has been created: a rigid geographic separation, with Palestinian citizens confined to ghettoes. Although these two Zionist organizations enjoy a quasi-governmental status, neither is subject to Israel's rarely enforced anti-discrimination legislation.

For other state land, officials concentrated on expanding the land-hungry Jewish farming cooperatives, the kibbutzim and moshavim, and on building a series of development towns to bring in significant numbers of poorer Jews, especially new immigrants from Arab countries. However, by the time Koenig was writing his memorandum, the Judaization program was running out of steam. Few new Jewish immigrants wanted to endure the hardships of life on a kibbutz, and the development towns were becoming economic blackspots tarnished by their proximity to Palestinian communities. As Koenig argued, Judaization needed a new lease of life and found it a short time later.

In 1977, Ariel Sharon, Agriculture Minister in a new rightwing Likud government, warned of the threats to the Judaization program: "the region is again the Galilee of the gentiles [i.e. Palestinians]. I've begun intensive activity ... to prevent control of state lands by foreigners."[14] During 1978 he established the first of fifty small Jewish communities called *mitzpim* (or "lookouts") scattered across the hilltops of the Galilee. The mitzpim were aimed at a new kind of settler—mainly middle-class left-leaning professionals, very different from the dedicated pioneer settlers. The mitzpim offered a move out of the cities and overcrowded center of the country. Though small, their power was great. Through regional councils they controlled vast swaths of countryside, much of it owned by neighboring Palestinian communities. In this way, a significant portion of the 3 percent of land in Israel owned by Palestinians was effectively taken out of their control.

The resistance of the three Palestinian communities at the center of the Land Day strike—Sakhnin, Arrabeh and Dier Hanna—had forced the government to return their land, but it also spurred Sharon to devise the mitzpim as a new way to contain Palestinian communities. Predictably, the three villages were the first to be surrounded by mitzpim. Today, 29 mitzpim, known as Misgav Regional Council, have seized control of the returned land, and Misgav receives the land taxes levied on the villages' farmers.[15] In addition, Jewish doctors, bank managers and teachers in these "lookouts" have been turned into unwitting spies, watching over their Palestinian neighbors and ensuring no "illegal expansion" occurs.

Separate and unequal

The state's methods of controlling the Palestinian minority did not end with the confiscation of land. Many other policies, including those advocated by Koenig, have been pursued to:

- marginalize or exclude Palestinian leaders who resist the system of control;
- recruit leaders who can be persuaded to cooperate;
- and keep the wider Palestinian community isolated, poor, uneducated and feuding so that its members cannot fill the leadership vacuum or form alliances with Jewish sympathisers.

Despite Israel's self-definition as an ethnic state, most observers assume it is a democracy because its Palestinian citizens vote. However, political participation has never been as free or open as it appears; independent Palestinian parties were blocked until the early 1980s, and even today Arabs elected to the Knesset must pledge an oath of loyalty not to their country but to Israel as a "Jewish and democratic" state. Parties campaigning for constitutional reform—particularly the party led until recently by the exiled politician Azmi Bishara, which demands that Israel become a "state of all its citizens"—have been hounded by the security services.[16] An unshakeable Zionist consensus holds that Arab parties be denied any voice in government. No Arab party has ever been invited to participate in Israel's coalitions.

In local government, most Palestinian communities were deprived of municipal representation for many decades, thereby failing to qualify for basic services. In 1976 only one Palestinian village had a sewerage system, and half were without electricity.[17] Hatim Kanaaneh discusses the obstacles he faced trying to get sewerage systems installed in Arrabeh and other villages. The same hardships continue for dozens of unrecognized villages: some 90,000 people in the Negev, for example, still do not have electricity.[18] Unequal budgetary allocations from central government exacerbate the deprivation and perpetuate the minority's political marginalization. Most government ministries allocate less than 7 percent of their municipal budgets to Palestinian local authorities. Unsurprisingly, more than 95 percent of Palestinian councils were in deficit in 2002, with two-thirds in deep financial crisis.[19]

Israel has marginalized and intimidated another potential source of leaders, those heading civil society organizations. Hatim Kanaaneh helped found one of the first and most important, the Galilee Society, in 1981, dedicated to improving the health and socio-economic conditions of the Palestinian minority. His struggles are detailed in his memoir, but similar problems continue today for non-governmental organizations (NGOs). With international funders treating Israel as a first-world country, Arab NGOs inside Israel are rarely eligible for the development grants their community's actual socio-economic conditions should warrant. Instead they are dependent on a few progressive Zionist American-Jewish foundations, which either demand apolitical activity or severely circumscribe the nature of the work the NGOs can undertake. In addition, the authorities scrutinize the every move of Arab NGOs, threatening legal action, and denying them permits to recruit overseas volunteers. The most important Arab NGO, a legal organization called Adalah (Justice), which has mounted many challenges to state-sponsored discrimination in the courts, has been subject to regular investigations and campaigns against it in the Hebrew media.[20]

Even the best-educated Palestinian citizens are often forced into menial jobs. The country's trade union federation, the Histadrut, has worked tirelessly to exclude the minority from having a voice in workers' issues. In the 1970s, at the height of its power, not one of the Histadrut's hundreds of firms or factories was located in an Arab community.[21] In 2005, of the country's 56,000 civil servants less than 5 percent were Palestinian; most working in lowly positions in separate "Arab" sections of the education and health ministries. Under-representation in the state monopolies, such as the telecoms company Bezeq and the Israeli Electricity Corporation, is even worse. Nachman Tal, a former Shin Bet advisor, reported that in 2004 there were only six Palestinians among the 13,000 staff of the electricity company.[22] Palestinian workers are almost never employed in Israel's vast "security-related" public industries. The average monthly income for a Palestinian family is today about 60 percent of that of a Jewish family, though the Palestinian family is typically larger than the Jewish one.[23] Two and a half times more Palestinian families than Jewish families are in poverty.[24]

A separate and inferior Arab education system has underpinned the state's exclusion of the minority from the economy and prevention of later interaction with Jewish citizens. Israel's justification of segregation to protect the minority's language and culture might be persuasive had Israel invested in Arab education. But Palestinian schools are a pale shadow of Jewish schools, with severe shortages of teachers, classrooms and books, and government interference in the curriculum to marginalize Arab culture and Palestinian history.[25] Education funding continues to be starkly different. A 2001 survey revealed that, excluding teachers' salaries, the money allocated to the education of each Arab student was less than a quarter of that for a Jewish student.[26] The domestic security service, the Shin Bet, also controls Arab schools. Hatim Kanaaneh observed these problems from his own brief experience as a teacher in the 1950s. Such interference was denied until 2004, when a senior official admitted: "The Shin Bet not only determined and intervened in the appointment of principals and teachers, but even decided who the custodians and janitors that clean the bathrooms in the Arab schools would be."[27] The policy was supposedly ended a year later.[28]

Higher education is not segregated, but has nonetheless been an effective arena for marginalizing Palestinian intellectuals and encouraging them to emigrate.[29] According to a report in 1971, in a Palestinian population of 400,000 there were fewer than 500 with university degrees.[30] When families could afford to, they sent their children to study abroad. Scholarships available from the Communist party, meant most attended universities in the Soviet bloc. Unusually, Hatim Kanaaneh headed in a different direction: to the United States. He also returned. In 1976, 18,000 other Palestinians who left the country, many presumably to study, did not.[31] Despite years of lobbying, no public university has been established in a Palestinian community; no university teaches in Arabic; fewer than 1 percent of academic staff are Palestinian;[32] and though Palestinians of university age are a quarter of their age group, they form only 8 percent of the student body.[33] That such discrimination is intentional was revealed in 2003, when culturally biased psychometric tests governing admissions were briefly dropped, in an attempt to help "weaker sections" of the population. That apparently referred to recent Jewish immigrants, not Palestinian students. When the Committee of University Heads learned that the number of Palestinians gaining university entrance had risen sharply, the tests were immediately reinstated on the grounds that "the admission of one population [Palestinians] comes at the expense of the other [Jews]."[34]

The Israeli Arab "timebomb"

From Israel's inception, ways to limit the growth of the remnants of the Palestinian population, while increasing that of the Jewish population, were sought. Monetary prizes, child allowances, even the provision of family planning clinics were devoted to this end, as Hatim Kanaaneh's daughter, Rhoda, a scholar now living in the US, notes in her book *Birthing the Nation*.[35] But after the second Intifada, concern about the country's demographic trends reached new heights. The Herzliya Conference, an annual security convention, was launched in late 2000, its theme the threat posed by the growth of the Palestinian minority. From this conference new kinds of legislative assault on the citizenship of Palestinians emerged. In 2003 the government amended the 1952 Nationality Law, to bar a Palestinian citizen from bringing to Israel a spouse from the occupied territories. Officials feared such marriages might allow a Right of Return for Palestinian refugees "through the backdoor."[36]

It was not surprising that opinion polls soon showed similar worries from the Jewish public. A large survey in 2003 showed that 57 percent thought Palestinian citizens should be encouraged to emigrate, through inducements or force.[37] In a follow-up poll in 2006 the figure had risen to 62 percent.[38] In another survey that year 68 percent of Israeli Jews said they did not want to live next to a Palestinian citizen.[39]

These racist views have been encouraged by leading journalists, academics and politicians of all persuasions, who now regularly refer to the Palestinian minority as a "demographic timebomb." Many advocate drastic action to save the state's Jewishness. One favored measure is a policy of "transfer," or ethnic cleansing of the Palestinian minority. Such talk has been heard from revisionist historians like Benny Morris, and former prime ministers Binyamin Netanyahu, Ariel Sharon and Ehud Barak.

Leading the charge in promoting "transfer" is Israel's far-right, particularly Avigdor Lieberman, a Moldovan immigrant and leader of the increasingly popular Yisrael Beitenu party. Lieberman, once director-general of the Likud party, has been promoting the "Separation of Nations" whereby mutual transfers of territory ensure Jewish settlers in the occupied territories are inside an expanded Israeli state, but as many Palestinians as possible are relocated to a future Palestinian state. He has powerful allies in Washington, including former US Secretary of State Henry Kissinger.[40]

Lieberman has exhumed the idea of transfer from the dark recesses of Zionism, freeing Israeli politicians to speak about it openly, especially as part of a potential peace agreement with the Palestinians of the occupied territories. He has made respectable the idea of transferring the Little Triangle, a small area of Israeli territory close to the West Bank and densely populated with 250,000 Palestinian citizens, to a future Palestinian state. He also proposes a loyalty oath for Palestinian citizens who remain inside Israel, not to their country but "to the State of Israel as a Zionist Jewish state."[41] Those refusing would presumably be expelled.

In October 2006 Prime Minister Ehud Olmert appointed Lieberman to his cabinet as deputy prime minister. Two months later Lieberman made a trip to Washington to promote his "loyalty scheme." He told American Jewish leaders: "He who is not ready to recognize Israel as a Jewish and Zionist state cannot be a citizen in the country."[42] In January 2007, for the first time, the government backed loyalty legislation proposed by a rightwing legislator, under which Israeli citizenship could be revoked for participating in "an act that constitutes a breach of loyalty to the state"—i.e. loyalty to Israel as a "Jewish and democratic" state. The Justice Ministry, now in charge of the bill, had not released its version at the time of writing.[43]

It seems clear that the consensus is now behind the Lieberman approach. Shortly before the Annapolis peace conference in November 2007, Israel's foreign minister, Tzipi Livni, observed that a Palestinian state would be the "answer" to Israel's Palestinian citizens: "They cannot ask for the declaration of a Palestinian state while working against the nature of the State of Israel as home unto the Jewish people."[44] Earlier, in August, President Shimon Peres, in a post intended to embody the nation's unity, proposed exchanging settlement blocs in the occupied territories for Palestinian areas inside Israel.[45] All these ideas are in line with the political instincts of Olmert. He has repeatedly stated the goal of two states for two peoples, Jews and Palestinians, though every indication is that by "Palestinian state" Israel means a patchwork of ghettoes in the West Bank and the besieged prison of Gaza.

The outlook for the Palestinian minority is today possibly even bleaker than it was in Koenig's time. For those of us who wish to learn how Israel reached this point, Hatim Kanaaneh's memoir provides an invaluable insight.

Jonathan Cook
Nazareth
February 2008

Notes

1. The more usual translation, "Israeli Arabs," fails to connote the possessive quality conveyed in the original Hebrew phrase.

2. Ian Lustick, *Arabs in the Jewish State* (University of Texas Press, 1980), pp. 9–10.

3. Fouzi el-Asmar, *To Be an Arab in Israel* (Frances Pinter, 1975) and Sabri Jiryis, *The Arabs in Israel* (Monthly Review Press, 1976).

4. All the quotes from the Koenig Memorandum are taken from *Journal of Palestine Studies*, Vol. 6, No. 1 (Autumn 1976), pp. 190–200.

5. Simha Flapan, "The Palestinian Exodus of 1948," *Journal of Palestine Studies*, Vol. 16, No. 4 (Summer 1987), p. 16.

6. Reinhard Wiemer, "Zionism and the Arabs after the Establishment of the State of Israel," in Alexander Scholch (ed.), *Palestinians over the Green Line*, cited in Rhoda Kanaaneh, *Birthing the Nation* (University of California Press, 2002), p. 35.

7. Jiryis, *The Arabs in Israel*, p. 262; Lustick, *Arabs in the Jewish State*, p. 177.

8. From the minutes of a debate in the United Nations Security Council, November 1, 1976, available at: http://domino.un.org/unispal.NSF/eed216406b50bf6485256ce10072f637/f67d4d633a025cf685256fd3006449ca!OpenDocument.

9. Nur Masalha, *A Land Without a People* (Faber, 1997), p. 151.

10. "The other Israelis," *Haaretz*, July 5, 2002.

11. Jiryis, *The Arabs in Israel*, chapter 4.

12. The report of the Gazit Committee in 2000 found some 30,000 illegal "structures" in Palestinian communities, mostly because of a lack of master plans to legalize them. Hussein Abu Hussein and Fiona McKay, *Access Denied* (Zed Books, 2003), p. 270.

13. "In Watershed, Israel Deems Land-use Rules of Zionist Icon 'Discriminatory'," *Forward*, February 4, 2005.

14. Lustick, *Arabs in the Jewish State*, pp. 317–18n.

15. "Unacceptable norms," *Haaretz*, September 26, 2004.

16. See *Silencing Dissent*, by the Arab Association for Human Rights, October 2002; and my "The Shin Bet and the Persecution of Azmi Bishara," *Counterpunch*, June 5, 2007.

17. Lustick, *Arabs in the Jewish State*, p. 191; Jiryis, *The Arabs in Israel*, pp. 228–9.

18. Ibn Khaldun, *Civic Developments Among the Palestinians in Israel*, November 2006, p. 17.

19. Ibn Khaldun, *Civic Developments Among the Palestinian-Arab Minority in Israel*, June 2004, pp. 35–7.

20. See, for example, Adalah press release, August 13, 2002.

21. Lustick, *Arabs in the Jewish State*, pp. 96–7.

22. "Even the Shin Bet is against discrimination," *Haaretz*, May 25, 2004.

23. Ibn Khaldun, *Civic Developments Among the Palestinians in Israel*, p. 17.

24. "Government report: 1.65 million Israelis living below poverty line," *Haaretz*, September 5, 2007.

25. HRW, *Second Class: Discrimination Against Palestinian Arab Children in Israel's Schools*, September 2001.

26. "Report: Haredi school spending twice as much per pupil as state schools," *Haaretz*, August 6, 2005.
27. "Even the Shin Bet," *Haaretz*.
28. "Shin Bet will no longer scrutinize Arab educators," *Haaretz*, January 6, 2005.
29. "The great brain drain," *Haaretz*, May 25, 2004.
30. Jiryis, *The Arabs in Israel*, pp. 209–10.
31. Lustick, *Arabs in the Jewish State*, p. 280n.
32. "Know thy neighbor—but don't hire him," *Haaretz*, July 12, 2001.
33. Ilam, *Alternative News Briefing*, No. 25, September 7, 2006.
34. "Numerus clausus," *Haaretz*, December 16, 2003.
35. University of California Press, 2002.
36. See my *Blood and Religion: The Unmasking of the Jewish and Democratic State* (Pluto Press, 2006), chapter 3.
37. "The Democracy Index: Major Findings 2003," Israel Democracy Institute, available at: http://www.idi.org.il/english/catalog.asp?pdid=288&did=50.
38. "Poll: 62 percent want Arab emigration," *Ynet*, May 9, 2006.
39. "Poll: Israeli Jews shun Arabs," *Ynet*, March 22, 2006.
40. "A new opening for Mideast peace," *Washington Post*, December 3, 2004.
41. "Israel Beiteinu's Political Position on Settlements, Peace Negotiations and Jerusalem," *Foundation for Middle East Peace*, October 23, 2006.
42. "Lieberman: The unfaithful cannot be citizens," *Ynet*, December 10, 2006.
43. "Gov't to support bill on revoking citizenship for disloyalty to state," *Haaretz*, January 7, 2007.
44. "FM Livni: Palestinian state should satisfy Israeli Arab national desires," *Israel Insider*, November 18, 2007.
45. "Abbas opposes exchange of populated territory with Israel," *Haaretz*, August 26, 2007.

1
Cat and Mouse

Land Day memorial in Sakhnin.

November 1, 1977

On the return leg of my trip things turned a bit farcical. It all began with the *halva* I was taking back for my children. The box in which the Oriental delicacy was packed set off the alarm of the metal detector at Tel Aviv airport. At that point one of my fellow travelers—an elderly woman—stepped in to take matters into her own hands. As I was explaining to the security officials that I had bought the halva in the

Palestinian city of Jenin in the occupied West Bank, she interjected. Israel produced the best-tasting halva around so there could be no reason for me to go to Jenin except to bring a bomb to the airport. When I ignored her comments and joked to the security officials that if they wanted to take the halva away for closer examination they had better promise not to eat it all, she demanded they bodysearch me and check my shoes for explosives. The officials were more than happy to oblige.

I was returning to Los Angeles, and then on to Hawaii, after a two-week visit to see my family in my home village of Arrabeh. It is an Arab village in the Galilee, one of about 120 Palestinian communities that were not erased in 1948 by the war that established Israel on my homeland, a land once called Palestine. As I took my seat on the plane, I realized that my elderly friend could see me from where she sat provided she turned her head back. She must have ended up with a very stiff neck by the time we landed eleven hours later, when she was finally relieved of her terror watch. Throughout the flight she observed my every movement and followed me wherever I went; she accompanied me to the door of the bathroom and on my frequent strolls in the aisles. Mischievously, a couple of times I waited till she started to doze off before leaving my seat; then I watched from a distance as she panicked on waking and rushed around the aisles looking for me. By the end of the flight, I had developed a certain intimacy with the woman and even felt a little bad for being so mean to her, reduced to playing cat and mouse in the most childish way.

I had arrived for my short stay in Israel, back in August, in equally unwelcoming circumstances. As the aircraft touched down at Tel Aviv airport, I found myself singled out from the 261 mainly Jewish passengers by the security agents who boarded the plane before we had a chance to disembark. They took me off for a three-hour interrogation solely on the strength of my Arabic name. When I eventually emerged to be greeted by a dozen waiting relatives and friends, Ahmad, my eldest brother, could see how angry I was about the security agents' *a priori* determination that, from my ethnicity alone, I must harbor ill intent and plot harm. He tried to lift my spirits: the humiliating treatment was a sign of the respect shown by an Israeli security service threatened by my international connections. I felt like explaining that both they and he are way off the mark, that I hold myself above their thinly-veiled assumption of my potential for intrigue and violence. But I hold Ahmad in higher respect than to contradict him on matters of feeling. I simply dropped the subject.

I returned to Arrabeh in fulfillment of a promise I had made my family and myself not to stay away for more than a year in Hawaii, where I was working as a family physician. I sought to reclaim my peace of mind and inner balance to sustain me for another year away. We drove to the village in great excitement but, after an absence of a year, I was surprised again by my repugnance and dismay at the squalor of the Arab villages we drove through and the obvious poor health of the people. The hot and dusty air, the flies everywhere, the garbage-strewn, sewage-drenched alleys, the overcrowding, and the innumerable children in the streets scrambling out of the car's way, with scabbed impetigo lesions on their bare skin, mocked me and my Harvard medical degrees. These were the conditions awaiting me if and when I decided to return from the US—testimony to my failure to make a dent in the community's dismal health care, despite the six years I had already invested in the attempt before I left for Hawaii. It was enough to instill despair in my heart—or redouble my commitment.

Those six years had proved to me beyond any shadow of a doubt the enduring hostility shown by "my" state towards the one in five citizens who are not Jewish but the natives of the country, its Palestinian minority. Even during my brief time away, there had been new and troubling developments. One of the most concerning was a shortage of drinking water in many Arab communities in the Galilee.

"I am becoming the laughing stock of my own community," the mayor of Arrabeh, a former schoolmate of mine, tells me. "For most of the day the water supply to Arrabeh is turned off by Mekorot.* It shows the degree of ill-will the state bears us. How else can you explain the fact that Yodfat, the Jewish settlement next door, never lacks water for its cattle, cotton fields and green lawns?"

"But you must have raised the issue with government officials, haven't you?"

"You know who it is I report to, don't you? Israel Koenig! It takes me months to get an appointment with the little dictator and whatever topic

---

* *Mekorot:* Hebrew for "resources"; the Israel National Water Company, a government corporation with near total monopoly over the country's water resources and allocation.

I bring up he winds up chiding me for failing to do my duty; he wants me to limit the number of births in Arrabeh. He claims that Mekorot can no longer provide enough water for the Arab communities' needs because of the rapid natural growth rate of our population."

Such acrimonious exchanges had apparently intensified after the leak of a secret report written by the District Commissioner of the Galilee, Israel Koenig, who had recommended to his superiors in the Interior Ministry that, among many other apartheid measures, Arab women should be forced to have their fertility limited. This, of course, is meant to protect the Jewish character of the state. To my dismay, at least half a dozen women in our Kanaaneh clan have apparently come off the pill I had started them on. Two of them I spoke with mentioned Koenig's infamous report as a background to, if not the direct cause of, their decision to get pregnant again.* They approvingly cited a popular gesture made by Toufiq Zayyad, the poet mayor of Nazareth. On the birth of his most recent child, shortly after the leaking of the Koenig Report, he telegraphed a birth announcement in the form of a message of condolence to Mr. Koenig.

"And it is not just one sick official we are talking about," Arrabeh's mayor explains; "imams in mosques and folk singers at village weddings are being interrogated and even jailed by the Shin Bet† for making traditional pronouncements that have nationalistic overtones. Yousif here can tell you what happened to him and to his fellow Arab workers the other day," he adds as he beckons to a young man to join us. Yousif, a strapping muscular young man, comes over and without any further prodding bashfully relates to me a recent incident in which he was caught up. Apparently a civil defense exercise was recently held in the vegetable market of the nearby city of Haifa. The police, rehearsing what to do in the event of an explosion at the market, rounded up a few dozen Arab men, including Yousif, who were waiting in a neighboring square in the hope of being hired for casual labor by small-time contractors. A crowd of Jewish shoppers, agitated by the arrests, mistook what they saw for a real security incident and attacked the Arab laborers with their bare fists and spat at them. Things got so

---

* *Koenig Report:* See Foreword.
† *Shin Bet:* aka Shabak, the Israeli General Security Services or Secret Police, often operating outside the limits of accepted international conventions and of the country's own laws.

out of hand the police had to hide the Arab men in their headquarters, where they were detained "for their own protection" till after sundown. Yousif ends his story with a shy giggle, his eyes fixed to the ground, as if somehow feeling guilty. Ali, a younger haughty relative of mine confirms Yousif's story but adds proudly:

"Those day laborers are pitiful. You need smarts to get by in the city. I saw it all. I was working at my boss's falafel stand in the market. No one there knows I am an Arab; I go by the name 'Eli' and I speak better Hebrew than most Jews."

Now, as I weigh up the consequences of leaving the comfort of Hawaii to return to live in the Galilee, I can't help but consider what happened in 1970, the first time I went back after an absence of a decade. During that decade I had obtained degrees in medicine and public health from Harvard University and completed an internship at the Queen's Medical Center in Honolulu, Hawaii. I was Arrabeh's first son ever to leave to study abroad, a historic moment made possible by my father's agreement to sell some of his farming land to pay my way and by the charity of a childless American couple, Byrd and Amie Davis of Clarion, Pennsylvania, who had become my pen pals after meeting me during a visit to Nazareth. They sponsored me through college and, at the end of my studies, offered to adopt me and leave me their considerable fortune as an inheritance should I agree to carry on the family banking business in their hometown. Tempting though the offer was, rejecting it did not delay me long. As soon as I had reached the point in my medical training where I mustered the skill and fortitude to stand before another human and tell him or her what to do with their body, I rushed home to play God to my friends and next of kin. I had studied medicine so that one day I could return to repay the debt to my community. I was committed to the professional life of a physician, to a life dedicated to healing bodies, to guiding and uplifting spirits, and to improving the living conditions of my village—a life, in short, dedicated to saving humanity through serving my people. More than a little optimistically, I thought I was going to change the world.

In the summer of 1970, on the way back from the US, I had spent a pleasant month camping across Western Europe, in the company of my seven-month pregnant wife, Didi, in a brand new VW Kombi minibus that we had pre-ordered in Germany. It was difficult not to wonder at the wisdom of turning our backs on my promising medical career in the US, and on the paradise of Didi's native state of Hawaii, where we had for a time considered settling. But head back to the Galilee and Arrabeh we did nonetheless. After all, that was why I studied medicine; any other decision would have robbed me of the rationale for accepting a profession I would never have chosen on my own. People in Arrabeh tell of the village simpleton who bought a donkey. When asked why he needed a donkey, he answered:

"To carry loads of grass from the fields."

"But you own no cattle! What do you need the grass for?"

"To feed my donkey, of course!"

That is how it would have been for me to have settled and practiced medicine in America.

The Harvard name opened at least one door on my return. When I applied for a position at the Ministry of Health, a fellow Harvard alumnus, Dr. Hedy Frank-Blume, the chief physician of the Acre sub-district, picked up my letter and responded positively, against all the racially and politically unfavorable odds in an Israeli bureaucracy resistant to employing Arabs for anything more than menial tasks. Deciphering her motives was harder: was it simply the Harvard connection that spoke across the ethnic divide, or did she somehow approve of my stated intention to help my people by trying to reverse in whatever ways I could the neglect and hostility shown them by their state?

I started off with two jobs: as an official in the Ministry of Health and as a family physician in my own community of Arrabeh. My first day in the latter role was sobering. Here was a suspicious, needy and hardened rural village all too ready to judge me if I did not deliver on its expectations of me. There was not a single nurse in the village to help. The challenge of tending to the villagers seemed insurmountable: every man smoked; the elderly wheezed and complained of arthritic pains; every child looked malnourished and anemic, their skin covered with impetigo sores; every father was overweight; and every mother seemed overworked, and visibly exhausted by her phenomenal reproductive rate. It was summer and diarrhea was rampant. And everyone was after a magic cure by a single injection, and would not take "no" for an answer.

I looked at my wife's diary and saw the daunting list she had made of objectionable things she had already noticed in her new environment:

1. Immigration officials discriminate.
2. Khalid, a fifteen-year-old nephew, spent a week in jail in a "tiger cage" for loitering in Naharya, a Jewish town.
3. Malnourished children, deficient in iron, protein and vitamins. I will buy them milk if the mothers provide eggs.
4. Impetigo and rheumatic fever everywhere.
5. A relative's child has pneumonia.
6. No garbage collection.
7. Innumerable flies.
8. The village's only medical clinic stinks.
9. Sanitation abhorrent; bathing infrequent; children play in dirt.
10. Prescription drugs sold over the counter in shops.
11. No refrigeration; food poisoning common.
12. Babies are bound tightly and kept out of the sun. No vitamin D supplement.

The problem of being an Arab in a Jewish state had confronted me even before I set foot back in Israel. In preparation for my first return to Arrabeh, after a decade of studying in the US, I sent my passport to the Israeli consulate in Los Angeles for renewal. The officials replied with a standard package of information for returning students that included details of interest-free loans readily available from offices across Israel to help with my re-absorption into my community. Once in Arrabeh I tracked down the nearest office in Haifa. It was actually the office of the Jewish Agency, where no one had ever come across a similar case of a returning Arab student demanding that his government honor its promise to him. A few visits later, a kindly lady there made a phone call to the Prime Minister's Advisor on Arab Affairs to set up an appointment with Yorum Katz, a seemingly pleasant young Ashkenazi who claimed to know some of the Kanaaneh elders. Unfortunately he was very open that he saw this meeting as a chance to recruit me as an informer in exchange for securing me the promised loan:

"Scratch my back and I will scratch yours," he told me in fluent Arabic.

"My itch is gone," I told him and walked out.

Back in Arrabeh people knew Yorum Katz well. Ahmad, my brother, gave me a piece of his mind for even thinking of getting a government loan:

"You might be a doctor alright, but you don't know beans about this country. Yorum Katz is probably the man behind the military order banning me from entering Gaza to sell and buy and make a living. Don't let anyone know that you've met this guy or else you will be considered another lackey. You don't want to shame us all. I want to continue holding my head high when your name is mentioned!"

I expressed my frustration to my brother:

"Ahmad, I am a good doctor; I know what needs to be done here, but I don't know how to go about it."

"Now you are making sense. The task you assign yourself is nearly impossible. But you have done the impossible before, you have become a doctor."

"Thanks in great measure to your support and to that of our late father."

"Don't lose faith, then; don't give up on me! I have already found you a temporary place for a clinic, right across from the hillside where our parents are buried. In a month or two I will start building a permanent clinic for you."

So, there I was, having realized my impossible dream of old, but now embarking on a collective nightmare. Fully conscious and in full command of my senses I committed to meeting the immediate curative health needs of friends and relatives in the hope of enlisting them on my side in the battle to arrest further deterioration in our communal spirit and collective health. I felt like a trained athlete jumping to clear the bar, only to realize in mid-air that the rules had been changed and the bar was now too high for me, or anyone else, to clear. The political climate in the whole of the Middle East was, and still is, not conducive to better health and development for us. It takes a redirecting of the dominant winds of ill will and enmity, a friendlier atmosphere of care and solidarity, to change our fortunes and health conditions, caught as we are on the wrong side of the Arab-Israeli conflict. And that change, alas, is still an impossible dream.

A sense of despair finally overwhelmed me at a feast Ahmad had prepared for village elders to celebrate my return. I ran from the crowd of well-wishers and locked myself in my mini-camper. I drew the curtains, turned on the motor and, with its noise for cover, sobbed loudly. And I had not yet had to deal with the most formidable opponent to my long-cherished dream of bringing public health to my community: the Israeli Ministry of Health.

Over the next six years disillusionment set in further as I struggled to cope with my multiple roles: as a primary care physician, as a community leader, and as an official in the Ministry of Health. Repeatedly I had to endure casual insults from Jewish colleagues. Take, for example, the time I accompanied "my" health minister, Victor Shem-Tov, of the socialist Zionist party, Mapam, on a tour of Western Galilee. During a meeting with council members of the Jewish city of Naharya to celebrate the construction of a new hospital wing, he declared proudly: "I am against the policy of land confiscation, except for the public good. But for building a hospital like yours I am willing to confiscate private land not only from Arabs but even from Jews." Afterwards, we met the sixteen department heads of the Naharya Government Hospital, not one of whom was an Arab. I raised the issue of a memorandum submitted to the hospital's director, Dr. Avigdor Einhorn, by the mayors of neighboring Arab villages requesting the appointment of an Arabic-speaking clerk in the emergency room to help the Arab 60 percent of its clientele understand instructions and find their way around the maze of hospital corridors. In response, Dr. Einhorn blamed the recent death of a Jewish department head, shot dead by a disgruntled Jewish patient, squarely on the violent nature of Arab patients. The violence was especially uncontrollable among Druze patients, he added. Unlike Christians or Muslims, the Druze served in the Israeli armed forces and therefore, he claimed, had full rights and privileges in the state, just like Jews.* Hence, they could not be prevented from entering the

* *Druze:* A conservative semi-secret sect that broke off from Islam in the eleventh century. Its more than half a million followers live mainly in separate mountain villages in Lebanon, Syria, Jordan and northern Israel. Though fierce Arab nationalists elsewhere, in Israel the Druze concluded a deal with the Jewish forces in 1948 and later on accepted the drafting of their young men into the Israel Defense Forces. In

hospital and behaving in a rowdy manner. The Health Minister meekly accepted these observations without a word of protest. I stormed out of the meeting, but am sure no one noticed or cared.

It was no less dispiriting to be a community leader in Arrabeh struggling to make the state meet its obligations to its Arab citizens. Faced with the obstructions placed in our way by the authorities, the slightest step forward required superhuman efforts and considerable financial sacrifice. In those six years Arrabeh waged many battles for its rights: to be connected to the national electricity grid, to have its main street paved, to get a second school built, and to be connected to the telephone network. As a member of the Electricity Committee in Arrabeh, for example, I quickly realized that the villagers' limited financial means was not the only, or even the main, hurdle to actualizing the project. They simply didn't trust Israel to ever care enough for its Arab citizens and hence didn't subscribe to the project. To break the impasse I offered a special deal to everyone in the village for three months: any patient who showed up at my clinic with a voucher proving they had made the down payment for electricity would be treated free of charge. It worked wonders. Of course, eventually the villagers would have come around of their own accord, but my scheme speeded up the process. When people from neighboring villages started showing up with receipts for electricity, or even water, I had little choice but to honor those as well.

And finally, of course, there was the overwork of providing preventive health services to a quarter of a million people, two-thirds of them Arab villagers, and of running a rural solo general practice around the clock. When I was home for a meal or nap, it was Didi who handled patients that came knocking at our door. Elderly patients expected to be received and hosted while waiting, a task often entertaining but always demanding. Almost daily, Didi would report to me the various conversations she struck with the village folks, the minor misunderstandings, and the frequent *faux pas* because of the language barrier. Among those were the first time an aunt handed her a live rooster

---

return for their collaboration their villages were spared evacuation and demolition in 1948, though their land has not been spared from massive confiscation and their socio-economic status, like other Arabs in Israel, lags far behind that of Jews. Despite some objection from within the Druze community, Israel relates to it as culturally and racially non-Arab.

in payment for my fees, the man who accused her of hiding me and who barged in to look for me in bed, and the food gifts from thankful mothers whom she would advise on the care of their children. To me patients often sang the praises of my wife, what a gracious hostess she was, and what a traditional obedient wife she must be.

After one particularly grueling night, in November 1975, at three in the morning, half asleep, I wrote bitterly:

> Arrabeh has reached 8,000 residents, two-thirds of whom are under sixteen years of age; it promises to double in size in another fifteen years. Our infant mortality rates remain double the rates for the Jewish population whose homes our men build, whose roads our men pave, and in whose factories our men toil, all at an average of half the pay Jewish workers receive. And we live in a democracy and have the right to vote, they tell me! Our leaders are kept out of breath, the outspoken ones shouting against the intended confiscation of another swath of our land and the kiss-ass lackeys denying such "rumors."

Not long after, I started to admit defeat and to think the impossible: we should escape the insanity we were living. I was rapidly making up my mind to leave, when my state delivered the final blow. On March 30, 1976 I woke up to a sight I had never seen before: soldiers and tanks less than a hundred yards from my house. My two young children, Rhoda and Ty, and their cousins were screaming and running to the bathroom with diarrhea. A neighbor was shouting from his window that his wife had gone into labor and needed help. I stepped out of my door waving my stethoscope at the soldiers. They responded by taking aim with their guns. I hurried back inside and told Didi:

"That's it. Israel is not meant for peace-loving people like us. We will move back to Hawaii."

"But Arrabeh still needs you," Didi responded trembling and her voice cracking with fear.

"The need is temporary; soon other village sons studying medicine in the Soviet Union will return to fill the void."

"How about your Health Ministry job?"

"This appalling violation of our right as citizens to protest against the state's confiscation of our land is perpetuated by the very same bureaucracy to which I belong. How can I maintain my self-respect and credibility within my community while working for a state that is prepared to do this to them? Any state that commits this kind of violence against its own citizens is not worthy of my service. How can I keep my dignity in my own eyes? Or in yours for that matter?"

That day, known forever more as Land Day,* was the first time the Palestinian community inside Israel tried to stage a general strike, to protest against the extensive and continuing confiscation of its farming lands by the government. Until Israel's creation, rural communities like Arrabeh had depended on their land and agricultural skills, both for subsistence and to earn a living. Without the land, villagers had been pushed into poverty and casual labor, working cheaply in Israeli quarries, factories and, as hired hands, in what were now declared as Jewish farming communities like the *kibbutzim*, often on the very land confiscated from Arab villages. The state could not countenance defiance from its Arab "citizens"; so to break their will it responded with massive violence against villages like Arrabeh. It imposed a curfew and deployed its tanks, turning our peaceful streets and fields, for the first time in living memory, into a war zone. Six unarmed demonstrators from Arrabeh and neighboring villages were killed in the ensuing clashes. The army, of course, emerged victorious. In nearby Sakhnin, a few dozen Golani crack troopers linked arms in a circle and danced the Hora to their own chants of "*A'am Yisrael hai*—The people of Israel lives" on the very spot where they had shot dead two young villagers.

I submitted a letter of resignation to the Ministry of Health, both in protest at the state's violence on Land Day and at the lack of support for my efforts to improve health conditions in Arab communities. On the face of it, the step carried more weight than I had expected, securing me two meetings with the Health Minister himself. He rejected my letter of resignation and asked instead for a detailed list of the steps that would be necessary to improve the health of the Arab minority in Israel. He granted me an extended leave without pay. It took a moment for me to realize that this was political maneuvering, that his promises were empty. My absence would be used as an excuse for delaying the implementation of any serious measures I would suggest.

So in 1976, shortly after Land Day, we moved back to Hawaii. But it wasn't long before I was contemplating my return to Arrabeh. Didi and I were unhappy with the risks to which we were exposing our two children in America: schools where drugs and violence were on

* *Land Day*: See Preface and Foreword.

the rise; streets so unsafe that parents accompanied their children to school for fear of molestation or worse; and our inability to control our children's TV viewing and prevent them from consuming a diet of sex and violence. We started romanticizing the technological backwardness of rural life in the Galilee, and to idealize the traditional extended family where all adults care collectively for the safety and behavior of its youth.

February 20, 1978

I like the exotic mix of humanity that passes through my examining room here in Hawaii. Still, my relationship with my patients never transcends their episodes of illness. I request routine laboratory tests, write prescriptions or referral notes to specialists or to the hospital. But I miss the all-empowering confidence and dependency my patients in Arrabeh had on me. And I miss my involvement in the life of my community.

On Halloween night, Didi and I joined a group of parents for dinner as our children went trick-or-treating. I was struck by the glut of toys in the house, which in turn brought back memories of my childhood when the only toys were carriages we fashioned out of cactus leaves and handballs we rolled out of rags. Soon I was recalling days when I was restricted to no more than one onion per meal and the admonition from my parents as we, the children, competed for the contents of the shared dish set before the crowded circle of the family: "*Sawa, sawa! Awadim!*—Share together like good humans!" Suddenly, separated from the rest of the company in Hawaii by a veil of memories, it dawned on me for the first time that I still bear on my body the stigmata of childhood malnourishment. My notoriously big head as a child was nothing but the "frontal bossing" of rickets, and my "barrel chest" and "double maleoli," persistent as part of my physique, confirm the diagnosis beyond doubt. Two very young siblings I lost in early childhood must have suffered from protein-calorie malnutrition, Kwashiorkor, and one of them from severe vitamin A deficiency. At the time, family elders explained their deaths by telling stories about how the evil eye had felled them: one, it was said, had lost his sight overnight after a jealous neighbor admired his beautiful eyes; and the other's health deteriorated so rapidly he died a week after another jealous relative apparently admired his full face and round belly (signs of protein malnourishment mistaken at the time for signs of good health). Sitting there at the dinner table in Hawaii, I now began to wonder if my late mother had prolonged her exclusive breastfeeding of these two sons to avoid more pregnancies in her fifth decade of life. It all fell into place as I absentmindedly refused another serving of pork. The hostess wondered if I was feeling okay, but I was unable to share my thoughts, not even with Didi, for fear of ruining everyone's fun.

"Quote me a price and I will carry the message up the Kaiser Permanente system for you," says the head of my unit as I inform him of my intended departure in half a year. "Each of us has a price; tell me yours." But I change the subject. Nathan, a colleague of mine, comes up with an alternative plan:

"Why don't we two take on the Kahuku clinic? I hear it is on offer by the Kaiser management and it is the next best thing to solo practice in terms of independence. The beach is just great, a combination of wilderness and plush new development. Your ego will be readily massaged by the combination of near total independence as the primary physician and of serving a deprived population of former plantation workers. And it is very safe for raising kids."

Nathan's suggestion resonates well with me.

Apropos of such an attractive option I start picking supporting hints, as if targeted at me by some intelligent supreme manipulator out there. A walk-in patient, a model father figure by his demeanor and kindness, objects to my warning against the possibility of him getting addicted to the Valium he takes.

"It is the principle of it," I explain to him, "I am your physician; I have to warn you."

"I am past forty and hence I am no longer constrained by principles. I am in transit, you could say, and all that matters to me is the tranquility and pleasure of the moment. Take it from me, son!"

I find that wise. The thought registers as another beguiling justification for my possible moral copout. I am forty! Serving my people is no more than a matter of principle, nil and void as per this wise man's attractive dictum.

The moment my wise customer leaves I ask my nurse for a cup of coffee and take a half-hour break. I lock my door and sit down at my desk to counter his magic with another. I write a letter to a man at home I admire and respect who would surely offer a different counsel. In the letter to Dr. Sami Geraisy, aka Abu-Farah to his fellow Nazarenes, I intimate my commitment to return to the Galilee. I follow it with another to a colleague and fellow Ministry of Health employee from the Galilee offering him encouragement to stick around so that soon, when I return, we can join hands in setting an example of commitment and professional dedication for all the prospective young professionals returning to their Arab villages in the Galilee. With this willful emotional exercise I maneuver myself back in line. The falsity of Nathan's glittery option is revealed: No one in Kahuku expects my help. People in Arrabeh invented the myth of my destiny as their healer; their expectations are binding on me forever. Commitment to the deprived in Hawaii would be empty of mutually binding expectations and hence lacking in emotional charge. It would be a breeze, a toil lacking in challenge and meaning. Only in that hell of oppression and inequality that I witnessed again on my trip in August can the mettle of my dedication to humanity be tested.

2
A Second Homecoming

Remains of the Effendi's guest house in al-Zeeb overlooking the Mediterranean. (Photo by Moslih Kanaaneh.)

September 23, 1978

We landed in Haifa on board a Greek ship we took from Athens to the expected harassment and the usual insults. Under the guise of security precautions, I, my wife and two children, aged five and eight, were rudely questioned about every item in our car and luggage, about the daily itinerary of our two-month camping trip in Europe on our way back from Hawaii, about our family history and our future plans,

16

about our views on current and past events in Israel and Palestine, about the price of our children's toys, and about the color of the flowers that the seeds we were bringing with us would produce. We were shifted back and forth between security agents at the port who discussed their findings, compared notes and consulted with more senior officials before releasing us to the mercy of the customs officers and their multiple forms and stamps.

Early in the proceedings we were joined in the extra security line by another traveler with an Arabic-sounding name who had also brought a new car on board. Once his Moroccan Jewish identity was revealed, he was cleared through within half an hour. We, however, were accorded the full attention of the law. The ordeal took us over five hours, with family and friends waiting across the hallway, waving and shouting their hellos every time they caught a glimpse of us. Finally we joined them for a warm and raucous welcome and a lengthy round of hugs and kisses that required the intervention of the ever-vigilant security agents to clear the area of our intolerable loitering.

On the way to Arrabeh, our new VW camper—an improved version of the vehicle we had parted with two years earlier, this one gleaming metallic green with a magical pop-top—got the usual coat of dust and a couple of solid bangs from the potholed road. Rhoda and Ty were disturbed by the dirt and flies and by the barren and rocky terrain. Upon arrival they were temporarily overwhelmed by the attention of so many children their own age, as well as aunts, uncles and neighbors. The calm that enveloped the village at night belied its geopolitical position in the midst of the Middle East conflict. No one spoke of, or seemed disturbed by, the civil war raging in Lebanon only two dozen miles to the north, or by the news that Israel's and Egypt's leaders, Menachem Begin and Anwar Sadat, were at Camp David. Our return and our comfort loomed as the only topics of conversation in our little neighborhood.

The next week I returned to the Ministry of Health. I sat with my former boss and mentor, Dr. Hedy Frank-Blume, who sprang a surprise offer: she wanted me to be her deputy in Nazareth, the seat of the Northern District, serving a racially mixed population of more than 500,000 people, half of them Jews and half Arabs. I suggested that someone in the Ministry's hierarchy would undoubtedly object to my assuming a middle-management position. Then I launched into a frank discussion about racial discrimination. The total denial and assumption of moral superiority by the Jewish majority in Israel regarding the dismal treatment of the Palestinian minority, and the concerted effort at hiding even the existence of such a minority from the eyes of the world, was what I found daunting, I told her.

In conclusion, I reminded her of the lengthy position paper on the health development needs of the Arab minority in Israel that I had submitted to her and, through her, to the Ministry's head office in 1973, and of the paper I submitted to the Health Minister in 1976 after Land Day. I reminded her of her evasive written response: "We need time and modernization to take their natural course before 'we' can impose our interventions." This time, I insisted, my core duties at the Ministry of Health must include exposing inequality and discrimination, and fighting against them. As her deputy, would she permit me to address such sensitive topics or did she intend to keep me under her thumb?

During my speech, Dr. Frank-Blume fidgeted nervously with paperclips, shredded a page from her writing pad into tiny pieces, busied herself at length with cleaning her table, and ordered another round of coffee for the two of us. When I finished, she launched into the standard polemics of liberal Israelis about the special situation of the country and the primacy of security considerations in all state institutions. She admitted she was aware of anti-Arab discrimination permeating the system at all levels and intended to fight it by pushing my candidacy for her own position when she retires in four years. I began to point out that, for my own reasons, that was not something I aspired to when she interrupted to tell me of a recent TV program about Nazi Germany and its treatment of Jews. Knowing her family's history of suffering and extermination at the hands of the Nazis, I fell quiet. A palpable sense of discomfort and inappropriateness descended over the two of us that forced me to shift the discussion instead to practical considerations about the job offer.

A few days later I visited the office of Dr. Shukri Atallah, an Arab colleague who had recently taken a position of responsibility at the ministry. We spoke at length about the pros and cons of assuming such a role in a system that shows clear evidence of enmity and mistrust towards its Arab citizens, so much so that Jewish nurses are encouraged to carry handguns in their handbags along with the usual vials of immunization serum and bottles of vitamins. We pronounced words of support and encouragement for each other and patted ourselves on the back for being leaders in our fields who set an example of daring and self-sacrifice for other Palestinian professionals in Israel.

On Sunday I escaped with the family to the beach at Achziv, just south of the Lebanese border. We found it had been attractively developed into a modern tourist resort with a children's playground, trees offering shade and an expansive grassy knoll topped by an imposing sealed building of local stone in the traditional style of crossed arches. Not far from this was another structure smaller in size but similar in style, except that it was gutted, leaving only the four arched pillars of stone meeting to form its ceiling. The two buildings stood as silent monuments to some mysterious past not explained by the historical note affixed by the Israeli Parks Authority to the cashier's stand at the entrance. Next to these monuments a small sunken area has been cleared and shaped into a mini-amphitheater suitable for parties and dances, with a bandstand to one side of it. A couple of repaired old stone structures had been converted into bathrooms. All across the grassy knoll young lovers were embracing, others playing racket ball, while children frolicked and happy parents roasted lamb and mixed *tabouli* salads to the music blaring from their radios.

To the west, the grassy knoll sloped down to the Mediterranean with a steep stairway constructed out of recycled local building stones. A millstone or two were strategically located on the way as quaint decorations, adding to the idyllic scene. The stairs led to freshwater showers and a protected swimming enclosure that was safe enough for us to allow our children to splash around it unattended. To the left, along the seashore, were the grounds of the exclusive Club Med resort with innumerable bungalows further supplemented by many old-looking stone buildings, some of which were partially damaged and others extended by tarpaulin canopies. To the north was a large enclosure, mainly of rubble and stone, with warning signs of "Private Property," "Entry Prohibited" and "The Independent State of Achzivland."

Amid this confusing scene, as we watched a rapturous sunset from atop the grassy hillock, we listened to an alternative history of the place recounted by a local Arab man not much older than me. Claiming to belong to the place by birthright, he snuck in daily to watch the sunset. We were sitting, he said, in what was once the center of the prosperous Arab fishing village of al-Zeeb before the 1948 *Nakba*, Arabic for catastrophe, when the Palestinians were dispossessed of their homeland under cover of war. The grassy expanse and seaward slope were the main residential neighborhoods of the village, he told us, which were bulldozed clear of rubble. Some of al-Zeeb's homes now housed the Club Med resort for international vacationers, while others had been claimed by a Jewish squatter, Eli Avivi, who had collected a great many household items, especially ceramic jars and stone implements, left by the Palestinian residents who were driven out from the village to Lebanon by the Jewish forces. Mr. Avivi was reputed to have created a beatnik and hippy drug commune attracting stray youth from all corners of the earth. The sealed structure was once the village mosque, and the dance amphitheater its former front yard. The second remaining building on the hill, the gutted structure, had been the guest room of the village head, the Effendi.

As we departed, we noticed a sign next to the mosque: "No Trespassing! Sacred Site!" I reread the informative sign posted by the Parks Authority at the entrance:

> Achziv is an important archeological site dating back to the days of the Phoenicians, with significant remains from the eras of the First and the Second Temples and from the days of the Crusaders. The Israeli Antiquities Authority has recently excavated the site and maintains it for your enjoyment; so, please keep it clean and refrain from damaging its archeological treasures.

Some thirteen centuries of Arab presence in al-Zeeb, now Achziv, was apparently of no historical significance to the Parks Authority. Those Arabs must have been very good people, for they came and lived here for more than a millennium and then in 1948 quietly packed up and left peacefully, without soiling it or ruining its valuable archeological remains. They did not add a thing or detract from the sanctity and value of this historic gem. But how to explain that sealed structure, the mosque, on top of the hill?

As we drove back in the company of a young Jewish colleague, his American wife, and their two unruly children with whom we had enjoyed our outing to Achziv, we wondered about our own sanity. How were we to maintain it in the face of this hurricane of contradictions and negation raging around our very existence here? The other family suggested extending the neighborly get-together by visiting our home. The doctor and his family are part of a Jewish communal settlement near Arrabeh that was established recently by a group of nature enthusiasts who subscribe to vegetarianism and living in the bosom of nature. These settlements, of which there are many springing up across the Galilee, are exclusively for Jews and have been built on land confiscated from local Arab villages. In the state's view, their purpose is to "Judaize"—make more Jewish—areas of Israel like the Galilee where there is a large Arab population.

I first got to know the young man some years ago, when he came to my clinic for a physical examination as part of the requirements for admission to medical school. As usual, I did not charge for the service, considering it the first gesture of collegiality to a future fellow physician. Sure enough he was now a full-fledged MD, a competent and devoted family physician in training. He was currently tending to the medical needs of the residents of all these little settlement outposts designed to Judaize the Galilee.

The doctor had expressed disapproval of the dishonest ways, such as at al-Zeeb, in which government agencies were skirting around the truth about Palestinian history. But once in our home, he switched topics. Prefacing his comments with reassurances about his professional commitment and natural idealism, he explained his reason for wanting to visit us:

"I know now that much of the land for the settlements [inside Israel] was taken illegally [from Arab communities] and I know about your legitimate complaints that led to Land Day. At that time we were misinformed; officials of the state and the Jewish Agency simply lied to us. I am dismayed by the amount of false information still accepted by much of the Jewish public as the truth. Your land has been stolen from you by force, lies and treachery."

But he had more to tell us:

"That said, as a Zionist, I consider it my duty to contribute to the success and progress of the settlements that have been already established. I suppose you can explain that by my commitment to the Zionist ideal of 'redeeming the land' and by my upbringing and training in the Zionist youth movement. I respect Zionism and I subscribe to the principle of Judaizing the Galilee. I start with the facts on the ground. I accept what already exists as a reality and proceed with my duties from there. I am here to serve that higher purpose. I personally did not prostitute my integrity. I did not do something wrong or illegal. I did not lie to you or spread false information. But if someone else does it, I am in no position to reverse that. My field is health care and that is what I stick to."

He added that he was genuinely interested in fostering coexistence and friendship with the Galilee's Arabs, his neighbors, including me and my family. After all, we now shared the same space and would just have to learn to live with each other.

The readiness to appropriate the moral high ground while encroaching on other people's space and rights, when practiced by an entire system, is an old colonial tactic. In Israel, when practiced by individuals, especially the young, with the appropriate degree of aggressiveness, it is considered the height of cleverness. It is encouraged socially and appreciated to such a degree that it is exported internationally—under the brand name of "*chutzpah*"—as a magical ingredient in the Israeli ethos. But I felt insulted and dehumanized hearing these sentiments from someone who counted himself a friend and owed me a favor. I told him sarcastically that it was nice of him to consider putting up with the natives, but having taken that gracious decision he should realize that I was unlikely to commit wholeheartedly to his lofty Zionist ideals. I showed him the door, sure he would never enter my home again.

Lying in bed at night, Didi and I wondered if we were bound by our duty towards world peace and our humanitarian ethics to love these neighbors. And again, if so, how should we maintain our grip on sanity? We wondered if our children would grow to love or even to tolerate their children, or theirs ours.

At my private evening clinic there has been no end of impetigo cases and the usual complications. Just last night I hospitalized two children with life-threatening acute glomerulonephritis, a kidney affliction secondary to the curse of impetigo. In addition there is the never-ending scourge of summer diarrhea among children, with the occasional deadly complication of dehydration and the frequent accompaniment of serious malnutrition. This together with rheumatic fever are very much routine. But there have been surprises too. An outbreak of typhoid fever is peaking, I hope, in one extended family in the village. I have hospitalized nine children with it in the past week, three of them after they had been mistakenly diagnosed as strep throat and treated with daily penicillin injections.

God forbid anyone thinks I made such an elementary medical mistake. I was simply picking up the pieces left by a local pediatrician, a recent Russian immigrant working for the clinic run by the General Sick Fund, Kupat Holim Klalit. Whenever I try to sweet-talk her or her equally incompetent compatriot, the GP working alongside her, into developing a reasonable working relationship, they give me hell for sticking my nose into their business. When I approached her for help in reviewing the records of the typhoid cases she had seen, she was very condescending, as I expected. I had to beg her forgiveness before she would agree to show me the standard one-line entries in the children's records. Given her uncooperative response, I simply bypassed her and talked to a local nurse who was able to give me the information I needed to track down the cluster of cases. It is enough to persuade me of the rumors that all these Russian immigrants forge their professional documents on the way over to Israel.[*] Not only are my two Russian colleagues totally uninformed about the community in which they work, they also lack the skills to communicate to their patients directly. Neither speaks Arabic and both reside in the city, showing up at their clinic as total outsiders. Their main interest and first concern is to get patients in and enter their name on the ledger to swell the daily performance statistics that form the basis of their monthly bonus payments. It seems clear that Arrabeh and similar end-of-the-line localities serve as the dumping ground for rejects from the medical centers in the city.

That is why for me it is back to the salt mines. The fourth patient to interrupt my sleep tonight has just left my treatment room at home. Her husband carried her in, both hyperventilating, asking for

[*] *Russian immigrants:* More recently, especially in the 1990s, over a million former Soviet Union citizens, mostly with higher education, utilized Israel's Law of Return to immigrate to Israel, including many whose Jewishness is questionable. While their recruitment was justified on the basis of demographic demagoguery, their impact on Israeli society has raised some questions.

a "piece of paper" so that he could take her to hospital. But I managed to "cure" this trusting relative of mine on the spot. The hospital emergency departments won't see anyone without a referral from a doctor, a formality that helps to make life so much more miserable for community physicians. Three years ago I sent a young man from Arrabeh with hypertension and an impending stroke to the hospital, about 25 miles away. Somehow on the way he inadvertently lost his referral letter that I had given him. Without an ambulance service in the area, and given the limited and indirect public transport routes from Arrabeh to Naharya, it took him five hours from the time I saw him to the time he reached the hospital. In the meantime he had developed a full-blown stroke. He had to wait in the emergency room for three more hours. And finally when it was his turn, he was refused medical attention because he did not have a referral letter. The receptionist sent him back to get "a piece of paper." He had no one with him, and so was there alone, with a right-sided stroke and now very indistinct speech. Finally, a taxi driver, who was dropping off a patient, saw him slumped there and decided that this man needed urgent attention. He tried to intervene on the man's behalf but, without a referral letter and with his limited medical credentials as a taxi driver, he failed to persuade anyone. He brought him all the way back to Arrabeh to get another letter, and then returned with him to the hospital. The young man was admitted and stayed for several weeks. To this day, Salih al-Hajj is a hemiplegic who hobbles around the village with a cane, a living reminder to me of the shortcomings and callousness of the bureaucracy of which I am a part, especially when dealing with Arab patients.

October 12, 1978

At five o'clock this morning, as I opened my eyes, Didi told me that yesterday Ty's kindergarten teacher had slapped his wrist and pulled his ear. She is also concerned about the physical condition of Ty's classroom. It is a small basement in a neighbor's house with chairs and a blackboard; it has no playground and no other saving grace to qualify it as a classroom, much less as a kindergarten. Apparently, the only way you can handle forty kids single-handedly in such a small space is by regimentation, shouting, slapping wrists and pulling ears. Not much can be done in the short run.

And yet, the village life of Arrabeh is what we left Hawaii and the US for. I have to admit that I find Ty's behavior much nicer, more to my liking, than when he was in Hawaii. He is less rambunctious and unruly than before. When I play rough with him, I find him less ready to scratch and bite.

Just last night I saw one of our most influential school teachers. He brought his ten-year-old daughter because she started wetting her bed and has developed a nervous tick. When under pressure she blinks constantly and squeezes her eyes in a disfiguring manner. After talking briefly to the father and to the girl herself, it became obvious that these problems were a response to her home situation, where she gets constantly punished, shouted at and shamed for the slightest mistake, let alone her bed-wetting and blinking. With over a dozen other sick children in the waiting room I did not have the time, and presume I never will have the time, to dig deeper into the family's situation. Apparently the mother is a very domineering woman and the girl, the youngest of eight siblings, comes under much pressure. Knowing full well that it will not make much difference, I told the father that it was normal for a shy child to blink her eyes, and that probably it is a transient symptom. They should try to simply forget about it, and then she probably will too. Obediently, he said he would see to it that all of my recommendations were carried through.

It leaves me wondering what kind of understanding Ty's teachers have of child rearing and of educational methodologies. It is an open secret that the promotion of teachers is dependent on their service as collaborators with the domestic security service, the Shin Bet, and not on any consideration of competence. A few years back, a group of eighth-grade girls complained about a teacher sexually molesting them. That and his bad name as a Shin Bet agent—he was so reliable, he was even allowed to carry a gun—aroused much public consternation. Parents of the girls kept their daughters home for several weeks. In the end, however, they had no choice but to accept his continued presence at the school because government officials at all levels offered him their firm support and inundated the village with yet more agents. The one person in Arrabeh who kept his two daughters home for the rest of the school year, being forced to wait that time and go to court before he could enroll them in another school, was my brother Ahmad. He is a model of old-style village honor if I know one.

The other day I visited a Bedouin family in nearby Wadi al-Hamam with my nephew Khalid to check on his prospective bride. Khalid has known the girl, Rudaina, a nursing student at the French hospital in Nazareth, for a year and wants her for his wife. She wants him too. But an issue of at least equal importance is what both sets of parents think. Khalid says her family supports the idea. His family certainly does not. The girl has two counts against her: she is dark and she is Bedouin. My sister-in-law has some very basic qualifications she requires from any daughter-in-law: she must be white and plump, and preferably tall with green or blue eyes. Apparently nobody fitting that description wants to come to live in Arrabeh, and such characteristics are rare among the village's home-grown stock—except for one albino family, but they seem to have run out of daughters on the strength of their skin color alone.

Khalid announced before we left that he would not accept anybody but his dark-skinned Bedouin love, and it was decided that his wish should be respected. I had been to Wadi al-Hamam once before, when I finished my high school studies and matriculated. I was dispatched as a rookie teacher to the refugee Bedouin community in the hope of opening a new elementary school there for their children. The school supervisor instructed me to convey his regards to the village chief, the *mukhtar*, none other than Rudaina's grandfather, and to ask for his assistance in the matter, as had apparently already been agreed. With no public transport to the village, I joined a gang of stone cutters from Arrabeh who work at the quarry in Wadi al-Hamam. In deference to my status as a teacher, they insisted on my taking the passenger seat of the truck, while they, all my seniors, sat in the back. We arrived at dawn. I hung around the quarry till after sunrise and then walked up the valley to the mukhtar's tin shack.*

---

* *Unrecognized villages:* Some 120 Arab rural localities in Israel, often Bedouin, retroactively rendered illegal by the 1965 Planning and Construction Law. Tens of thousands of homes, mostly Arab, outside the areas delimited in this law by a "blue line" are targeted for demolition and prevented from connection to water, electricity and telephone networks, not to mention any public services. Their land is coveted by

As I knocked at the corrugated iron sheet that served as the door to the single-room residence, the whole structure reverberated and a sleepy man emerged still tying his tunic around his waist. I delivered the good news about my teaching assignment. He politely invited me to sit on a small chair by the door while he prepared a fresh pot of delicious black coffee. I sat through a lengthy hour as he built the fire, roasted the coffee beans, rhythmically ground them, then ground the cardamom seeds, boiled the coffee and meticulously mixed and decanted the liquid down four different steps, each time adding just so much of the different grades of fermenting liquid from previous batches to the fresh pot, and concentrated it over the slow fire. This was the very same painstaking routine I had watched my father go through a thousand times without ever figuring out what made his coffee have that delicious bitter flavor.

By this time the rest of the family had woken, and the two of us were presented with a delicious breakfast of freshly baked bread, honey, goat yogurt cheese in olive oil, and black olives. Finally he proceeded to formulate his response to my mission. He was brief and to the point: "Please convey my respects to the good school supervisor and tell him that the folks of Wadi al-Hamam have changed their mind. We can't find rooms to live in. Where would we find rooms for a school?" With that I went back to the quarry and whiled my time watching the stone cutters do their back-breaking work till sundown and rode back with them to the village, this time in the back of the truck.

Our visit to the bride-to-be was a surprise. As soon as we arrived, two male family relatives, neighbors, came in and offered us coffee and the usual hospitality of fruits, nuts and seeds. A thousand children gathered around the car outside, so we asked an older boy to guard it for us. The first matter our hosts raised was the housing situation of their community. In very apologetic terms, they explained that they still lived in corrugated iron shacks because the government would not allow them to construct more permanent housing. In truth, I felt quite at home. Other than the building material itself, their housing conditions, the furniture and household amenities, as well as the overall

---

the state for settling Jews. Exceptional cases of such villages that have managed to gain formal legal recognition after a long and ardent struggle still lack most such amenities thanks to bureaucratic inertia and racist low- and middle-level bureaucrats.

socio-economic situation, resembled very much what I remember my
family's being as a child. Which is as limited as you can imagine, with
very few things to sit on. The house comprises two rooms, a guest room
and another for the entire family of I don't know how many members.
There are a few dishes, pots and pans, all stored in one cabinet inside
the guest room that obviously doubles as a bedroom. Every time the
women needed an item, they would send a boy who whispered to the
uncle, who reached over our heads to open the cabinet and get out
first the matches, then the tray, then the coffee cups, then the spoon,
and so on.

I could not help the feeling that this is poverty at its worst and that
this will be a factor on everybody's mind in arranging the marriage. As
if to balance the account, our hosts informed us that they came from
a big tribe and that before they lost all their property in the Nakba of
1948, they had lived in a well-to-do village in the Hula valley close
to the border with Lebanon. A good part of their family was forced
out into Lebanon during the war and still live there as refugees. They
added that in the "recent troubles"—the civil war in Lebanon—they
had lost sixty men from the family. Despite thirty years of separation,
they still count as "our men" people whom, for the most part, they
have never seen.

The wedding season is peaking in Arrabeh. With the exception of the
winter months, there is more than one wedding a day. I had heard that
the family of the two most recent cases of typhoid fever are having an
engagement party for their son. So, today, I went to see if I could go
into the home and give the family, especially the mother, some basic
instructions on personal and household hygiene; how to wash hands
with soap and water before handling the food for the family and the
guests; how to disinfect the bathroom area; and how to get used to
overusing water, plenty of water, "wasting water" if possible in the
kitchen and bathroom. That was the plan. Then my whole scheme had
to be scrapped. No one was there to listen to my sermon on hygienic
practices except a little girl; all the others had gone to visit their sick
children in hospital. The sweet girl explained to me that there was
no running water in the house. The only water pipe they have—for

drinking, cooking, washing, for everything—is outside in the yard, right by the enclosure used by the family to relieve themselves.

As I left the house, a neighbor, Mahmud al-Helu invited me into his home for the customary cup of coffee. He started telling me about his son, who departed three weeks ago to the United States to attend college somewhere in Oklahoma. Neither he nor his wife-cum-first-cousin know anything about the town, or the exact location or name of the college. Their son apparently is a serious, persistent, and ambitious young man, but at the same time very docile—a strange combination of traits. The parents say that before he obtained his student visa to the US, he had gone to the American Embassy in Tel Aviv 34 times. On each occasion he was rejected; either a form was missing or had expired or some official was not there.

The father finally used *wasta*, a go-between who had influence with the American Embassy. It was a police officer the family knew. Most likely, he had nothing to do with anything, but to placate or impress the family, gain favor, or for some form of payment, he told the father: "Yes, I'll do it for you." By whatever coincidence, the son was accepted to a college in Oklahoma and received his visa. He did not receive a scholarship, however. The family is paying the college and living expenses out of their meager income. The father says all of the income from his watermelon crop this year covered the expenses of the trip, with $2,000 left over for his son. He was hoping that that would be enough for the first school year. I doubt it will be. But I tried to sound encouraging. He said soon he would be through collecting the olive crop, and would then exchange the money from the olives and their oil into dollars and send it on. The son has already called the village council, the one telephone line in the village, to say he has arrived safely and is staying at a hotel next to the college while waiting for the dorm to open.

During the discussion, the mother asked repeatedly about the weather in Oklahoma and how cold it would be sleeping outdoors. At first I did not catch on. But then the father, full of pride, started relating to me the story of how his son attended the University of Tel Aviv for a year while waiting to be accepted in the United States, and what a hardy and determined boy he was. Once he made a decision nothing could deter him, he said. While in Tel Aviv, he had spent much of the year sleeping on the grass on campus. The reason, according to the father,

was that he was evicted from his room at the beginning of term. Within
24 hours, the police had arrested him, holding him for two days, after
a neighbor complained. It happened to be a religious Orthodox Jew
who did not like having a young Muslim living there. With a name
like Mohammad on the contract, his identity could not be concealed.
Although the boy had a signed rental agreement, the police tore up the
contract, gave him back part of the money he had already paid and told
him not to come back. From that point on, he slept in a grassy nook
on campus until one of his professors, an Ashkenazi woman, saw him
there one evening and intervened on his behalf.

The father related these details to me in a deliberate manner, his
voice booming with pride at his son's determination in the face of
adversity. He seemed to take it for granted that it was right for the
police to behave in the manner they did. He intimated no objection,
no sense of bitterness, no hint of resentment, not even any expression
of indignation. All he wanted to convey was that his son took it all in
his stride, that he stood tall throughout. The mother, however, cursed
twice as her husband was telling the story.

She also wanted reassurance about her son's chances of making it in
America. As the local expert on living in a foreign land, I was expected
to respond. I have a standard sermon I deliver on such occasions. Any
young man, fresh from high school in an Arab village, who winds up
being a laborer in a Jewish city, as most of our young men do, and
who can survive that, emotionally and physically, to come out of it
unscathed and in one piece, maintaining his sanity, is capable of survival
just about anywhere in the world, including at the South Pole and
the darkest jungles of Africa. That's what I recall telling a couple of
nephews and their parents as they weighed the possibility of striking
out to study abroad. And I tried to say the same to the parents of this
boy. If he had survived Tel Aviv under such conditions, he could survive
in the United States.

The father's final comment, said in mock accusation as I got up to
leave, was: "Well, you opened the door for everybody. You were the
first one to strike out. You started it!"

3
Legends of the Diwan

Abu-Faisal, my cousin and nominal head of the Kanaaneh clan, at al-Zawieh with two guests, 1950. Note the prayer niche in which he sits and the coffee set on his left.

October 12, 1978

Today I visited my old cousin, Abu-Faisal, who is the nominal head of the Kanaaneh clan though he has little actual influence these days. Every morning he still prepares a new pot of black Arabic coffee and sits in the clan's traditional guesthouse or *diwan*, al-Zawieh, handed down since my grandfather established it. He shares his coffee with his daily circle of visitors, his elderly friends, and with the occasional passer-

31

by: a door-to-door salesman or a Bedouin visitor. They sit, sip coffee, smoke, stare into empty space, and exchange grunts. Occasionally they talk about the affairs of the village at their own outdated level of understanding of it and reminisce about the good old days. When they are really bored, they play *manqala*, the popular local board game.

Occasionally I drop in at this old-style nook on my way to work. Every time I do, someone seeks my medical advice on behalf of the group, either half-jokingly about their diminishing sexual potency or, more seriously, about common ailments such as headaches, hemorrhoids, low back pain and insomnia.

Can you believe it, but the Shin Bet once tried to get me to inform on this group. Shortly after I assumed responsibility for the Acre sub-district in the Ministry of Health, I received a formal letter congratulating me on my new position and inviting me to meet with the representative of the Prime Minister's office in Haifa. Only after I arrived and entered the bare-walled room furnished only with a small coffee table and two chairs did I realize what kind of "representative" the young man receiving me was. Among other things, he wanted to know how I would react if people in a traditional *diwan* in Arrabeh were to criticize the government of Israel. I insisted that we talk about health only. He pointed out that "the health of the state" should concern me as well. I called his trump by asking him not to light his cigarette while I was in the room. He promptly ended the "interrogation."

The old regulars at al-Zawieh are not unaware that such "spying" goes on. A story is told about Abu-el-Kamel, a traditional man of the old religious school who holds precariously on to his teaching job, having never qualified in accordance with the "modern" requirements of the Department of Arab Education. One Friday morning he was the center of attention at al-Zawieh, telling for the umpteenth time the local equivalent of the born-again Christian prophecy of the return of the Messiah. Traditional learned Muslims know the epic prophecy as al-Jafr, a text that few are reputed to have read. It predicts the rise to power of the Jews at the end of time under the leadership of the One-Eyed Imposter, assumed by most of these old-timers to be none other than Moshe Dayan. He and his followers will conquer the Muslim armies and enter Damascus. Then, and this is as far as Abu-el-Kamel got with his story, the Mahdi, the Islamic version of the reincarnated Messiah, will lead the Muslims to a glorious victory over the armies of the One-Eyed Imposter and finish them off. But as Abu-el-Kamel reached the climax of his narrative, a young man, assumed by all to be an informer, entered the *diwan* and greeted those assembled. He sipped the black coffee he was offered and returned the polite individual "*Marhaba*" greetings from each of those present. Then everyone turned their attention back to Abu-el-Kamel for the punch-line of the al-Jafr prophecy. But he froze in mid-sentence. He did not dare relate the dire prediction against the Jewish armies in the presence of the presumed informer. His job was on the line. When the company urged him to finish his story, he replied: "I took them all the way to Damascus. Go ahead and get them back if you dare!"

Days were when al-Zawieh was a lively place, the very focus of rural life. I recall it as a crowded gathering place in the cool summer evenings of 1948. It had the only radio set in the village, one brought by the family of my aunt Samiyeh Rustom, refugees from another village on their way to safety in Lebanon. Men of the village, young and old, would gather around, the elders seated and the younger and less landed crowding at the door to hear the evening news. "Radio Rustom does not lie!" we would say to convince ourselves that the impossible, the surrender of so many Palestinian cities to the Jews, was actually happening.

With the establishment of Israel, almost overnight, al-Zawieh lost its purpose and its chief occupant much of his authority. The loss of so much land through confiscation by the new state—and the resulting shift away from subsistence farming to casual labor—pulled the rug from under the entire land-based social structure that had given credibility to al-Zawieh and its influential chiefs. Suddenly landless laborers had cash in their pockets, more of it than their former masters, and did not need their favors. Any youngster could go to the city and work in construction; when he came home, he was not ready to take orders from his elders. These sudden changes played havoc with the social order of the village.

Al-Zawieh was first established by my grandfather, Ahmad al-Mustafa, a man whose name inspired respect and awe throughout the Galilee, if not Greater Syria—or so his ten children and dozens of senior grandchildren who knew him would have us believe. As a young man, he left the village and took on the responsibility of guarding the Banat Yaa'qoub Bridge, then the main route across the Jordan River between Palestine and the Golan Heights. He was in charge of collecting the transit fees on behalf of the Turkish Sultan from all those crossing the bridge in either direction. No one knows exactly by what luck he landed such a significant job, except that by doing so he single-handedly replaced a whole division of armed Turkish soldiers. He was reputed to be a marvelous and fearless swordsman, so much so that he came to be known to his contemporaries and descendants by the name of his rough hewn sword, *Abu-Shelfi*. His trusty horse cried tears of blood upon his death and refused food from anyone else, dying shortly after him.

At the end of his heroic seven-year assignment, Abu-Shelfi rode into Arrabeh with his double saddle full of gold coins. His first act was to build the *diwan* for the Kanaaneh clan. It functioned, and still functions in a diminished way today, as the center of communal life, the place at which all collective clan business is conducted. Government officials are received there, as are well-wishers on happy occasions and those paying their respects upon the death of any Kanaaneh clan member. Any traveler who arrived in the village after nightfall was welcomed into al-Zawieh and provided with food and shelter for the night. Guests of any member of the clan were accommodated at al-Zawieh, no questions asked, at least for the traditional three days of formal guest receiving. Every morning fresh coffee would be brewed and all the men folk of the clan would gather to consult and receive their respective tasks from my grandfather, a he-man if ever there was one in these parts of the Ottoman Empire.

One morning, it is told, an unfortunate pregnant woman happened to pass by on her way to the fields as Abu-Shelfi was making coffee in al-Zawieh and heard him clear his throat. The thunderous boom caused her to abort on the spot. On another occasion, the same act of him clearing his throat before passing sentence on a group of criminals from south Lebanon caught in the act of stealing cattle from Arrabeh caused them all, without exception, to wet their pants. That's how ferocious my grandfather was.

A while before Abu-Shelfi returned from his seven-year guard duty, eight beautiful girls arrived in Arrabeh with their devout Sufi father, driven out of the Arabian Peninsula by the new Wahabi rulers. The father, Idrees al-Najdi, died shortly thereafter and was buried not far from the Kanaaneh cemetery. The girls, all fair-skinned and green-eyed thanks to their distant European roots, were the responsibility of a rival Arrabeh clan, the Yasins, after the head married the oldest among them. He had his own *diwan*, al-Qabu, still maintained by his descendants to this day. Idrees al-Najdi must have been held in high regard by his new hosts in Arrabeh for they accorded him the high honor of burial in a specially constructed mausoleum right next to the revered village holy site we knew only as *Qabr-es-Saddeeq*—the holy man's grave—till the Israeli Ministry of Religious Affairs built a wall around it and prohibited the village folks from entering its vicinity. It turns out that es-Saddeeq was a Jewish rabbi, Hanan Ben-Dosa. It is ironic that after this attempt at protecting its sanctity it has lost all significance to village people. Times were when every family crisis—a sick child, an absent son, a barren wife, or a failed crop—would rate a visit to *Qabr-es-Saddeeq* to dress the grave with green silk cloth or to light an olive oil lamp. Those limited of means or asking small favors would just give the site a good sweeping and sprinkle it with rose water. Now, under lock and key, it is totally abandoned except for the occasional religious Jew arriving on the holy Shabbat or on high holidays. For me, the site is doubly significant, or triply so since my father and mother are both buried on the same hillside as well.

After his return, Abu-Shelfi sent a messenger to the Yasin clan asking for the hand in marriage of Haji, the most beautiful of the daughters. The head of the rival clan demanded what he thought would be a prohibitive bride price, upon which a bag of gold, more than the asking price, was promptly delivered and the marriage contract sealed. That was his first wife, my grandmother, "*Sitti* Haji," whom I know only through tales of wonder and grace. Later on, he married two more wives: one with the excuse of needing a helper around the house, as the work animals and farm hands had become too much of a chore for one wife to handle; and the second, a beautiful young cousin, very late in his life, to sweeten the days of his waning health.

Upon his death, shortly before the end of Turkish rule in Palestine, his extensive land holdings were divided between his six sons with an equal share held in perpetuity for the maintenance of the guesthouse. His daughters received nothing. Although, under Islamic law, women are entitled to inherit a half-share of what the men receive, traditionally, and even to this day, daughters do not inherit in the Galilee. Their inheritance right is never exercised. And, in fact, most women are not even aware of their entitlement. The idea, presumably, is that it should work out equitably, as a woman's husband does not have to worry about the loss of part of his inheritance to his sisters. Still, it reflects a continuing patriarchy which often has severe negative repercussions for women, especially for single women. When a woman is "not marriageable," she is supposed to be cared for by her brothers. That means in practice that she usually ends up being a servant to them, their go-for.

My uncle Salih inherited two generous shares—his own and that assigned for the guesthouse—and became the boss of the Kanaaneh clan and an influential figure in the wider Galilee. He was reputed to be a wise and courageous man, adept at solving conflicts between the villagers. He acquired sufficient influence and the necessary number of clansmen to make his decisions enforceable and to offer protection to anyone who was in trouble. He was sought out from far and wide by anyone who had committed a serious crime, say a murder, theft, or transgression against a woman's honor. The name of Salih al-Ahmad would be enough to afford such a refuge-seeker protection while my uncle arranged for the traditional truce period needed for peace-making. This was in the days when government did not function properly and the arm of the law did not reach far into the rural countryside. Villagers from around the area would pay their debts in gifts of parcels of land and by swearing allegiance to the man. Or, perhaps, he would grab the land, and the owner would feel so indebted and intimidated that he would not dare to refuse the arrangement.

Despite being functionally illiterate and a villager, Uncle Salih apparently was a dapper and clever man, an intrepid social climber who moved in the circles of the *effendis*—notables—of Acre; he befriended several influential figures, including Shoghi Effendi, the Guardian of the Bahai Faith; the nationalist Bishop Hajjar; the head of the Sufi sect in these parts, Sheikh al-Shathli; and a young lawyer and rising star, Ahmad Shukairy, who later became the founder of the PLO. Early on, Uncle Salih took a second wife whom he kept in Acre, a citified cousin and the widow of a high-ranking Turkish officer and hence experienced and graceful enough to measure up to hosting such dignitaries.

Herbert Samuel, the first British High Commissioner of Palestine, once visited my uncle at al-Zawieh to announce the reduction of taxes from 12 to 10 percent of the farmers' annual crops, thus further increasing my uncle's recognition and influence throughout Palestine. In 1936, during the Palestinian uprising against the British Mandate and the Balfour Declaration,* Uncle Salih befriended the revolutionary firebrand Ezzidin al-Qassam. Nonetheless, he continued to deal with the Mandatory authorities, presumably acting as a double agent in the rural hinterland of the revolt.

I remember Uncle Salih as a tall man, very fair-skinned with blue eyes, which made him resemble the master race, the British. That, very likely, was not far from the truth, considering all the miscegenation, rape, and fence jumping that must have taken place in these parts during the Crusades. Towards the end of his life, shortly before the establishment of Israel, he rated an occasional visit from an Armenian physician from the city, Dr. Ardikian, who would bring with him a new magic injection called insulin. His grandson and the current heir-apparent of al-Zawieh has severe diabetes mellitus, requiring multiple daily insulin injections. He seems proud of it; even his grandfather's diabetes is worthy of emulation. The young man conducts himself with aplomb, speaks and walks in a manner implying awareness of his social rank and expected special role, a rank and a status that exist only in old people's memory. Even when seeking help at my clinic he takes umbrage at having to wait his turn and tries to pull rank over others. I am not above giving him the occasional pleasure of some special attention, for his psychological benefit and for keeping the peace in my waiting room.

Today, on my visit to al-Zawieh, I met my cousin Salim, one of the founders of the Communist party in Arrabeh and the first young man in the village to dare to walk in its streets without the traditional headgear. The majority of Communists in the village are simply political activists rather than ideologues. Among the Palestinian minority, it is impossible to speak out politically except through the Communist party, which has Jewish activists too. But even if outspoken villagers like Salim are not formally Communists, they are labeled as such by the authorities,

---

* *The Balfour Declaration:* A 1917 formal letter issued on behalf of the British government to the London Zionist leader, Lord Rothschild, by its foreign minister committing it to supporting the establishment of a Jewish homeland in Palestine. The country's native Palestinian community was mentioned only incidentally.

who want them pushed to the margins. Toufiq, my closest village friend, started out in carpentry as a furniture maker. For a couple of years, during the period when I was a teacher in a neighboring village, he worked in a workshop with cousin Salim, who was constantly under surveillance by the Shin Bet and the military government and spent much of his time in jail for his political opinions. In fact, Salim had learned carpentry during one of his extended jail terms. It was considered so dangerous to associate with Salim that some of Toufiq's friends abandoned him because they feared he was tainted just by sharing the same physical space. I was not that cautious but certainly I had no desire to be tainted with Communism as I stood at the threshold of applying for a student visa to America. I kept my distance from the party members, adopting the policy, as the saying goes, of *"Ibi'id a'n al-sharr aw-ghaneelu*—Cheer for evil from a distance."

On one major aspect of our community's development, the Communists deserve sole credit. The Soviet Union extends benefits to the Israeli Communist party in the form of scholarships for loyal youths selected by the party, usually children of its well-established local members. The first such cadre of physicians, engineers and lawyers—who have studied in Soviet states—are back and active in our towns and villages, both in their professions and in politics. They are fast becoming the main source of our up-and-coming intelligentsia. In the absence of accessible places of higher education for our youth in Israel, the party is attracting many who otherwise would never make it to college. Enrollment in Israeli universities is nearly impossible for most Arab citizens; witness my own experience: good enough material to win a scholarship at Harvard but not to enter the Hebrew University. Universities in neighboring Arab countries are totally out of reach, of course, because of our Israeli citizenship.

4
Present Absentees

Abu-A'atif, a present absentee,
on Keren Kayemit guard duty.

February 18, 1979

One of my cousins, Afif, is building our home for us. Relatives and
passers-by keep offering their unsolicited advice on the construction
of my house: "Oh no, but the Jews do it differently," or "I worked on
a house in Tel Aviv and it has a much nicer style." Many are builders

themselves: one has done the roof on the home of a Jewish doctor
in Herzliya, or planted the garden of a Jewish multi-millionaire in
Raa'nana, or plastered the penthouse of a Jewish contractor in Savion.
All tell me it is a great shame that I am doing my house or garden in
the way I have chosen and not like those Jewish big shots. But I want
my house to be part of Arrabeh, not look like it should be in Herzliya
or Savion.

After inspecting the finished part I point out some of the defects to
my cousin, the master builder.

"What do you expect?" he tells me half joking. "It is *avodat
aravim*."

He is alluding, of course, to the widely held view in the Jewish
community that Arabs are capable only of menial work—and shoddy
work at that. The racist Hebrew expression literally means "Arab
handiwork." The assumption that Arab labor is worthless and
intrinsically defective very much accords with the Israeli Jewish view
of the country's Palestinian community. Needless to say, I reject such
racism. The first time I heard the expression it infuriated me. I and some
twenty male high-school friends were spending the summer working
at Kibbutz Mishmar Haemeq. In exchange for eight hours of daily
labor in the fields, we got free room and board in the exotic communal
atmosphere and the chance to feast our eyes on teenage girls in shorts
and skimpy open blouses. The project was marketed by the socialist
Zionist Mapam party as an exercise in brotherhood and coexistence
between Arabs and Jews. Even then the scheme reeked of manipulation
and fake humanitarianism, but it beat spending another boring summer
in Arrabeh. At the time, when I overheard a kibbutz member refer to
our work with the derogatory term *avodat aravim*, I made enough of
a fuss that he had to formally apologize to me in the presence of my
friends. Nowadays such insults are common, and Arab workers are
likely to lose their job if they open their mouth in protest. Most of my
fellow villagers learn to expect such abuse, and worse; they deal with
it by adopting it as part of their own language, incorporating it in the
jokes they crack with their Jewish bosses and by giving it expression
in concrete and stone. It is a sign not only of our village mentality but
also that we have accepted and internalized a sense of inferiority as
Arabs in the Jewish state: we are unwelcome, disenfranchised, and
unworthy even in our own eyes.

"If you want a perfect house, go ahead and buy one in a Jewish city," my cousin Afif tells me. He knows I don't qualify. There have been several cases of Arabs trying to buy a house in a new development area such as Upper Nazareth, a Jewish city built on land next to, and confiscated from, Arab Nazareth, provoking strong objections from prospective neighbors.* "Try your luck. You are a doctor. Maybe they will accept you."

Then, bitterly, he launches into a monologue about the troubles of the Arab worker:

"Construction workers like us build all the new housing in the cities and settlements. Without us the Jews wouldn't be able to put one stone on top of another, or build a concrete wall one inch high. They don't want to do the hard part, and they don't know how to do it either. If we were to leave them alone, they would still be living in tents in their immigrant absorption centers. All they are good for is drawing maps and bossing us around. And as soon as the sun sets, you have to clear off the site. Once we Arab workers finish those high-rises and fancy new neighborhoods, we are not allowed to take shelter in them even for one night, much less dream of living in any of them. And the big contractors and their inspectors are so finicky! The slightest uneven surface and you get docked twice the cost from your pay. And we get shouted at and derided for doing 'avodat aravim.' They don't know what they are talking about. As long as it looks nice on the outside, you can do whatever you want with the foundations and the parts they can't see. *Allah jaa'ilha tihdim a'ala rus-hin inshallah!*—May God bring it tumbling down on their heads—Goddamned dogs! They have reserved everything for themselves: interest-free loans, scholarships for their children to study, well-paying jobs in government offices, and social security payments every time they sneeze. And their monthly child support payments are twice as much as we get.† If you haven't

---

* *Land confiscation:* Over the years since its establishment Israel has promulgated and enforced some three dozen different laws designed to deprive its Palestinian citizens of their land. Today these citizens make up close to one fifth of the total population of Israel but own less than 4 percent of its land area, down from close to 25 percent in 1948.

† *Welfare payments:* At various times Israel has adopted different pro-natalist policies including, for example, National Insurance Institute child support payments for a fifth child that reach five times that for the first. To deter Arabs from taking advantage of such policies, full child support payments were linked to service in the armed forces.

served in the army or you are not an immigrant, you don't qualify for anything. You, Hatim, are educated and have a diploma half the size of this wall, I am told. And you work with the Jews in a nice office. Tell me, how can an Arab get anything in this country? Can you get anything like they do?"

February 25, 1979

Yesterday I had a sixteen-hour day organizing a program of typhoid immunization at Arrabeh's schools. My three nurses gave over 2,000 shots without the benefit of automated equipment. A thousand more school children have been held back for another week for research purposes. I and Prof. Sarah Navo, a geneticist from Haifa University, are investigating whether there is a possible genetic element in the predisposition to getting sick when exposed to the typhoid bacterium, *Salmonella typhi*. But the way Prof. Navo analyzes her data—putting the children into categories of Muslim, Druze and Christian—is not to my liking. You would think epidemiology and genetics are neutral sciences. Yet in this country, they are tainted by racial politics. All official national statistics are categorized by religious affiliation in a persistent attempt to avoid assigning a national identity to us, the Palestinian citizens of Israel, as a minority in the country. There is an aversion in all official circles in Israel, and academia slavishly follows suit, to using the term "Arab" (not to mention "Palestinian") except in patronizing and negative ways, included the politically loaded phrase "Israel's Arabs."

I still recall an official complaint I received several years ago from a certain Dr. Suliman, a Jewish immigrant from Turkey and a senior psychologist at the Ministry of Health, against a French physician, Dr. Simone Boulus, who had married into a well-off Arab family from Acre and "sinned" by referring to her in-laws as "Palestinians." In his complaint, Dr. Suliman claimed that referring to "Israel's Arabs" as "Palestinians" violated the public's sensitivities to such an extent that it warranted imposing professional sanctions against the young woman, including rescinding her medical license. Indirectly, Dr. Suliman presumably was also objecting to my own occasional use of the term "Palestinian." I recall meeting with Dr. Boulus in my office, and, over coffee, allaying each other's fears.

Later, talking with my three nurses in Arrabeh, the subject of Prof. Navo was raised. The nurses heard that she had lost her son in the 1967 war. They say they can see the anger and fear in her eyes whenever she finds herself in a crowd in Arrabeh. This observation triggers a wider discussion about the meaning of our existence here as Arabs in a Jewish state. Toufiq Khatib, my close childhood friend who is married to one of the nurses, Zainab, offers his own reaction:

"Deep in my heart, I empathize with a mother who has lost her son—and for that reason alone I might be able to overlook her share of the blame for the continuing conflict. But I certainly cannot do the same for the Israeli public at large, hawkish, aggressive and opinionated as they are. The explanation for it varies, but the feeling of enmity for all things Arabic is pervasive: it is in the media, in people's expressions, in their body language, and in their actions. You can cut it with a knife in the air around you in the Jewish street. For us to live with that and maintain our sanity is nearly impossible, although it is good to try for the sake of our own integrity. Personally I find it easier to rationalize a lot of these things away and try to forget about them rather than mull them over endlessly in my head. The Jews suffered a great deal and they are deeply anxious about their future. But why should I bear the brunt of their anger and anxiety? It is hard enough for us to survive physically here, but to expect us to live out a one-sided commitment to non-violence and neighborly conduct is not humanly possible. We live in the midst of a group of people that, much as we would like to understand them, truly does not like us, a group that truly hates our guts."

One of the nurses, an aggressive young Israeli-trained woman, chips in:

"We have to distinguish between this kind of 'ordinary' prejudice and the well-entrenched and widely practiced discrimination against Arabs that is legally sanctioned by the state. This state was established for the Jewish people. The state historically and to this very day takes our existence into account only in the negative sense, as a hindrance to be overcome. This attitude is so well entrenched that it permeates the whole system from public leadership to policy makers, administrators, lowly bureaucrats to the man on the street. One way or the other, everything is connected to the overriding Jewish purpose of the state. Whatever is done has to contribute to this goal, which in essence is racially defined and hence discriminatory. You better get used to that, doctor!"

I know all this, of course. If an Arab community is ever to benefit from a scheme aimed at its development, such a project can only be advanced through the system if it can somehow be justified in terms of the state's over-arching goals. This is the stated policy and routine practice of the entire system of administration here, and to function within it you have to toe the line or the system will throw you out on to its rocky shores among its refuse. I am experiencing this even in the supposedly neutral field of health care. There is no possibility of official approval or financial support for any project in my area unless ultimately it serves the national goal of "developing the Galilee," the new phrase meaning "Judaizing the Galilee," settling Jews in the region with the inevitable negative consequences for the area's Arab citizens in what is always a zero-sum game of state-organized land theft. If you plan to open another mother and child health center in an Arab community, you had better throw in family planning as part of the proposal to get approval.

I give the nurses another example:

"Geriatrics is fast becoming the new flagship of the Ministry of Health, investing ever more of its resources in this field. I am constantly bombarded by circulars from my head office and letters from specialists working in geriatrics in the Jewish community demanding my time and attention. And yet, everybody forgets that in the Arab community childhood diseases are the major health threats. We are overwhelmed by the more pressing issues of deficient sanitation, child malnutrition, infectious diseases, the absence of school health services, lack of medical insurance coverage, inadequate housing, and infant mortality rates twice the national average. When I can show that inadequate sewage disposal is killing children in Arrabeh, that ought to be enough to persuade someone in the Ministry of Health to do something about it. And yet routine immunizations is the only concession I can squeeze out of the system for my community. That is why of late, as I agitate for improving sewage disposal in Arab villages, for example, I have started pointing out to my superiors that the current situation of neglect poses a danger to the Jewish population as well, because it will lead to the contamination of the water table and damage the national water resources."

"A community is the sum of its members. The attitude of its individuals gives you the bottom line," Toufiq adds. "Any time you discuss politics, human rights or issues of equality with Jews you touch a raw nerve. After you finish the discussion, each of you sticks to his position, a little diminished in the eyes of the other and totally unconvinced. But even Jews who are hawkish and ultra-rightist behave like reasonable human beings at the individual level. The other day, we were fishing in Lake Tiberias alongside a very obviously conservative Jewish family. They caught some fish and we caught some fish; they ate theirs and we ate ours. They came over to borrow some salt and we started talking about our families and life in general. We played football together and they were very nice and fun to play with, to fish with and to eat with. But not to talk to, not seriously, not about politics and who belongs where. That's the kind of thing that I don't understand. They are not stupid or crude people socially. How can they fail to see the truth? How can they miss the justice of our cause?"

"What about your friends in Naharya, the Petrokowskis?" interjects Zainab.

It is worth briefly mentioning the peculiar circumstances in which I first got to know the Petrokowski family. It was through Said Nassar, a friend in Arrabeh who landed himself a job at the Naharya Hospital laboratory. However, his employment was terminated when a jealous relative and well-known Shin Bet collaborator identified Said as a security threat. After his dismissal, Said sought help from the newly formed Jewish-Arab Coexistence Circle in Naharya, to which some influential Jews belonged, including Dov Yerimyah, the pre-1948 commander of the Haganah forces that conquered most of Western Galilee, and his wife, Menucha, who grew up on Kibbutz Nahlal surrounded by such legendary figures as General Moshe Dayan. The group used its connections to get Said reinstated. Said was aware of my own problems as the sole doctor in Arrabeh, and especially of my desire to spend one night a week with my wife and children away from the village so that we could get some undisturbed sleep. Until then we had been escaping every Sunday to a hotel on Naharya's beachfront, but the cost was becoming prohibitive. Said put us in touch with the Petrokowskis, members of the circle, and our two families clicked.

"The Petrokowskis freely offer you the use of their guest room once a week as a sincere gesture of friendship to you as an Arab," continues

Zainab. "We too have visited them, and they have been to our house. They are as mild-mannered, refined and kind-hearted as any individuals I have met. And yet, they do not really find fault with their community's attitudes. They feel sorry for the Palestinian refugees in the camps in Lebanon and they donate excess clothes, blankets, and canned food to them through the Red Cross. But they continue to grow exotic semi-tropical fruits on the land from which those refugees were driven. They are liberal enough to share the first custard apples and persimmons of the season with you as 'their Arab friends,' but part of their fields probably belonged to your aunt's family, the Rustoms, before they were driven from neighboring Dannon in 1948. My guess is that the fact that the Rustom family live in el-Buss refugee camp, across the border in Lebanon, is not allowed to disturb the precarious equation of friendship between you and the Petrokowskis. The contradictions inherent in their position do not enter their consciousness, and you swallow your pride and indignation, pushing it aside in exchange for the convenience of one night a week of uninterrupted sleep at their house. In the final analysis, whether consciously or not, the Petrokowskis actually confirm the overall attitude of hostility among the Jewish community to Palestinians."

I have little to say in response except to point out that the same kind of argument could be made in the other direction. Many Arabs work in Jewish communities and have "friends" there, yet the deep distrust continues. "Neither Said nor I feel comfortable in the Coexistence Circle to which the Petrokowskis belong," I conclude, rather apologetically.

"But the Palestinian Arab community in Israel lacks any political influence," adds Toufiq, who was trained as a Communist party functionary in the Soviet Union and does not easily concede a point in a debate. "We have no say in the drafting of laws or administrative regulations, not to mention in shaping judicial pronouncements. We lack the clout to make demands on the system or to have a marginal influence. All we can do is react with the same measure of distrust and collective hostility shown us by our Jewish neighbors. In fact, our general attitude towards the Jews is one of admiration and envy. In terms of our recent behavior, we have done very little to justify the hostility shown us by the Jewish majority. Had we dared to do something, at least we could lay claim to a degree of heroism—which might have halted the downward spiral of negative self-image among our youth. Obviously in 1948 the situation was different: we were in opposite trenches. But once the war was over, from that time till now, I know of no real reason to believe that the people of Arrabeh, for instance, should be feared or distrusted by their Jewish 'friends'."

A couple of days ago I picked up a young Arab man who was hitchhiking home to his village of Sha'ab. Although his family is originally from the village and live there to this day, they are classified by the authorities as refugees. The family belongs to that peculiar class of Palestinian citizens in Israel known as "present absentees"—one of Israel's more Kafkaesque contributions to the democratic world's lexicon.* After the young man had buckled his seat belt and stopped inspecting my car's interior, I surprised him with a direct question:

"How do you get along with the people in Ya'ad?"

Thrown off balance by a question about the Jewish settlement springing up next to Sha'ab and stealing much of its land, he started stammering. I rephrased the question:

"How are your new Jewish neighbors? How do you get along with them?"

He took his time, glancing again at the back of my VW Kombi, a strange and luxurious vehicle compared with most of the cars in Sha'ab. He gave me the blank look of a child concocting a lie: "We get along fine. They're alright."

"How do they treat you?"

"Fine. No problems. We're good neighbors."

"Well, do you get to see each other? Have you tried to establish a relationship with one another?"

"Oh, yes! As a matter of fact we are planning to have a party in a couple of weeks to get to know each other."

"Do you find them agreeable?"

"Yes! Great, great. No problem."

---

* *Present absentees:* Internal refugees; Palestinians who, during the war of 1948, left their homes but did not leave the country as refugees. Though they became citizens of Israel, they lost their homes, land and bank accounts for the benefit of Jewish citizens. They and their descendants make up around a quarter of Arab citizens in Israel and half of Nazareth's residents.

Throughout our exchange he was looking at me and at the back of the car. He probably thought I was one of the many engineers freshly arrived from South Africa to work in the large weapons industry complex under construction near Ya'ad—and for some inexplicable reason I knew Arabic. So I reassured him:

"Listen, never mind all the bullshit, I'm from Arrabeh."

"Yes, sure, I knew that. But your questions are unusual. Are you with the Shin Bet?"

I told him my name and that I am Arrabeh's doctor.

"Of course I know you. I brought my mother to your clinic once."

As he began reminding me of her medical story, I interrupted to repeat my question about Ya'ad.

"Well, you know just as I do that very few Arabs love Jews, and very few Jews love Arabs. What kind of relations do you expect between us and these newcomers in Mia'ar?"

He used the name of the destroyed Arab village on whose remains the new Jewish settlement of Ya'ad is being built.

"One relationship is that they have our land, the land we're driving through right now, the land of Mia'ar and Sha'ab, including my family's land. Now it is illegal for us even to pick mushrooms or gather greens from our own land. They have used about eighty of our villagers for trespassing on 'their' land, which is in fact my land and my father's land. If I try to pick mushrooms, I am taken to court and fined. What kind of relations do you expect?"

"What about the party, then?"

"That's bullshit. Nobody is having any party. I made that up for you before I knew who you were."

Present absentees, it is clear, learn to be pragmatic. They are easily intimidated, they lie low and are willing to make up stories on demand. They kiss ass to make a living or to get a job, or to hitch a ride home.

"You know, I work with the Jews in Kfar Ata all week, and, believe me, there's no love lost between them and us," he added before thanking me and leaving the car.

No wonder there is a common perception among Jews that the average Arab is *tzavoa*, a play on words that has a double meaning. Initially, it sounds like reference is being made to the Arabs' ability to change color, or their lack of reliability and transparency. But the hidden reference is to a hyena, a dangerous and treacherous scavenger.

I have another connection to a "present absentee" from Sha'ab: Wahsh al-Sha'aby, aka Abu-A'atif, who is married to my cousin Samiyeh. Last week I spoke with him about getting a colt for Ty in the hope that it will take my son's mind off toy guns. Abu-A'atif is a traditional sort of guy, born and raised in a very respectable Sha'ab family during the British Mandate days.* He is very proud of the fact that he owns an Arabian horse from a good line, though it has to be admitted that nowadays he cuts a pathetic figure on it. Once he owned a lot of land, mainly olive groves, having inherited it all from his father because he was the only surviving son. He was given the name Wahsh (Beast) to protect him from the evil eye that had felled all his brothers in their infancy.

In 1948, during the Nakba, Sha'ab was one of the Arab villages that surrendered early to the Jewish army. The natural place for Abu-A'atif and his family to escape the fighting was to Arrabeh and his in-laws. Except that his old mother, out of an attachment to Sha'ab, adamantly refused to leave her home. She was in danger of being killed but took the view that she had lived long enough: she had seen her only son married and have a good number of children. If Sha'ab was going to be destroyed, then life had no purpose anymore—or so she told her son. Abu-A'atif never stayed away from his mother or his home in Sha'ab for more than a day or two at a time. He feared marauders could rob the old lady, or worse. So, in fact he never abandoned his house and property. Within months, as some semblance of security returned to the area, he and his wife started living there for periods of time to be with his mother. Within a year or so they finally returned permanently to their home in Sha'ab.

But as far as the Israeli authorities are concerned, Abu-A'atif and his family are "present absentees," refugees who have abandoned their home and thereby forfeited their right to it. So Abu-A'atif no longer

---

* *The British Mandate:* From 1918 (defeat of the Ottoman Empire in the Second World War) to 1948, Britain administered Palestine under a mandate as per the Sykes-Picot agreement of 1916 with France. This was reconfirmed in 1922 by the League of Nations. Britain took upon itself, as part of this mandate, the establishment of a Jewish homeland (Balfour Declaration) to the disadvantage and displeasure of Palestine's native population.

owns any land in Sha'ab—or rather, the state holds it in trust while he
seeks justice in a judicial system designed to legitimize the theft of his
property. But while the infinitely slow wheels of Israeli justice turn, he
continues to live in his family's home, a house which officially he does
not own. In short, Abu-A'atif is a squatter in his own home, which
now belongs instead to a state bureaucrat, the Custodian of Absentee
Property. This proud "landless landowner" is unable even to fix the
roof over his head without a permit from the state, and the state always
refuses to grant him a permit because it does not recognize him as the
house's rightful owner.

Abu-A'atif has one hope of being recognized as the house's owner: if
he signs away his claim to the family's extensive farmland, which he also
no longer officially owns, the authorities will allow him to rent his house
from the state for fifty years at a nominal price. He continues to fight the
case in court, like so many other internal refugees. Not one of them has
ever won his case. But unlike Abu-A'atif, many have signed away their
property in exchange for minor concessions from the state, and a small
easing of their constant mental anguish and physical suffering.

Abu-A'atif is tall and has a thick moustache and booming manly
voice. Despite all his woes, he acts ferocious and speaks big. Anyone
who mentions land hears his well-rehearsed story: "When I was all by
myself and my children were hungry and little, I did not kneel before
Israel and did not accept its terms. Now that all my children are grown
up, all my sons are big strong men and earn a good living, now that
they are well-off and I have all the money I need, I am not about to
knuckle under and be defeated by Israel." His sons are all plasterers,
like their uncles in Arrabeh.

Abu-A'atif is very proud that he has resisted the system—his "*sumud*"
or steadfastness. But in truth he was defeated many years ago. Long
before his children could make a living, he had to earn one. The job
that he found and holds to this day satisfies his sense of pride and his
nostalgic yearning for the good old days. He is employed by the Jewish
National Fund (Keren Kayemit Liyisrael) to guard the olive groves,
including his own, now rented to Jewish agricultural contractors, and
to guard the "national forests" that have been planted on his own
land and the lands of other refugees from Sha'ab and the neighboring
destroyed village of Mia'ar. "There is no sign of Mia'ar anymore," he
says in a forlorn and lowered voice, "except for few fig trees and the

remnants of the cactus hedges on the outskirts of the village. I used to come up on my horse to visit friends in Mia'ar and in season we would eat delicious figs and many other fruits from the orchards there. Believe me, now when I try to eat from those same fig trees I can't swallow. The fruit has turned bitter since those pigs took it over."

I have heard this one before! It was in Acre from the old patriarch of the Ashqar (blond) family, apparently named in pun for their clearly African features. I was with a Jewish nurse collecting blood samples to conduct a survey of sickle cell anemia in the area. After the kindly old man welcomed us into his seaside shack by the industrial zone south of Acre I explained the reason for our visit. He was suspicious:

"You are collecting blood for the Israeli army. Ask someone else for blood donations. I have none; *nashafu dammi*—they have dried my blood up. I was born and raised on these sandy shores of Acre's Sea and my children and grandchildren have survived thanks to its generosity. I have savored its daily gifts from the day I was born; I swam before I could walk. Ever since 'your army' conquered these parts and started harassing us fishermen, even the fish in the depth of the sea have changed. I swear to you by the graves of my father and mother, the fish I catch have lost their flavor; they have turned foul tasting."

So paradoxically, Abu-A'atif is making a living guarding for the JNF the very same land he is fighting them to reclaim. He rides his thoroughbred horse, perhaps no longer so proudly or with such an upright posture, from one place to the other, checking that nobody has harmed the trees with their bitter fruit or the crops planted on the land he still claims as his own. And the party he does not recognize as the land's rightful owner, the JNF, pays him for his labor. While he refuses to accept that the land is not his, he is forced to admit it to the extent that it offers him the chance to earn an honest living. What he does is the reverse side of the same coin used by the state: it will recognize his rights to his land only in so far as he is prepared to sign away his ownership of it.

Abu-A'atif, in his booming voice, promised to give me the next pony his horse delivers so that I can raise it on my own little piece of land.

Another tragic hero from Mia'ar's yesteryears is Abu-Ahmad, who brings his Jewish friend, Swisa, to my clinic to be treated for a cold.

I have more than a passing acquaintance with Abu-Ahmad. His son, Ahmad, now a school teacher, was a classmate of mine and one of my best friends when we both attended high school in Nazareth in the 1950s. To all his classmates he was known as Ahmad al-Mia'ari, a reference to his village of origin in the Galilee, the same Mia'ar now destroyed and whose figs have turned bitter to Abu-A'atif's palate. Today he is called Abu-Hatim, because he named his firstborn son after me.

I remember visiting his family's encampment in the fields of Mia'ar one spring in my teenage years and, in my innocence, finding their life enviably romantic. During the Nakba of 1948, when Mia'ar was completely demolished by the Jewish army, Ahmad's extended family refused to leave the area, even though their homes had been destroyed. They put up tents and makeshift shacks in a secluded hillside close to the village that was out of view of the Israeli authorities. Somehow, they eked out a living from their land, although they were not allowed to farm it. They stayed on the hillside, persevered, and multiplied. They are now a big family. One of the children, Hasan, works as a cook for the nearby police station, the same police that have given the family no end of trouble trying to remove them from their encampment and to prevent them from planting crops on their former lands. So, not unlike Abu-A'atif, Hasan finally found a job making an honest living working for his persecutors.

After the destruction of Mia'ar, the authorities began establishing a new Jewish settlement, before Ya'ad, called Segev. It was planned as a farming community, mainly for Jewish immigrants from Morocco and Yemen. These immigrants were given homes and land but abandoned Segev and left shortly afterwards. Most had been brought over from cities where they were merchants, traders and craftsmen. They were city dwellers, not farmers. Although they tried to make a living by growing vines on the land they had been given by the JNF, they failed. The JNF was forced to reclaim the abandoned vineyards and, to make sure the former Arab owners did not return, planted a pine forest on the fertile land.

Although the family of my friend Ahmad al-Mia'ari was living close by throughout this failed experiment, they could not participate for obvious reasons: they were not allowed to farm their confiscated land after 1948. But that changed when they made the acquaintance of the Swisas, one of the Moroccan families that remained in the area despite the failure of the vineyards. Over the years I have come to know this family well, especially old man Swisa himself. Abu-Ahmad is always bringing him to me to be treated for minor illnesses. It seems almost as if, when old man Swisa has a fever, Abu-Ahmad gets the shivers. He begs me to take good care of his friend and do my best to preserve his life. Abu-Ahmad is always reminding me that he was a personal friend of my late father, who had maternal cousins in Mia'ar.

In fact, Abu-Ahmad has a vested interest in old man Swisa's continuing good health.

Abu-Ahmad, who has no land, loves farming and that is what he knows best; old man Swisa has access to the land but does not know how to farm it. So the two families have found a living arrangement based on mutual trust and tacit understanding. Old man Swisa lets Abu-Ahmad farm the fields that were stolen from Mia'ar and passed on to him. Together they have found a way to bypass the racist discrimination at the heart of Israel's system of land control.

It works like this. Abu-Ahmad cannot rent his land from the JNF or the state because that might suggest that it actually belongs to him—an outcome that cannot be allowed. Official regulations do not permit Arabs in general, and internal refugees in particular, to rent state or JNF lands. Such restrictions are all the more strictly enforced if an Arab has an outstanding claim to the land in question. So, old man Swisa rents the land from the JNF under his own name instead, and then lets Abu-Ahmad and his family farm it without a written rent agreement. In return Abu-Ahmad pays old man Swisa the equivalent of rent and some of the profits from the produce he grows each year. As a result, the two families have developed a neighborly symbiosis and closeness. They live conveniently, even happily, side by side, despite all the ethnic hostility the state's official ideology, Zionism, tries to engender. One family, the Mia'aris, are not supposed to live where they do but have done so against all the odds; and the other family, the Swisas, are not capable of living where they do but have also done so against all the odds. Which just goes to prove that, if you put two families together out in the sticks, they had better find ways to be friends!

I reassured Abu-Ahmad that his neighbor, old man Swisa, would survive the cold. He thanked me warmly and offered to pay for the clinic visit. I refused for old time's sake. Later I found paper money slipped under the door.

5
My First Shaheed

Military Area Nine stretching between Arrabeh in the foreground, Sakhnin to the left, the Jewish city of Karmiel at far left, and Dier Hanna and Wadi Salameh at far right.

May 25, 1979

My friend Mahmud al-Musa, a civil engineer trained in Czechoslo-vakia, has planned our house and overseen its construction without payment. He has also come to my aid with a cash loan to finish the project, free of interest.

I became friends with Mahmud's late older brother, Mohammad, in the village elementary school. Our relationship grew closer when Mohammad lost his father in the first traffic accident in Arrabeh's history: two farmers were riding to market on top of grain in the back of a truck when the vehicle went off the road, killing both of them. Afterwards, his mother was even more welcoming to us, the friends of her firstborn son, to the degree that half a dozen of us almost became part of the household. We would spend most of our after-school hours playing in their backyard, a spacious empty field famous to this day in the village's collective memory as the place where passing gypsy bands set up camp, the men shoeing horses and trading in donkeys while the women danced at weddings and the children begged door-to-door for food. I remember the delicious greens that Umm Mohammad would gather from the fields and cook for us, and the freshly baked bread from her outdoor oven, the "*taboun*," savored dipped in olive oil and lightly sprinkled with salt and served with a few green onion leaves. These, together with various lentil and cracked wheat dishes, were very much the standard mainstay of every family's diet in the village. Yet Umm Mohammad's meals were special, with her hovering over us offering more of everything and edging us on to eat so we would grow up healthy.

Mohammad was tall and muscular. He would wrestle me down every time we competed, and he would occasionally even defeat the gypsy boys that no one else could. They were champion wrestlers by virtue of their style and agility, not bulk. Mohammad and I were among the half-dozen children from the village who attended high school in Nazareth. Not every one could. You needed money and brains for that. We competed in the national high school entry exams that determined how much of an exemption our families would receive on the fees demanded by government schools. As we arrived on the first day of term, there was a typewritten sheet on the bulletin board announcing the results. Our two names were at the top of the list, both 100 percent exempt. It cemented our friendship as we faced the new and intimidating environment of a city.

During our first spring vacation at high school, Mohammad joined a group of boys from his neighborhood looking for scrap metal near an abandoned military camp we called al-Kam that the British had once established on the northern edge of Arrabeh. We all did this regularly in those days, selling the shell casings and the shrapnel that we collected to the village's scrap metal merchant. That money was ours, extra pocket money to spend in the city. On this excursion, however, Mohammad returned in a bag. He joined the list of a few dozen village "*shaheeds*" (martyrs) killed by ordnance left by the British. Such deaths occurred while villagers were working in the fields, or tilling the land, or collecting greens, or tending the cattle, or collecting scrap metal.

By the time the British army cleared out of Palestine in 1948, they had opened in the village the first modern school up to sixth grade. They had also employed our men to build the first road for cars to our area, bringing it all the way to al-Kam, the military training camp they had set up on our farmland. The road terminated at al-Kam because that was its sole destination and purpose. But the thing everyone in Arrabeh remembers as the British legacy from the Mandate is the continuing menace posed by the extensive area claimed by the British army for their maneuvers and cannon firing. Not only have we been left with the live ammunition that intermittently kills our villagers, but the British army also offered Israel the precedent it needed to confiscate the same area, now known as "Military Area Nine," for its own dubious purposes.

In my family, there is another accursed memory of the British Mandate, an indelible black stain in our minds and hearts. In 1936, as they tried to suppress a Palestinian uprising against their colonial rule, the British army committed some of the most obscene atrocities in living memory. Though I had not been born at the time, I heard of the terrible incidents often enough from my parents and village elders to have a clear mental image: of troops breaking into single-room hovels and destroying everything in sight, breaking all the ceramic food containers and spilling out the meager stores of flour, grain, bulgur, lentils, fava beans and onions on the dirt floor, emptying over it the stored animal feed, and pouring the family's olive oil on top of the mix. (Did Israel's occupation forces in Palestine see this precedent as a challenge, one that had to be outdone? They now blow up Palestinian homes altogether, carrying the classic local ultimate ill-wish "*yikhrib beitak*—may ruination strike your house" to its logical conclusion.)

These violations and assaults were possible to bear, with much anguish, through communal solidarity and mutual support. People banded together and sought sustenance from the land or through the generosity of a neighbor whose house had been spared or a relative, such as my uncle Salih, who was favored by our masters. But my family could not share the pain and shame that came from the attempt by a British soldier to rape my pre-teen sister in our orchard, the spot where my own house now stands. Though she successfully fought him off, to this day she cannot hear or say that country's name without uttering a barrage of curses and prayers to God for its ruination. It was only after my father began reading each night to her from the holy Koran that she regained her mental balance and could sleep without the recurring nightmares that drove her mad for the best part of a year.

I carry the scars of that era on my body too, though my trauma was less painful. I have mostly managed to erase the memory, but if I dig deep a shiver runs down my spine recalling the incident that left me with a slight scar under my chin. Every once in a while I scratch it open while shaving, and that is when I remember what happened. I must have been no older than five at the time, walking home from our olive orchard, not far from al-Kam. An army jeep with two soldiers stopped and, using sign language, they offered me a ride. What child of my age would resist the chance to ride in an automobile in those days! As we reached the junction to the village, less than a mile away, I shouted for them to stop and, when they did not, I jumped out of the moving vehicle losing consciousness as I tumbled on the grassy shoulder of the road. I woke up to the tender touch of a village woman splashing water on my face from the jug she carried back from the *birkeh*, the adjacent communal rainwater reservoir. She washed the blood off my face and bare feet and took me home.

After his death, Mohammad's friends, myself included, continued frequenting his home and took on his three young siblings as our own. Khalid, the second boy in the family, soon joined us in high school in Nazareth and became especially close to me. On vacations we would gather at his mother's kitchen as usual and she would dote on us, indulging us even more than when Mohammad was alive. After high school Khalid tried his hand and failed at a couple of skilled trades, finally ending up as the head of a team of construction workers from his neighborhood. By the time I came back from the States, I found him well-off and socially prominent by village standards: a successful construction subcontractor, maintaining his position as supervisor with a road construction company while independently taking on small earth-moving contracts in the village.

I hoped Khalid would help me build my house and, given our close and long friendship, be happy to delay the payments for a while. I was disappointed by his less than enthusiastic response. At a deeper level, my disappointment probably stemmed from more than his lack of loyalty to me. He works for a Jewish contractor whose business is building settlements in the occupied Palestinian Territories and in the Golan Heights. He is not alone in this. There is much lucrative work to be done for the Israeli army, since the settlements always start as military outposts, and the beneficiaries are not only the major Jewish contractors but also small-time Arab subcontractors like Khalid. Ironically, the trickle-down benefits are sufficient to make a few "greedy" Arabs rich enough to gain prominence in their communities. This type of gainful collaboration is common in our powerless and deprived communities. To some degree, we all share in it. A popular joke among our neighbors in Sakhnin tells of a demonstration in Arrabeh against the prospect of peace negotiations between Israel and Syria. Why would we in Arrabeh be against a peace deal? Because if Israel were to give back the Golan Heights to Syria, where would we be able to collect the *a'kkoub* for our favorite dish? The wild thistle, plentiful in the Golan, tops Arrabeh's gourmet cuisine.

Khalid's brother Mahmud became a friend only after I came back from the States. I found that he had obtained his degree in civil engineering in Czechoslovakia thanks to a full scholarship from the Communist party.[*] Part of the sum he has agreed to loan me will repay a debt to another Communist, Musa Nassar, for a favor he and his Hungarian wife did us a couple of years back. Car prices in Israel are extremely high because of local taxes. Immigrants and returning students qualify for a tax-free car, but each is allowed only one purchase in the four

---

[*]   *Communist party:* Rakah, the only bi-national non-Zionist political party in Israel has served as the refuge for Palestinian activists in Israel. Its daily newspaper, the only Arabic language daily still published in Israel since before the state's establishment, has been a mouthpiece for the Arab minority in voicing its political opinion, complaints and demands. Swings in its popularity with this constituency reflected its alliance with or estrangement from Arab nationalist streams at home and abroad.

years after their arrival. My wife Didi and I had taken advantage of that benefit once before, in 1970, with our first VW camper. Musa gave us the chance to buy another car tax free by registering our second VW camper in his wife's name. They lacked the money to buy a car within four years of their arrival back from Hungary, where he studied, so they helped us defray the higher taxes on our car and in exchange we now pay them for the taxes on their cheaper car.

Musa Nassar is not a close friend, but we have known each other long enough to trust the other on a tax-evasion deal like this one, as long as it is a scam against the Israeli authorities and does not involve a third party from the village. "It seems self-evident that any way to save or retrieve any part of the one-way flow of the tax burden is morally justified," Musa tells me, justifying our action to both of us. He is another Communist well-versed in debate and dialectics. "Because not only do our villages never get their due share of government budgets, but also our taxes go to support the Israeli military that is killing and oppressing our Palestinian brothers and sisters." Neither Musa nor I needed to ponder further the morality of our tax evasion.

By virtue of being a car owner, I have befriended Musa's father, another Abu-Ahmad, who owns and operates the first gas station in Arrabeh. He is a man of high intelligence, very clever with his hands, a self-taught mechanic cum car and house electrician, an aspiring poet, political commentator and astrologer, and the all-round village intellectual. His poems, old ones memorized by heart or newer pieces scribbled on kerosene-soaked scraps of paper pulled out of his shirt pocket are read to me through my half-opened car window as I wait for my car to be serviced. Most are a mixture of Koranic classical Arabic and Galilee colloquial slang; they usually lack the required meter and frequently do not rhyme. As a child he learnt to read the Koran at the village mosque, and as a youth he was one of the first Communist party members in the village. Though he says he left the party in protest over its heavy regimentation and lack of imagination, his two oldest boys were loyal enough to the party's youth movement to win scholarships in Communist countries.

In listening to him, and he is a talkative man, oftentimes forcing me to start moving my car in mid sentence, I sense his presumption of a special link between the two of us as people of better understanding of world issues than your average villager. He is rather solicitous of my friendship, though he doesn't use my medical services, relying instead on his own herbal remedies when he is ill. Just recently he was extending the perimeter of the gas station and, in the process he pulled out a couple of ancient olive trees and used their trunks as stands for his mechanical tools. I expressed my real admiration for the improvised worktables. That afternoon he brought one over to my garden loaded on the back of his tractor.

Earlier today, my younger sister, Yusra, brought her baby daughter to see me, her seventh and last child, and one she bore against her will. She wanted to terminate the pregnancy but her husband objected. This time she had her tubes tied right after the delivery. Her baby has the hereditary skin condition which two of her other children already have: PPK or Mal-de-Meleda, a disfiguring condition suffered by our branch of the Kanaaneh clan. Yusra can already detect the first signs in the baby and is in denial; she comes to her doctor brother asking him to tell her it is not the case. I owe her. For two years, when I had just matriculated and was teaching, she drew water for me to bathe and baked fresh bread for me to eat. She also called her firstborn son after me. I hate to be the cruel bearer of bad news to my family, but I cannot lie to Yusra. Besides, in her heart, she already knows it.

In my teenage years, taking a cold splash bath was one of the few physical luxuries I could afford to enjoy every day. Unfortunately, as I returned home from a day's teaching, hot and bothered and itching for a bath, I would invariably encounter women huddled around my seamstress sister, Jamileh, as she operated her Singer sewing machine in our one-room residence. They would come in groups to collect dresses or to try on garments before the final fitting, then sit around inspecting and admiring other items commissioned at my sister's. The only other room, my father's guest room, was not available for my use, so either I had to forgo my bath or I had to endure the indecency of baring myself in front of these strange women. Usually, after much hesitation, I would opt for the latter. Yusra would draw me a pale of water, stretch a piece of cloth across the backs of two chairs to block off the distant corner of the room, and I would take off my clothes and bathe. I am not an exhibitionist, so I would turn my back to everyone and announce in advance that I intended to take a bath. Those who did not like the idea could leave. More often than not they stuck around and pretended not to look. Also, splashing a cold bucket of water on my listless body after an evening of arguing about nothing in particular with my village friends or of listening to a radio play or a live performance by Umm Kalthoom was the only effective way of putting me to sleep. I couldn't draw water from the cistern in our yard to save my life; Yusra always drew water for me.

After Yusra's visit, I received a call to see an old neighbor who had fractured her hip. On the way back I was sidetracked by another patient, an old man in his seventies, with cerebral palsy who in my childhood days was the village barber. He and the shoemaker, another severe cerebral palsy case, were good friends of my father and entrusted him with their meager savings. Both were never able to walk much, except to the mosque on Fridays, and now with age the barber is completely bedridden. Then the son of a third septuagenarian, the village cow herder, stopped me in the street. I am always impressed with the way the young man drives his new Ferguson tractor through the narrow alleys of the old section of the village, hart-al-Asli, where his father still lives, and with the nonchalant way he handles any minor mechanical problem that arises.

As I entered the family home, however, I was struck by the incongruity of what I have seen of the young man's technical skills and the deprived home in which he resides. Their ancient mud-thatched room is from a different century. I am back in the Ottoman era. As my eyes adjust to the darkness I can see the old man lying on a worn-out, narrow straw mat on the dirt floor with his wife stretched out next to him, campfire-side style, with her feet next to his face and vice versa. There is a flat tin sheet, the size of a plate, with ashes on it. By the look of what I have seen and the stench of their hovel, she has tried some traditional village remedy for him. The son tells me she has burned donkey manure for him to inhale, hoping it will help his dysentery. He has had dysentery for three days and, despite his wife's treatments, it has not improved. The old man has taken Epsom salts to purge the poison from his intestines but instead has nearly finished himself off. His state is so bad that he is seeking the help of a physician for the first time in his seventy-odd years. He is running a high fever, flies buzz all over him, and the dirt floor is damp from his wife's attempts to clean it. It is a hopeless environment in which to nurse somebody in his condition back to health. They refuse a referral to the hospital even when I offer to transport him in my own car. Reluctantly he accepts my advice to drink lots of fluids and my prescription of antibiotics. What he really wants is an injection and to be finished with it.

The old man tells me that he has had dysentery before but never like this. His condition is very serious indeed, but he finds it demeaning to admit to weakness. His wife is proud of his "strong physique" and that he has never seen a physician before. I do not know his exact age, and he does not know it either—only that he is approximately seventy, give or take ten years. Their age and past struggles with disease and deprivation have etched marks on their bodies and deeply furrowed faces. Both of them look emaciated; he has cataracts in both eyes, apparently from his childhood days; she has a cataract in one eye and two missing fingers; he has several scars on his bald scalp. Time has taken its toll, and now he needs a doctor.

I find it amazing that no one ever argues with a doctor, or at least not with this doctor, about his charges. There is no haggling or bargaining about prices in a culture where that is the standard procedure with all commercial transactions. It could be a legacy of the earliest Western missionary physicians to the area. One, a legendary Austrian doctor who worked in Nazareth, was reputed to physically attack his patients if they ever inquired about charges; that was a matter below his dignity, for the nurse, not for him. He was not working for money and they had better know it. A local Arabic saying dictates that only camel drivers and doctors collect on the spot. Don't ask me why these two professions are lumped together!

That is not my strangest house call of late. A few days ago I went to Naharya to treat Fritz, a young Swiss man who is volunteering on the farm that belongs to the Petrokowski family, our Jewish friends and weekend hosts. He is being nursed by Rivka, a German woman who married an Israeli Jew, converted to Judaism, and bore him two children, before they separated. She raises her two daughters in the Jewish faith and tradition. Some of Miriam Petrokowski's friends, who know that she has a soft spot for wayward lost souls, brought Rivka and her two children to Miriam, who gave them a little shack in the yard to live in. Fritz lives in a wooden shipping box that sits in the yard next to Rivka's shack. It is just big enough for one person to sleep in, and Fritz thinks it better than living on the street.

Everyone, including myself and my family, the old couple, their own two adopted teenage children, their huge dog Nimrod, and the vagrants in the yard are welcome to use Miriam's kitchen, which looks exactly as one would imagine: a constant mess. That day Miriam called to ask if I could make a special house call to see Fritz. As I arrive at the house, I am met by the grand old matriarch of the Petrokowski clan, Miriam's mother-in-law. She struggles to her feet to shake my hand, greeting me in the civilized, respectful manner that only old Germans know how to show a doctor. Alongside her are Miriam's two adopted teenage children, and their Jewish Moroccan biological mother. The boy does not see fit to introduce his real mother to me, so the matriarch nudges her towards me and she introduces herself, to the deep embarrassment of the boy who curses loudly in Hebrew, which the matriarch does not understand.

By the time I go into the yard to see Fritz, it is already late afternoon. I find him lying on a cot in the cool breeze under a huge eucalyptus tree in the backyard, with Rivka holding an ice pack under his inflamed swollen testicles. On a small stand next to him there is a glass of ice water and some fruits. I feel very peculiar, framed in this romantic scene as part of the paraphernalia. A Swiss young man volunteering on a farm in the Holy Land owned by two elderly Holocaust survivors who have adopted two Moroccan youngsters, being nursed back to health by a lost soul, a convert Jewess from Germany obviously trying to make up for her nation's collective guilt, and being treated by a local Palestinian doctor who is on good terms with the Jewish couple and takes care of them when they are sick. It is a wonderful mishmash of imagined ideals of international solidarity with Israel; of the collective guilt of Germans; of the oneness of the Jewish people, Moroccan and German immigrants alike; and of Arab-Jewish brotherhood. Becoming self-conscious that someone might use my goodwill as the raw material for such a twisted tale, spinning it out of its true context without my true concerns or views being taken into account, I feel unnerved. I start to imagine this story as the central plot of a Zionist-inspired political sequel to Exodus, with me painted in even paler hues than my actual pale self. I would be the servile Arab lackey admiring the cultured Europeans whose mere satisfaction and faint praise is my highest aspiration.

Panicking at the thought, I split as soon as I can get Fritz's fever down.

6
Lost in the System

A family home in Arab al-Naim that doubled one day a week as the Galilee Society clinic.

July 2, 1979

As I expected, a year after resuming my position at the Ministry of Health, my sense of alienation, boredom and disgust are quickly resurfacing. When I handed in my resignation after Land Day three years ago, I argued that it was not possible to bridge the large gap between my duties in a government department and my commitment to advancing the health of my community. Now I am living out that prediction in full, with all its painful details. Lacking any Zionist zeal,

I have a heightened awareness of the system's deficiencies, especially regarding my main constituency, the Galilee's rural Arab population. Much of my time and effort are spent dealing with the inequalities promoted by the system and made easier by the geographic segregation between the two communities, Arabs and Jews. I find my best efforts are self-defeating, if not stillborn. I am unable to overcome a sense of impotence when dealing with the problems I entered the system to solve.

I consider quitting again, but a colleague's chance discovery breathes new life into my official work. Since I took over as Sub-District Physician, I have noticed that each year the births in my area of about two dozen infants with the last name Sawaid are reported by the Interior Ministry to my office, but that they are never included in the lists used by my nurses for routine immunizations. Where do these children disappear to?

My health educator, Subhi Badarneh, stumbled across the answer to this puzzle while buying a baby goat for his children. The Bedouin man who sold him the goat invited him to his home in the mountains, an isolated community of corrugated iron shacks located on the far side of Jabal Abu-Qarad. The hill, north of Sakhnin, falls inside Area Nine, land set aside for Israeli military maneuvers and off limits to civilians. The Bedouin tribe, comprising 500 people, is called Arab al-Naim. I visited the village, just a short distance from Arrabeh, and was shocked by what I saw: a collection of metal shacks strewn between massive boulders around a clearing with no access road and no communal amenities or infrastructure whatsoever. The tribal elders tell me that before the Nakba they had permanent stone residences but after the war the Israeli army blew up all the houses and has prevented them from building new ones. "They ruined all our drinking water cisterns by exploding hand grenades in them," they said. "Our women carry water on their heads from Sakhnin."

And in Arab al-Naim lies the answer to all those missing children. Apparently, after 1948, the new Israeli Military Governor in charge of the Galilee's Arabs assumed that the villagers were a branch of Sawaid, the dominant Bedouin tribe in these parts.* The name stuck in

*   *Military government:* From 1948 till 1966, 90 percent of all Palestinian citizens of Israel were placed under military rule, a draconian form of martial law promulgated originally by the British Mandate in 1945 to deal with Jewish terrorists. It prohibited

all official circles. Al-Naim's mistaken identity and semi-secret location led to its total neglect by all government departments, including the Ministry of Health. So although the children's births are recorded, as new Sawaids, they are forgotten from that time on. With the riddle solved, I am faced with yet another, related challenge: There are several small communities of Bedouin and internal refugees in the Galilee, including Arab al-Naim, that are deprived of all community services. They have no water, sewage disposal, electricity, telephones, roads, refuse collection, clinics or schools. And of course, their homes are all illegal. They are designated as non-communities and targeted for elimination by the authorities. Someone recently coined the term "unrecognized villages" for them. There are even more of them in the Negev. Much more needs to be done for them.

This is a kind of trap I set for myself, a form of self-flagellation. The harder the task, and the more obstacles in my way, the more rewarding and uplifting the struggle.

Perhaps that is why I find it more satisfying to work with Dr. Ted Tulchinsky whenever I have the chance. He is the recently recruited head of the Public Health Division of the Health Ministry, a fresh-off-the-boat immigrant from Canada with much to recommend him in terms of his progressive views on public health. To him a problem is a problem regardless of where it occurs within his area of responsibility. And he is willing to stick his neck out and say: "This is being neglected because it is in an Arab locality that lacks political clout." Recently I joined him and his two assistants as their guest on a visit to the Arab village of Umm al-Fahm, which is outside my district.

The subject of the field tour was sewage disposal, a particularly acute problem in this village and one that greatly interests me. Umm al-Fahm exemplifies all the difficulties related to sewage disposal: its terrain is steep, it is overcrowded, over three-quarters of its land has been expropriated by the government, and it lacks a town plan. Two- and three-story buildings have been grafted on to old structures from

---

the movement of individuals outside of their villages without a special permit from the Minister of Defense. Under other clauses of these emergency regulations confiscation of land was made possible. Subjects of the military government were denied access to civilian courts.

past centuries, and sewage pits drilled into its non-porous rock overflow and leak into the next person's home or a property further down the hill. It adds up to streams of sewage running in gullies and alleyways on to the main street, where children walk and play.

This is one of those glaring examples of discrimination: all Arab communities suffer from such sewage problems, and all Jewish communities do not. One can see similar sights in Dier el-Asad, Majd al-Kroum, Arrabeh, or in just about any Arab village if one bothers to look. But because of the size of Umm al-Fahm—it has a population of 18,000—and because of its extreme overcrowding, the picture is more striking than anywhere else.

The mayor, Hashim Mahameed, showed us written documents to prove that he and his predecessors have been trying to solve the village's planning problems but have been rebuffed by the authorities, or given false promises. As a member of the Communist-allied Jabha party, Mahameed's politics do not go down well with government officials. Therefore, the village is deprived of grants and subsidies that local authorities usually receive.

But so are all other Palestinian communities in Israel, as Dr. Tulchinsky noted. He is head of the Ministry's preventive health services, which includes overseeing environmental health. But the planning and financing of environmental health projects are in the hands of the Interior Ministry, which has other priorities. Dr. Tulchinsky himself is so hampered by the bureaucracy that he is fast acquiring a reputation for inefficiency and trouble-making.

Like Dr. Tulchinsky, I can exercise my authority in the Ministry of Health mainly in terms of what I can stop happening. I am authorized to block things but not to initiate or expedite them. My power derives from my ability to say "No." I commonly refuse permission to a village council to issue a business license to a small country store because it does not have running water or a sink for hand washing. However, there are entire communities where there is no running water—and I cannot influence that situation for the better. To put it at its most extreme, I can refuse a license to bury a dead child until his or her family complies with my demands for a post-mortem, but I have very little power to initiate meaningful action to ensure that the dead child's siblings do not die from the same cause.

This basic inability to pursue positive options, to act proactively, puts me on a confrontational path with my bosses. It sets my ethics and my job description on a collision course.

I have just completed a polio immunization campaign in which about 18,000 children in my sub-district were covered. The reason for the campaign is that this year there were fifteen proven cases of clinical poliomyelitis in Israel, a major outbreak of this preventable disease. Thirteen of the cases were Arab children, and two were Jewish. The directive issued by the Ministry of Health's head office states that there is an urgent need for a re-immunization campaign in "certain geographic areas." As usual, mention of Arabs and Jews is avoided, but everyone in the Ministry knows the meaning of such language. Speaking openly of the need to mount a special campaign for Arabs is considered politically incorrect; it breaks a taboo by admitting that the country's Palestinian citizens enjoy a lower standard of health and suffer from deficient medical services. It is tantamount to admitting not only the existence of Arabs in the Jewish state but also their second-class status.

It is therefore left up to the District Physician to decide exactly what "certain geographic areas" means and who will be covered by the campaign. Out of a real fear of exposing any child, Arab or Jew, to the risk of contracting polio, I have made the decision to cover the entire population in my area under the age of three, the age group that seems to be involved in the outbreak so far. In the Acre sub-district, contact between Jews and Arabs is close. The polio virus is unlikely to be racially prejudiced, despite its seeming forty-fold predilection for Arab children. What is it, then, that underlies its propensity to afflict children of one ethnic group over those of the other?

We have considered this question long and hard. At my insistence, three of the Ministry's heads of department came on a fact-finding mission to solve this mystery. We considered the possible routes of transmission of infection. The experts would doubtless be happy to shift the blame on to my office, or even to the victims and their families. They looked closely at every possible deficiency in the immunization routine as it is carried out in the afflicted villages and found none to speak of. They questioned the professional standards of my nurses.

Instinctively, I recoil from such a line of thinking, even though it is essential to the epidemiological investigation. Many of the young nurses in the mother and child health clinics in the Acre sub-district studied nursing through my personal intervention, whether with the nursing schools they attended or with their reluctant parents. The whole idea of having local girls providing care in their own rural communities was first vigorously opposed by the nursing division at my head office. They rejected my argument that local nurses would show greater commitment to their own communities. I suspected that the division's hostility sprang from an unwillingness of the Ashkenazi top staff to release the strangle-hold that their professional and educational superiority affords them over all others in Israel. Still, "my girls" are in a class of their own. Questioning their performance is beyond the pale for anyone in the system. And "they" all know it.

So what then, in the name of Jehovah and Allah, is the explanation?

It is community sanitation, stupid! Sanitation explains the failure by a good number of our children to gain immunity from infection with the polio virus despite repeated oral doses of proven active vaccine given by trained, conscientious nurses. The tamed vaccine virus fails to implant in the intestinal wall and take effect in some local children because of their chronic diarrhea. The oral vaccine goes in one end and out the other so fast it does not get a chance to do its work. The vaccination program cannot be fully effective until the sanitation in Arab communities improves. In restricting its mandate on polio and other infections to prevention by immunization, the whole preventive approach of the Ministry of Health sucks.

September 22, 1979

Dr. Frank-Blume has taken off for a two-month tour of Scandinavia, sponsored by the Ministry of Health and the World Health Organization. That leaves me in charge of the public health services in the entire Northern District. Though it was not stated openly, I suspect this will serve as a trial period to test my ability to run the show should I assume her position when she retires in two years.

The assignment is not too demanding. I handle only those issues from the entire Galilee region that filter through the lower echelons of the hierarchy to my desk, cases that need my personal intervention or decision. I am struck by the unequal distribution of my attention. In terms of demography, I should divide my time equally between Jews and "non-Jews," as the system identifies its Palestinian population. Professionally and ethically, I have an obligation to give higher priority to the Arabs, the group with the poorer health conditions, the less accessible health services, the weaker internal resources, and the lower socio-economic conditions. Yet, I find myself handling three times as many cases from the Jewish half of the district's population as from the Arab half. The almost total segregation of the two groups into separate residential locations brings the differences into sharper relief. Jewish local authorities and their residents are more demanding and better at bringing their problems to the Ministry's attention. They are better equipped and more adept at engaging the system. Channels are more open to them and to their concerns, which means they are more likely to reach the higher levels of authority.

In fact, the picture is even worse than it appears. Given the current cuts to our budget, the basic approach of all government offices, mine included, is to put out fires. We respond to pressure from our constituencies, with few if any planned development initiatives. By and large, the only proactive work being undertaken is by the major Zionist organizations, like the Jewish Agency and Jewish National Fund, whose mandates limit their activities to the Jewish population, even when their projects are heavily subsidized by the Israeli government. I find myself entangled in this web, there to preserve the discriminatory status quo.

As I contemplate my own culpability in working for a system that discriminates in favor of the Jewish community, a thought occurs to me that, I fear, reflects my own acceptance of the inferior self-image of the Arab. I rationalize the discrimination by suggesting to myself that, even though I have devolved much authority to my staff, the Arab workers may feel too timid to handle the problems of the Jewish population and so send them up to me, resulting in my greater involvement with demands from the Jewish sector. Then it dawns on me that all the heads of departments serving under me are Jewish. Rather than suspect them of favoring the Jewish population, I preferred to advance a theory that put the blame on Arabs. What first-class Uncle-Tomism!

December 9, 1979

Another wave of budgetary belt-tightening is upon us. The imposed cuts and rollbacks negate the proactive essence of real public health work. The directives from the head office actually translate into cutting development funds from the peripheral areas, where the infrastructure is weakest and the need most acute, while well-established and heavily subsidized services continue receiving their regular budgets as well as built-in annual increases. If ever I dreamt of developing rural health services in the Galilee, the newly imposed cuts have put an end to it.

In groping for my way around the bureaucratic maze I again turn to my friend and senior mentor Dr. Sami Geraisy, aka Abu-Farah, the grand master of quiet diplomacy and useful compromise. In his ICCI* office, over Turkish coffee and Arabic sweets we speak openly and try to strategize:

"As we both know," I commence pleading my case, "neither of us identifies with the overall purpose of the state. In better times I could at least persuade myself that by being in the government bureaucracy I was able to influence events sufficiently to bring some benefit to my community. In cruder terms, if I kissed ass sufficiently, I could obtain rewards for my people—the basic operating principle of all Uncle Toms. However, today, faced with the severe budget cuts and the racism of the ruling party and its ministers—including the Health Minister and his senior staff—the wicked balance no longer holds. I prostitute my feelings and principles, but there is no bounty to cheat my superiors of. Only the deceit and rancor remain."

"At least a middle-management position in the state bureaucracy affords you protection against the willful abuse of other, more invasive state agencies, such as the police and the income tax thugs," Abu-Farah advises.

"But again, a deal is involved, an even dirtier and less respectable deal, because it is based on fear and on an assumption of a quid-pro-quo reciprocity with similar scared sheep in wolves' skins."

"True, but there is also a different and more honorable benefit: from your position in the Ministry of Health you can keep your finger on the pulse of the country and see where things are headed. That way, even

---

* *ICCI:* The Inter-church Coordinating Committee in Israel, a member of the Middle East Council of Churches.

if you cannot proactively promote the interests of your community, at least you can safeguard them."

"I probably can do more for the Arab minority in Israel from outside the system," I protest.

"Nobody stops you from doing that simultaneously. I serve more through my position with the ICCI than with the Ministry of Labor and Social Welfare."

Abu-Farah then points to his recent invitation to me, as a government official, to sit on two advisory committees on health and social welfare as an example of the possible benefits of the inside track. After the storm that the Black Panthers have kicked up in the United States, some of the dust settled here in Israel, where young, alienated Sephardic Jews* emulated their black counterparts in the US by leading demonstrations and vocal protests. In response, the government appointed several committees to advise it on what actions it should take to quell the disturbances, and similar but separate committees to advise it on how to prevent similar disturbances from Arab youth.

"Had I believed that anyone would listen to us, I could have saved them a lot of trouble and expense. The youth in our community are too timid and poor to protest on issues of equality and life opportunities. Paradoxically, you need a bare minimum of confidence in the system you are challenging, and belief in your ability to change it, to set yourself the goal of reforming or even overthrowing it. The only time our youth really stood up to official policy was three years ago, on Land Day, and then the issue was the government's continuing confiscation of our land. But the response of the Arab community was prompted by nothing less than self-preservation. Land, to a people steeped in subsistence farming for generations, is life itself. That is why the Land Day protest materialized so spontaneously and defied the coordinated onslaught of the Israeli police and army under the personal command of both Yitzhak Rabin and Shimon Peres."

"So, why are we doing this, why continue with the charade of advisory committees?" I protest and then continue as if to answer my own question: "Although I feel far from comfortable in either committee, still I am finding it helpful to learn about the plans, or lack of them,

---

* *Sephardim:* Jews of Arab or Mediterranean origin. In Israel they occupy an intermediate socio-economic position between the culturally dominant Ashkenazim (Jews of East and North European origin) and the Arab second-class citizens.

at both ministries for improving services to the Arab population. I am interested in listening—or spying if you wish—for information that in any reasonably functioning democracy would be in the public domain. Normally, to get the inside story on these ministries' plans for Arab citizens I would have to cut through two curtains of secrecy: the first preventing me as an Arab from accessing any 'state secrets'; and the second sequestering all issues related to the Arab minority from the outside world and from the light of day."

"In the interests of guarding against the calamitous possibility that the Arabs might start to demand equal rights," Abu-Farah explains sarcastically, "a consensus exists in the government and state bureaucracy to keep these issues in the shadows, to shield them from the bright light of 'our democracy.' All discussions about the Arab population are handled in private and in consultation with the Shin Bet. In their view, secrecy and darkness befit Arabs and their affairs. After all, equality, not to mention equity, for Arab citizens might lead to them feeling empowered, and that in turn would—most naturally for Arabs, of course—lead to them engaging in subversive activities and endangering the security of the state."

"Your analysis cuts through a lot of fog," I add, enchanted by the master's dark humor. "You just articulated much of what I know to be true, having worked with government officials for nearly a decade. Regardless of how high we rise in the system, we are suspect by definition. I can sense it in my isolation within the system and the wariness of those around me, whether spelled out clearly or implied in thinly veiled accusations, sly innuendoes or slips of the tongue. I sense it in the rebellious tone I detect in the voice of my Jewish staff and in the patronizing attitude of my superiors as I raise another issue related to the Arab community. I heard it in October 1973 when my head nurse and closest colleague walked into my office a day after the outbreak of war with Egypt and Syria and angrily told me: 'This is what you do to us when we trust you!' And I heard it after Land Day in the dismissive reply from the Minister of Health when I demanded for my community health services equal to those in the kibbutz in which he lived. It is real enough that I sense it every way I turn: I see, smell and taste it, and can almost touch it with my open hand as I extend it to greet people on the street. I feel it in my bones. At professional meetings at the hospital, I can almost pick it up from the tabletop and submit it as a specimen to the pathology lab."

"And yet the world ignores all such insults and injustices suffered by all of us, Palestinians, so as not to be reminded of its own historical assignment of constitutional ill-will to the Jews, its deeply ingrained anti-Semitism. You can trust me, Abu-Ty," he addresses me respectfully as an equal, "through these six committees that I chair we will get the word out."

So far I have attended the first meeting of each of my two committees. We are scheduled to meet Dr. Israel Katz, the Minister of Labor and Social Welfare, a liberal politician and former academic who seems to understand the urgent need to address the plight of the poor. He has set up the advisory committees dealing with the Arab minority and called on his friend Dr. Sami Geraisy to coordinate them. I value Dr. Geraisy's opinion enough to take his word on the significance of my involvement. He has gathered together members of the Arab community who through their titles, official positions or past achievements have attained some credibility in their community. Our letters of appointment state that the initiative has the best interests of the target group at heart, yet no one is fool enough to believe that the advice we offer the government will be binding on, or even heeded by, the decision-makers. My prediction is that, like advisory committees everywhere, our recommendations will be used more as a fig leaf than as a working tool.

It is already obvious that the advisory committee on Arab education is not a serious undertaking. The other members, all educators, appear to have been selected for their meekness, if not their collaboration, like Arab teachers in general. In its efforts to co-opt and pacify its Arab citizens Israel has focused much effort on their education, setting a separate department for that. It is an open secret that the Shin Bet has the final say in who gets appointed or advanced in the Arab Education Department. My own nephew, Moslih, is one of three teachers recently dismissed from Arrabeh's high school. Apparently, as a college student he once appeared on TV and said something to the effect that he thought the Arabs in Israel did not enjoy equal rights.

The director-general of the Ministry of Education, who is an Iraqi immigrant, was there as a guest observer for the first meeting of the committee. Though he speaks Arabic fluently, and everyone else at the meeting was an Arab, we all had to switch to Hebrew for his benefit.

As the director-general, he was invited to speak and did not hesitate to let us know what was expected of us. He wanted the assembled group, mostly employees of his ministry, to reassure him that no harm would come from our deliberations. His minister, it is reported, has been trying to get the advisory committee on Arab education canceled. The bottom line, as far as the minister and director-general are concerned, is that they know what is best for the Arab minority, and that all Education Ministry workers should be guided by their wisdom. In other words, the minister and his director-general are advising the committee, and not the other way round. But their advice is not binding on me, of course, and is the reason I may stay on this committee against my better judgment, if only to see how this reversal of roles will finally play itself out.

For two years, between 1958 and 1960, shortly before I left to study medicine in the US, I worked as a teacher. I entered the teaching profession with my vision already set elsewhere. Under different circumstances I might have tried to make a go of it as I enjoyed sharing what knowledge I had with my students. But I found working in the Arab department profoundly unrewarding and morally repugnant, both because of the anemic curriculum offered to the students and because of the severe erosion of freedom of thought. The authorities' strict controls on what teachers could say or do in the classroom, in an attempt to limit the horizons of our students, made me deeply uncomfortable. Even on pay day, I failed to exude the sunny aura of contentment I noticed on the faces of colleagues.

It was during that period that three seventh graders from the school were suspended for several days because they had expressed pride in the Arabs' historic achievements in Andalusia. The school superintendent himself came to the school to remind us all of the policy of "strict apolitical discourse in the classroom." We never found out how the news about what those pupils said had reached the authorities. The more we teachers whispered about it in the school corridors, the more suspicious of one another we became.

At the weekly teachers' meeting, the principal would advise us to avoid the "wrong political parties." As the twelfth Independence Day of Israel approached, he reminded us of the need to appear individually at the residence of the Military Governor in Nazareth to offer him our congratulations. In the words of the principal, the Military Governor was "the man who rules supreme over the destiny of all of us and that of our families, the man who approves our employment as teachers and issues us permits to travel out of our villages." (The principal did at least cover my back when I failed to make an appearance by registering my name in the Governor's guest book and signing for me.) On another occasion the principal recommended that each teacher purchase a copy of the collected Arabic poems of Salim Sha'shoa', the Iraqi Jewish immigrant who was the Superintendent of Arab Schools. The principal explained that it was not compulsory, only "highly advisable." I did not buy the book, and did not stick around long enough to suffer the consequences.

I recall peeking at the diary of a fellow teacher in 1960 while we roomed together during a teacher training program. He had recorded verbatim the political discussions we had had earlier that day, including the names of teachers who had maligned the name of King Hussein of Jordan and of others who thought Golda Meir was not pretty. I came back from the United States ten years later, to find him well advanced in the system, having attained the senior rank of superintendent. Those mentioned in his diary were still stepping in place at the lowest rungs of the system.

7
The Evil Eye

Villagers in traditional garb in our neighborhood. In the foreground freshly installed water line in the sewage-drenched ground.

March 15, 1980

Dr. David Gilbert, a recent immigrant pediatrician from the United States, was supposed to replace me in Acre after I moved to Nazareth to be acting District Physician, but at the last minute he announced his resignation, saying he was escaping back to California. He was emotional as he took his leave from me:

"You know my concerns are about much more than the salary and the position. I just can't take the crookedness, the hypocrisy and the callousness." He left me his Physician's Desk Reference with a tender admiring poem he wrote for me.

I have enjoyed working with Dr. Gilbert. Not only is he a good public health physician, he is also a genuinely liberal one. I try to console myself with the thought that in the end he would have become just another Israeli "liberal." His last words to me were:

"It takes about two years from the time of immigrating to Israel for your typical Jewish liberal to convert to the local brand of liberalism and accept the general attitude of hostility to all things Arab. Except that in the case of 'true liberals' such attitudes become wrapped in multiple layers of pious explanations and self-righteous contortions, enough to make the racism palatable, at least to themselves. I personally prefer to deal with the settler types, the violently hostile Uzi-toting goons. They are scary enough for me to keep my distance from them and to convince myself that their views are trite and their threats ignoble. Easier to handle than the liberals' manipulations."

Dr. Gilbert had an admirable innocence and enthusiasm about him despite his age and experience. He was still open-minded enough to see things to which others seemed blind. The first time we went out together on a field trip, a policeman stopped our driver, who is Druze and looks it, and inspected at length the vehicle's license, engine and safety features. Dr. Gilbert asked me if more Arabs than Jews were stopped for these "routine checks." The only honest reply I could give was to relate my own experience with the *Haga*, the civilian militia who man road blocks across the country. Whenever I drive by myself or with my wife, I am never stopped. We look Western and there is nothing to identify us as Arabs. It probably helps too that the car has a "doctor on duty" sign displayed prominently on the windshield. But whenever any members of my family dressed in Arab attire ride with me, I am pulled over and the car searched thoroughly.

For its comic relief value, I told him about the time I scolded a Haga man, a tiny Yemenite with an oversized automatic weapon, who was pacing back and forth by the closed electronic gate of the Naharya Hospital. Pointing to the security clearance tag on my windshield, I shouted my demand that he open the electric gate immediately. He replied:

"The gate's guard went to the bathroom, and I don't know how to operate it. I am Haga. I stand here to scare the Arabs away."

On the way back, Dr. Gilbert commented on the fact that the Jewish nurses' terminology showed a negative attitude towards the Arab population.

"They repeatedly referred to the Arab villages as 'backward.' That is an expression of their deep hostility towards those villagers. I think that they just misunderstand the differences between the cultures and label it as backwardness."

What I did not tell him is that, unfortunately, such stereotyping as equating the Arab with backwardness has been internalized by most Arab members of the government bureaucracy including some of my nurses. Self-deprecating remarks are part of their daily "professional" discourse. Sometimes I even catch myself lapsing into this type of racist labeling.

Dr. Gilbert regarded it as his mission to help develop and advance the health status of Palestinian citizens in the Acre sub-district. Apparently he talked about this with his friends and neighbors in Haifa, and told me that he could not understand their responses.

"Their reactions vary from extreme hostility to utter ridicule. Most people cut me off, become hostile, and stop associating with me and my family. Others simply advise me against my plan. And the rest laugh their heads off. The attitude of the average Israeli intellectual towards the suffering of the Arab minority is 'Let them stew in their own juice.' Nobody seems to mind it or plans to do anything about it. 'Let them improve themselves; no one is stopping them; they have to learn to live with the situation and solve their own problems with their own means.' That sounds innocent on the surface of it. But in truth, Arabs have little that is their own. I mean, they are living in a society where the economy depends on aid from abroad, and much of the budget is centered on the defense forces and the military industries. If you exclude someone from all of these parts of the economy, then he is not equal."

He was apologetic as he made these observations, saying that he had not been through whatever hell his neighbors may have endured, whether Nazi concentration camps or the loss of a loved one in wars with the Arab states. He estimated that over 95 percent of the Jewish population considered Arab citizens deserving of their deficient health services and the other forms of discrimination they face. I have to admit, that is my impression too. It is very much the reaction of people as

enlightened as I once thought Dr. Hedy Frank-Blume was. After the first
year of working with her, in one of many memorandums, I pointed out
the connection between the poor socio-economic development of Arab
villages and the health of their residents. Her written response was:
"We should let these communities develop naturally." Which sounds
to me like a polite version of "Let them stew in their own juice."

Unfortunately, I could see that even Dr. Gilbert's aggressive liberalism
was mellowing a few months after he joined the system. He switched
from the arrogance of the visionary social reformer to the contemplative
doubter of our shared values. When he started at the Ministry, he told
me he wanted to work in Acre to help the Arab community. He had
worked with minority groups in the US and felt that was his mission
in life. He hoped to raise the health standards of this underprivileged
community in Israel and start making a dent in its infant mortality rate.
I could not have wished for a better professional to take my place. But
by the time he decided to leave, Dr. Gilbert had reached the point where
he appeared to have become resigned to the idea of the Arabs in Israel
as social misfits. Sooner or later, he argued, they would benefit from
the general progressive trends and improvements in Israeli health care,
and this was probably their best hope for improving their situation.
That approach, of course, did not require any initiatives or planning
or deep thought. He too was slipping across the divide, towards the
"Let them stew in their own juice" philosophy.

That brings to mind Dr. Yorum Matan, who for a time sat in Nazareth
as the public health physician in charge of the Northern District, where
Arabs make up more than half of the population. Shortly after he
retired, the Israeli press reported that he had written the following
words to a liberal politician with whom he did not agree: "After
we finish killing off all the Arabs here, we will start killing guys like
you." Such views are far from unusual in this country, and are hardly
shocking until you remember that this man was actually in a position
to do harm to Arabs through willful neglect if not through active
slaughter, somebody who was in charge of issues of life and death for
many of the country's Palestinian citizens.

Dr. Matan was reputed in Ministry of Health circles to hold a
particular loathing for dogs, and would swerve his car intentionally

off the road to try to kill one. I sometimes wonder what he would have done had he met me in person. I was the first Arab physician to join his staff shortly before he left. Fortunately, I was spared the pleasure of meeting him thanks to my boss Dr. Frank-Blume's protection. It is interesting to note that before I joined the Ministry, her cadre of mother and child health physicians for the entire Acre sub-district comprised one elderly Dutch obstetrician named Dr. Kahansius. She had planned to split the whole sub-district geographically between Dr. Kahansius and me. I offered to do intensive preventive work in Arrabeh and neighboring Sakhnin and Dier Hanna on a full-time basis and to collect half a salary. That must have been convincing enough; she agreed and shortly thereafter she offered me her chair as she moved up the totem pole to replace the retiring Dr. Matan.

June 15, 1980

The first proper dental clinic has opened in Arrabeh. The importance of the occasion parallels that of the opening of my own clinic in 1970. The dentist, Dr. Mtanis, is using the two extra rooms I have in my clinic. When he approached me about that I agreed on the condition that it will be a properly equipped permanent dental clinic, not another fly-by-night dentist arriving from the city with pliers and painkillers to pull teeth out. Dr. Mtanis is the third dentist in his own village to qualify and decided to come to a less competitive location. He mounted a mini-advertising campaign, pasting small announcements in several public places in the three neighboring villages about the clinic's opening hours.

He has also hung up a sign with his name and title over the entrance to our combined clinic. I suddenly realized that for all these years, ten years to be precise, I have never had one myself. Everyone knew it was my clinic and could easily find out the opening hours; if the door was locked, a patient would ask a passer-by where to find me or when to come back. To date, I have operated within the expectations of traditional village life: everybody knows everybody else and their whereabouts at all times. But now that the dentist has put up a sign, people may think that I have cut and run and that a new professional has taken over the clinic. So, finally I will have to put up a sign stating my name and opening times.

Things are changing in other ways. There are now two other licensed physicians working in Arrabeh, one in my clinic on alternate nights and the other in his own clinic. Two more recent graduates are doing their internships, and three or four will graduate in the next couple of years. What that means is that I have stopped being unique, or in such demand that I can afford not to advertise myself. I am slowly on my way to becoming just another general practitioner whose services are needed but can be rendered by any other. This is good for the community, but emotionally I have mixed feelings about it. Time to brandish my public health expertise.

Still, I am not sure how astute some of the new clinicians are. Last summer, on returning from a two-month vacation in Hawaii with the family, I found several medical cases in my immediate family mistreated. One young woman, the wife of a nephew, had been laid up for thirty days with fever and back pain, and had received a month's worth of twice daily penicillin injections for presumed acute rheumatic fever, despite the lack of any clinical evidence for the diagnosis. By the time I came back, the doctor had been persuaded by the arguments of the woman's mother that this was a classic case of the evil eye. After all, she is young and pretty and had recently danced at a relative's wedding to the envy of the other women present. The mother says she persuaded the doctor not only to stop all Western medications but also to participate in guessing who might have put the evil eye on her daughter. The young woman is now at the central regional hospital recuperating from an acute flare-up of her inflammatory bowel disease, a form of autoimmune disease not a whole lot better understood than the evil eye.

On a work visit to the maternal and child health clinic in neighboring Rama I had a chat with my colleague Dr. Anwar Awad, family physician par excellence and the first local Palestinian physician to graduate on a Communist party scholarship and hence a leading community activist. With his credentials I felt confident in approaching him directly regarding my new dream:

"My expertise is in public health, a field of never-ending frontiers and unlimited potential, especially for the under-served and less developed. I see bringing health awareness to the Palestinian community in Israel and empowering its members to improve their own health as my next assignment. Would you join me?"

"That is a serious challenge, and a dramatic change of direction," Anwar replies. "It also smacks of narcissism. You need a big ego to go on a limb like that. But yes, it is about time we start a process of repositioning ourselves professionally and socially."

"For the past two years I have toyed with the idea of creating an independent organization in which a few of us who share a mutual trust and concern for our community can start to collect and analyze data, publish reports, and try to take corrective action on its behalf."

"You know we are treading on very thin ice here," Anwar cautions. "As long as you are part of the system, a mid-level official of the Ministry of Health, you are privy to 'privileged information.' If you start making too much noise about what you learn from such resources, the information will doubtless cease to be available to you. This would be equally true if you were to leave your government post."

"Such information is not secret; it should be in the public domain."

"But calling attention to the picture that emerges from the raw data—putting two and two together—will be seen as subversive, if not treasonous. It is the subject matter itself, evidence of the discrimination against the country's Palestinian population, which is taboo."

"The raw data is everywhere if only we could manage to organize its collection and analysis. In terms of field research, be it in health, demography, development, economics or politics, the terrain is truly virgin and ripe for exploitation. The next step is to recruit partners, a few trusted colleagues, to lead the process of launching a community-based non-profit organization with us."

"Just remember, we have our families to support. You know, like the saying goes, we are like grazing sheep, every time you say 'baa' you lose another mouthful of grass."

"I have enough leeway at the Ministry of Health to start acting on my new vision. If you agree I will sound out one or two more colleagues and we can get started."

February 15, 1981

I have started attending rounds at the Rambam Hospital in Haifa. Yesterday I also attended the outpatient clinic at the hospital. I introduced myself to the first resident to arrive at the clinic, a young Arab doctor, and told him that I would be joining him for the afternoon. The elderly patients and their families in the waiting room were so generous with their praise for this young physician that I started wondering about their motives. But indeed, from his rounds in the department, it is obvious that he is one of the good ones. Between patients we chatted about some common professional concerns:

"It is very demanding to be an Arab graduate of an Israeli medical school," he tells me as if I didn't know that. "We have no choice but to excel; to begin with, the fact that we were admitted to an Israeli medical school makes us a very select group. Arab university applicants are at a great disadvantage. Our primary and secondary schools are poorly equipped, poorly staffed and systematically neglected. And we have to compete against veterans of the Israel Defense Forces who get first priority. Given that, those good enough to be admitted are the top 1 percent of the students from the Arab educational system competing against the top 10 percent of students from the Jewish one. Once we pass the initial period of familiarizing ourselves with college life we face the prejudices, the discrimination and the negative stereotyping of our professors and classmates. It takes much stamina, perseverance and inner strength to handle all that and still come out as a humane health-care provider at the end."

"I know! Succeeding despite your minority status means that you really shine, more so even than us, the few who escape the discrimination to study abroad. We too have to be ambitious and self-reliant to make it, but we do not face the same kinds of psychological and social stresses. I would guess that any young man or woman who goes through your kind of experience comes out either terminally alienated and embittered or mortally defeated, and perhaps co-opted."

"When you came onboard we expected you to join us on the floor as another resident, but you show up only for rounds. How did you arrange that? Such a convenient arrangement would not have been possible without *protectsia*."

"I don't know if I would call it *protectsia*. The director of hospitals at the MoH, a fellow public health specialist, arranged it for me."

"Bribery and influence-buying are common in our health care system, especially in hospitals. It is an open secret that to enjoy the best hospital care you must first show up at the private clinic of the head of a

hospital department or his deputy. He or she will then admit you
to their departments at the expense of regular non-paying patients
belonging to the various sick funds. The practice is not permitted, nor
openly admitted in any formal document. But it is the way the system
works and everybody knows it."

"Protectsia is particularly applicable in this country in the case of
the Arab minority," I added. "We lack the temerity to demand what is
rightly ours in a system that disowns us. We wind up needing someone
to intercede on our behalf for the smallest of favors."

"Rumor has it that one of our semi-literate politicians who was
appointed to a nominal position in the Ministry of Transport regularly
and successfully interferes on behalf of his fellow villagers who want
telephones installed in their homes. All sides in the deal seem to miss
the fine distinction between the Ministry of Transport and the Ministry
of Communication because, as you know, in Arabic both words are
derivatives of the same root."

On leaving the hospital, I meet my niece Afaf, who is shopping in the
Hadar, the ritzy commercial center of Haifa. It is windy and raining so
I seek shelter in a protected corner of the busy entrance to a high-rise
building while she shops nearby. Suddenly, an elderly street cleaner
starts sweeping in my corner, intruding rudely on my solitude. Then he
takes off his plastic raincoat, turns it inside out, lays it on the ground he
has just cleaned, takes his rubber boots off, places one on each of arm
of the raincoat, lays his broom across its bottom edge and commences
to perform his noon prayer, prostrating himself across his private clean
space, totally oblivious to the hubbub all around. A Muslim sweeper in
a Jewish market place! For some inexplicable reason I find this image,
at one and the same time, disturbing and awe-inspiring, something to
remember and to be proud of, almost a cause for celebration. Nearly all
the street sweepers in Haifa, as in other cities in Israel, are Arabs. Might
this man be the father of the young physician I just left in Rambam
Hospital? Such incongruities are not unheard of among blacks in the US
or among minority groups elsewhere in the West. But in our situation
discrimination is spiced up with the enmity engendered by a continuing
war, in which the warring parties divide along ethnic lines. It allows
for a clear conscience as one hates or enslaves the other.

March 28, 1981

Yesterday I attended a meeting in Nazareth at the office of the Reverend Riah Abu-al-Asal of a pressure group lobbying for an Arab university in the Galilee. The idea has been debated for a long time but now we seem ready to tackle the logistics of it: the location, funding, staffing, accreditation, and so on. Above all, what we need to master are the legal maneuvers necessary to get the authorities to approve the plan, something they are not favorably disposed to. There are nationalistic overtones to this project, and no one is making a secret of the fact that we want to open an Arab university that will teach the Arabic language and Palestinian culture as they should be taught. This would be in addition to all the other standard subjects taught in Arabic.

One of the first departments of this planned university would be a nursing school. What more could I ask for!

8
Galilee Folkways

Composite family portrait, 1960; front row: my father, Abdul-Kader, between brothers Mohammad (left) and Ahmad; back row: author between brothers Mahmud (left) and Sharif. My mother and four sisters are not included!

May 2, 1981

The residents of Sakhnin, Arrabeh's larger neighbor, are known for taking much pride in their village. As in communities the world over, Arab villagers like to construct negative stereotypes about each other. In the Galilee, frictions between Sakhnin and Arrabeh are legend. Sakhninis look down on us for lacking both valor and the traditional

Arab generosity when receiving guests. In return, we find them haughty
and contentious. Their men strut around, noses in the air and head
dresses (*hatta-wi-iqal*) tilted to the side, walking in the middle of the
road with an obvious chip-on-the-shoulder demeanor. We refrain from
blowing our car horns at them for fear of starting a fight. Even my
mother-in-law, coming from half way across the globe, calls Sakhnin
"the sassy village."

In such social milieux, the clan, or *hamula*, identity counts for much.
My friend Subhi, a learned man and aspiring health professional,
recently married a pretty young woman from another clan. Subhi, it
emerges, has not only snatched his bride away from a large number
of her eligible cousins but also has commenced constructing his house
on part of their shared land. Land inheritance is always a sensitive
issue in rural communities, but to Palestinians it has added value
as a symbol of belonging and secret code for nationalism. So, over
this intimate issue of building a family and a home, my friend could
have sparked a clan feud that might have dragged in over half of his
village and resulted in considerable harm. He was playing the risky
traditional game of betting his own clan against another, equally large
and influential. Fortunately he did not have the support of his father,
a successful modern farmer thoroughly versed in the importance of
land and in the ways of traditional conflict resolution. To help calm
the clans' overwrought passions, I also brought in Sa'id Rabi, a man
with much influence and stature, being that rare breed: an Arab who
works in the head office of a government ministry in Jerusalem, in his
case my own Ministry of Health. The three of us eventually managed
to resolve the dispute peacefully.

At least, there are accepted ways of resolving these "traditional"
cases of conflict. What is becoming a source of ongoing and permanent
clan enmity are the recently introduced local elections, in which the
Shin Bet is able, behind the scenes, to incite rivalries and awaken
dormant feuds. The security services are putting old social structures
to new and evil uses. Our communities have not yet learned how to
quell the disputes inspired by this kind of intrigue, or how to rise above
them or avoid them in the first place. An example is the recent feud
between the Khalaileh and Abu-Yunis families in Sakhnin following
last year's municipal elections in which the two sides aggressively

supported different candidates. The damage to property in poverty-stricken Sakhnin was estimated to run into the millions of dollars.

Subhi is like a son to me. I love the guy since the days I taught him in elementary school and later I helped him get a scholarship to study for his Masters degree in Public Health. At the time, the Deputy Minister of Health was Mr. Abd-el-Aziz Zu'bi, the first and only Arab to attain that rank thanks to his long service in the Zionist socialist Mapam party. He once visited my office in Acre to tell me he would be happy to help advance my position in the system. Then as now, I was the only qualified Arab public health physician in the country and I remember feeling insulted that this politician, who lacks any professional credentials, thought he could patronize me. I told him that I did not need any personal favors, but that he could easily advance the health of the Arab community in the Galilee in two small ways: first, by securing a scholarship for one of my young sanitary inspectors, Subhi, to study health education at the Hebrew University; and second, by getting the government telephone company to install a line to my clinic in Arrabeh. The second measure would have saved the Ministry of Health a small fortune by ending the wasteful practice of sending a driver in an official car to Arrabeh every time my secretary needed to pass information on to me at the weekends or after hours. Mr. Zu'bi promised to take care of both matters but so far, eight years later, has delivered only on the scholarship for Subhi. Was the subversive act of bringing a telephone line to Arrabeh overruled at a higher level?

June 11, 1981

Today I have to make obligatory appearances at two social occasions in the village. One is at my cousin and neighbor Abu-Hisham's house. His son, Hisham, was married yesterday, and today I will drop in for a cup of coffee. Abu-Hisham makes excellent traditional Arabic black coffee and I am always game for the burst of flavor that the one sip of bitter brew at the bottom of the cup one is offered gives. The women of the extended family will be gathering to sing and celebrate with the bride, while the men gather around and enjoy coffee and sweets without any formal role at this stage. The official congratulations come later as each family visits privately, bearing the appropriate monetary gift or a household item. Now, all that is expected of me is to show my face, have a cup of coffee, gossip, and maybe even argue about current politics, about the Israeli attack on the Iraqi nuclear plant, about what Qadafi said to King Hussein and what Hussein said to Sadat.

The other event yesterday was the funeral of Hasan al-Shalash, the father-in-law of my niece Samiyeh. She delivered another baby boy about a month ago and named him Hasan after his grandfather, not an unusual practice here. Except that in this case they knew full well that the older Hasan would be dead in no time. I avoid funerals at all costs but today I have to make an appearance at the Shalash family to pay my respects. I will go with my brother Ahmad, who is a neighbor and also Samiyeh's father. Ahmad will be expected to invite the men of the Shalash clan to his house for lunch or supper today. It is customary for the bereaved family to be fed by neighbors for the first couple of days. The neighbors take turns inviting the men for food while the women and children stay home and food is carried over to them. It is not unusual for little children in the bereaved family to be taken away from the immediate vicinity of the death, the mourning and the singing of dirges, to the house of a distant relative.

Didi's and my presence as part of the host family is expected, almost mandatory. Between mealtimes, members of the family sit in their home, men and women apart, and receive visitors who come to pay their respects. A young member of the family offers black Arabic coffee, cold water and cigarettes to the guests. Sweets, almost always dates, are offered only if the dead person is elderly. It is a kind of offering of thanks to God for having granted the deceased such a long life. Or, perhaps, it is a gesture of grateful acceptance, sweetening the occasion of the timely departure. Normally, after the drinking of coffee, one returns the cup and says "amar," a single word that conveys much: "May this house flourish and remain this prosperous forever." You always say "amar" after drinking coffee except on the occasion of visiting the family of a dead person, where you return the cup and say nothing or mumble an "*Allah yirhamo*—God have mercy on his soul." But the combined physical act of returning an empty coffee cup and blurting out the word "amar" has becomes so ingrained and inseparable to me that it takes special vigilance to avoid making a terrible faux pas at funerals.

June 15, 1981

A while back it was the wedding of Ihsan, my late brother Mahmud's eldest daughter. I owe much to my late third brother. But for him, I might well have been one more plasterer in Arrabeh. In 1948, the year of the Nakba, when the accursed war threw everything out of balance, my father had the wisdom to keep us from leaving the village as refugees and to counsel other village elders to stay put. In the meanwhile we all lost a year of schooling. But my brother Mahmud didn't forget his dream of continuing his education. The danger of the war had hardly diminished before he had devised a scheme to earn money for the school fees. In his own unorthodox and impractical way he imagined joining a fruit picking gang of village boys to make the needed money. He was the poetic type, not much on planning. So this was dismissed out of hand by my father as another unworkable scheme of his dreamy son. It was not only impractical but also extremely dangerous. The fruit picking was in the citrus orchards of Jaffa and under the supervision of cruel Jewish bosses, the very same heartless monsters who had just finished butchering Palestinians and driving them out of their homes, or so it must have seemed to Palestinians of my father's generation. How could my father allow such a dangerous venture? Besides, further schooling was out of the question. Even if the fees for the first semester were to be secured, who is to pay for the rent of a room in Nazareth and for food, books, proper school clothes, and the bus fare to come home for vacations? This was not a reasonable plan and the dreamy kid should get it out of his head.

But Mahmud did not listen to reason. One day he struck out; he ran away and joined a gang of fruit pickers. After several weeks, two age-mates from the next village, Dier Hanna, brought news that he was well and earning good money. There was no danger to their lives. The only danger was that the Histadrut, the Jewish labor union, sent its own gangs to look for the cheap Arab laborers and would beat them and drag them to jail whenever they caught them. The father of the two boys came calling and tried to intercede on behalf of Mahmud. By the time my father relented, Mahmud had already registered and paid his fees at the Nazareth Municipal Secondary School, the closest high school to Arrabeh. My father made his peace with the strange idea of his son becoming a scholar, in fact the first boy from Arrabeh ever to attend a secular high school. Father traveled to Nazareth and with the help of his nephew and niece, members of the respected Nazarene Safadi family, he rented a room and got his son properly settled for serious academic work.

My late father was a man of purpose. Once convinced, there was no stopping him. After two years, Sharif, my fourth brother, joined Mahmud and two years after that I followed suit as well. During all those years father had to skimp on all other family expenses and cut corners to make ends meet. For seven long years the family afforded to eat meat only during holidays when we came home, and for seven long years no one but us three students bought new shoes or clothes. Sister Jamileh became a veritable artist in performing alterations on everyone's clothes. She particularly excelled in maintaining my dad's formal village style outfits, rendering her patchwork somehow presentable and even fancy. For a total of seven years he had to cover our not so negligible expenses. For that entire period he stood the shaming and the social pressure brought on him by relatives and peers to change his ways and to refrain from selling his land to support this venture of his. By the time I graduated he had only one last piece of land in the Battouf Valley, the village's fertile source of livelihood. Even that last piece he had to sell to pay for my ticket to travel to the States in pursuit of my own wacky dream. But he was the one to blame; he was the one to install the thought of studying medicine in my head in the first place. Would he have had the willpower to sell part of the olive orchard too had my two late younger brothers survived? God was too merciful to put him to that test. One thing I know for sure: He was proud to receive news of my success and high grades in my first year of college, the one year he was alive after I left.

On the day of Ihsan's wedding, again, I had to play the role of the surrogate father, the responsible decision-maker who has the last word in approving all the fine details of preparation and social charade that custom compels a bride's father to go through. But at the key moment of the ceremony it was Ahmad, as the oldest living uncle, who had the honor of escorting the bride to her in-laws' waiting car. They had brought with them the local *qadi*, or Muslim religious judge, when they came "to collect their property," as he put it to us. He is a known collaborator, a drunkard, and an Uncle Tom if there ever was one among the Palestinian minority.

That is the rule now in Israel: Muslim religious judges are appointed by the Jewish bureaucrats of the Ministry of Religious Affairs, obviously under the direction of the Shin Bet, and thus are specifically selected for their contribution to dishonoring their religion and ethnic group. Because these *qadis* automatically accept any government demand, the country's highest Islamic clerics have sanctioned some notably un-Islamic tasks worthy of Allah's hottest hellfire. For example, the *qadis* are handsomely paid to attend all sorts of dubious occasions, such as the laying of a corner stone or the initiating of a commercial project on Islamic *waqf* (religious endowment) land, thus sanitizing, and justifying such trampling on our collective rights and sensitivities. In return, they get to curry influence with the authorities and make a lucrative business from intervening on behalf of others with officialdom—the *wasta* system, our own watered-down version of the Israeli Jews' *protectsia*. For our *qadis*, such favors have been justification enough to keep silent about, if not actively promote, the sale of Islamic cemeteries in Haifa and Jaffa to Israeli development agencies. The only *qadi* who is a possible exception to this rule that I know of is my friend Fareed Wajdi al-Tabari, or Abu-Jareer, a decent man who had to remain studiously neutral on all political matters before securing a job as a religious judge—even though he hails from a long line of *qadis*, dating back to the days of the Ottoman Empire.

The *qadi* at Ihsan's wedding entered the house and, without any introduction or social pleasantries, demanded in a most arrogant way: "We are in a hurry. Let us go. Give us what you owe us." Brother Ahmad almost blew his top. He would have had it out with the man there and then if I had not taken him aside and begged him to be magnanimous and do what was expected of him socially, despite the judge's impolite and infuriating style. The *qadi* clearly hoped to fuel dormant tensions between the two branches of our family, the Arrabeh and the Nazareth Kanaanehs, a standard village-versus-city feud. He thought he could set the two groups at each other's throats, knowing that the embers of discord are still smoldering since Ahmad's son was rejected earlier as a suitor by Ihsan's mother.

It is a sad state of affairs when the highest religious authority in the community is an open informer and trouble-maker in the pay of the Shin Bet. You no longer know who to trust and who not to. I remember experiencing a similar inner disquiet walking between the sage bushes in the Wyoming desert, when I joined a team of roughnecks drilling for oil during my summer vacations. One had to be constantly on the lookout for rattlesnakes; you never knew from which bush the next one would slither, even when you could hear its rattling.

Also on the home front, through sheer obstinacy, my niece Wafa'a has forced us all to agree to her engagement, early, to her high-school sweetheart, Ahmad Khalaileh from Majd al-Kroum. A few months ago the boy's family sent a good friend and medical colleague to sound me out, as her surrogate father, on the matter. At that time I felt Wafa'a and her mother were not ready to reach an agreement. But the deal is now on and so Ahmad's family came on the traditional formal mission of asking for Wafaa's hand in marriage. For that purpose they had to enlist the services of a recognized personality or village elder who could head the *jaha*, or group of weighty respectables, and speak on their behalf. I told the father that if he was going to do it formally, as he must, then he should bring with him the same medical colleague he sent on the first round of sounding out.

Unfortunately, perhaps because I hold a high position in the government, the father brought with him Mr. Abu-Yasir, a known collaborator of the gun-toting type who is the advisor on Arab affairs to the Minister of Education. I was very upset and seriously weighed the option of not letting the man into my home. That would have ruined the whole deal, and complicated matters beyond repair. I love Wafa'a too much to allow myself to break her heart. My brother Ahmad, the formal head of our family, was equally outraged and left the room, having to be cajoled into returning and keeping quiet. I maintained my composure with a minimum of the required decorum until something totally unexpected and unorthodox happened to sweeten the proceedings for me.

Along with my medical colleague came his uncle, Abu-Bakri, a Communist leader in their village who brims with self-confidence, speaks in a clear loud voice, and has a permanent combative stance, especially when in the presence of co-opted lackeys like Abu-Yasir, who has to hide his gun under his shirt when in decent company. The two occupy opposite ends of the social and political spectrum within the Arab minority in Israel: the one a known informer and high political appointee, and the other a card-carrying Communist, and therefore on the government blacklist.

At the right moment, after coffee had been served, Abu-Ali, the boy's father, offered a standard poetic cliché appropriate to the occasion:

"Like bees, we in the Khalaileh clan always choose to visit only the most fragrant and sweetest of flowers, and it is our great pleasure this day to land in the most respectable domicile of the grand old family of the Kanaanehs." Then he turned to the elders of the jaha and asked that one of them speak for the group. After the customary round of each protesting his humility and asking others to do the honors, Abu-Yasir commenced performing his expected role. He cleared his throat and started:

"Ahem ... ahem ... Speaking for my self and on behalf of the Khalaileh clan, it is indeed a great honor to approach you ..." But before he had finished the sentence, his nemesis, Abu-Bakri, decided to contest the social honor. He, in turn, cleared his throat and raised his voice even louder:

"We are here on the honorable assignment of asking for the honor of engaging our son ..."

Then Abu-Yasir raised his voice a few decibels to make himself heard, and there followed several seconds of explosive tension as the two fought their vocal dual before Abu-Yasir accepted defeat, lowered his voice and then went silent. Abu-Bakri boomed the rest of his presentation and I and my brother Ahmad acknowledged their kind words and assented to their request. The group silently recited "al-Fatha," the opening verse of the Koran, to bless the contract. Wafa'a then came in and offered all the assembled men sweets so they could get a good look at her and judge her graces. The conversation became much less formal. Others in the group sang the praises of the groom to us. Dr. Wa'il Fahmawi, another colleague and acquaintance of mine in the jaha, gave his "unbiased" opinion of the young man. He attested to his good health and manners and pointed out that he was the best player in the football team of Majd al-Kroum.

Early one recent morning, at about sunrise, a couple from a neighboring village knocked at my door. Their fourteen-year-old daughter was having severe abdominal pain and was in great distress. I took her into my examining room in the house. Within two minutes it was obvious she was in labor. As is my way in such cases, I spoke with her alone and then with each parent separately. The father did not have a clue, or did not want to have a clue. The burden of dishonor would be too much to bear. The mother knew and pleaded with me to save the girl's life, not from expected medical complications but from certain honor killing by the male members of her immediate clan whose honor she had besmirched. I called both parents in and, in the girl's presence, explained that she has what we doctors call "an acute abdomen" and needed to be hospitalized immediately. I offered to take the girl to Rambam Hospital, where I claimed to be heading in an hour's time. They left the girl in my trust and went home. I had had experience in handling such cases and knew where to go, who to involve, how to keep inquisitive relatives at bay, and how to cover the girl's tracks for her three-day absence from home.

But there was a problem. I had worked long and hard to schedule a meeting at my office that morning with all the big shots in the area to discuss a project I wanted to launch on limiting the number of infant deaths in the region. I could not possibly stay away from the meeting. I checked the girl again and convinced myself that she had several more hours of labor to go. Didi was not home so I called my trustworthy niece, my right hand in my private practice. I explained to her that she was to stay with the girl until I returned at eleven. In the meantime she was to look after the girl and not let anyone into the house. I woke up the children, fed them breakfast and sent them off to school. I told my niece how to contact me if anything went wrong. I also explained this to the girl, who had stopped crying and writhing the moment her parents left. I gave her a painkiller and drove over to Acre with one thing on my mind: how to cut the meeting short.

About an hour and a half into the meeting, my secretary, who had instructions to screen my calls, rang. My niece was on the line, very agitated: "Come right now. She has delivered." I excused myself and fled home. I made it in eighteen minutes, a record time. The fourteen-year-old, in full control, had wrapped the dead fetus and placenta in a towel and placed them in a bucket, cleaned herself up and was having a snack of bread, *labeneh* (yogurt cheese) and olive oil. I hugged my ashen-faced niece and reassured her. I checked the girl and took her and the bucket to my trusted friend and colleague, Dr. Hans Bernath, at Nazareth Hospital. He, in turn, reassured me that the fetus was not viable in the first place. Four days later I took the girl, a perky and pleasant teenager, now miraculously cured, back to her welcoming family. The mother took me aside and reassured me that "my secret" would always be kept. As expected, I have not seen or heard from the family since. Their sense of shame guarantees they will avoid me till the next crisis.

9
Galilee Panoramas

Brother Ahmad, his wife and eight of their nine children, 1962.

June 20, 1981

Here is a scene I observed from the village taxi stand, located at the edge of a central open space known as "*al-Marah*—the resting area," a name derived from its function in times past when the work animals would be gathered here before being taken out to communal pastures by the collective cowherd attendant. Each farmer, or more commonly one of his children, would bring the animals, mostly cows, to this location and leave them under the watchful eye of the cowherder. I recall as

99

a child bringing our donkey here. We were never much of a farming family, my father renting out our fields to landless sharecroppers from the village. I also remember the cowherder's daughter, about my age, showing up every evening at our door to collect the standard payment for her father's services, a loaf of bread or a small share of whatever my mother had cooked that day, slopped into the girl's *keshkool*, or bucket. To this day, in the Galilee we use the term "like a cowherder's meal" to imply a messy hodge-podge of things or events.

Al-Marah also stands out in my memory as the village square where the conquering Jewish forces gathered all the men of our village in the summer of 1948 to choose the most physically fit and line them up against a wall, the same one I now look at. One soldier knelt behind his Bren gun poised to mow them down, or so everyone assumed at the time. We had heard that such massacres had occurred in other villages. Instead, the men were spared and put in trucks to be taken to hard labor camps as prisoners of war.

My father was not taken as a POW, probably because of his age and frail build. The fear and anxiety of the moment has totally evaporated from my memory. What remains is a sense of anger and revulsion at the way those soldiers manhandled my father, insulting him publicly with a slap across the face that sent his traditional headdress, the seat of a man's honor, rolling in the dirt. The next day they added a further insult, undercutting his authority within his own private domain. Our traditional walled courtyard with its gate opening on the village square was selected to house the cattle looted from the village farmers overnight till the army trucks arrived to haul them away. Though two armed guards stood at the gate, one old woman made her way in and wouldn't stop embracing her milking cow, calling it by its endearing name "*Hamami*—pigeon," and begging my father to free her cow for her. When he tried to interfere with the two soldiers he was insultingly shoved back into the one room our family was cooped in. The old woman spent the night with us singing dirges for her cow till day break when an army convoy arrived and she saw her Hamimi forced with a rude twist of its tail up a wooden plank to the back of a truck and driven away. Her wailing and beseeching of my father—"Please, Abu-Mohammad, make them let Hamami go!"—still rings in my ears.

For weeks afterwards, I would take packages of freshly cooked food to my three brothers who had followed my father's wise advice and hidden in the woods, sleeping in caves and whiling their days hunting birds or collecting *zaa'tar*, the local herb, for the family. Every few days, when an army Jeep approached Arrabeh from the west, we, the young children, would run to the eastern outskirts of the village shouting at the top of our lungs: "*Khara wawi*—jackal shit," our secret codename for the Israel Defense Forces.

It is interesting that the young man in charge of the taxi stand has a wireless communication gadget far in advance of anything commonly available in the village. He is from a family of refugees originally from a village in the Jordan valley. He and his older brother were part of the same group of boys I joined for two summers volunteering on a kibbutz. When I came back from the United States, I was shocked to hear that the older brother had abandoned his wife and two children and settled for a new life as a Jew in a religious neighborhood of Haifa. An even stranger twist of events befell a third member of our kibbutz coexistence group, this one the son of a family from a destroyed Palestinian village in the Jezreel valley. According to "reliable" rumors, he converted to Ultra-Orthodox Judaism, married a Jewess and to this day works as a "*shohet*," a religiously authorized kosher butcher at a chicken slaughterhouse in Bnei Brak. Now that is wild!

The Arrabeh taxi stand manager is an ambitious young man, judging by his energy, hustling and salesman-like smile. Paradoxically, in front of him is an ancient hand-written sign preaching the anti-Protestant work ethic: "Contentment is an everlasting treasure." On the other side of the street are the two village butchers—old man Musa Hailak and the younger Mansour Salih al-Mansour—preparing to kill a cow they have just bought from the pick-up truck of a Bedouin man.

Some years ago, the village council enlarged Musa's cesspool so he could slaughter animals at will and the blood would not flow down the village main street. The concrete roof of the cesspool used for slaughtering the animals is designed in such a way that the blood drains inwards and not out on the road. The council assumed that he would empty it regularly before it overflows, but paying for a tanker to empty the cesspool is clearly beyond his means. So Musa waits for rainy nights and pumps out his cesspool on the street. The way the council-owned, tractor-drawn tanker disposes of the sewage from the village's cesspools into the open fields is another story—one only suitable for those with a strong stomach.

On this occasion, old man Musa is clad in his work outfit of an old yellow damascene *qumbaz* over a white *sirwal*, both shiny with old blood stains, and a hand-woven skullcap covering part of his salt-and-pepper unshaven head and face. Two of his young sons hover around him waiting for his orders; the family has been cursed by schizophrenia and no one has figured out the source of the plight. With him is the younger, muscular butcher, Mansour, one of my classmates at elementary school. His father, who associated with my own, figures in the village's collective memory as a leader of the 1936 Palestinian uprising against the British and their favored subjects in Palestine, the Jews.

The family is also renowned for Mansour's uncle, Hajj Yousif, who earned the title *hajj* for making the pilgrimage to Mecca, then a religious achievement of heroic proportions. Hajj Yousif was a very respectable man, and a regular in my father's narrow circle of friends on the rare occasion that he was in the village. At one point, my father even considered giving the hand of my second sister to him in marriage. The hajj figured prominently in the 1936 Palestinian revolt too, though he was more of a loner, given to spending his time alone in the mountains with his gun. He was a follower and personal friend of Ez-eddin al-Qassam, the inspirational leader of the revolt.

There is a well-known and romantic story featuring Hajj Yousif. He is said to have fallen instantly in love with a girl from the neighboring village of Nimreen, which was totally wiped off the face of the earth in 1948, the grounds then used as a military installation. Nimreen was near Hittin and Lubyeh, two larger and more famous Palestinian villages that were also destroyed in 1948, and not far from Meskana, another transformed Palestinian landmark now known as the Golani Junction, named after an Israeli army brigade. The story goes that one day, while out seeking to quench his thirst, Hajj Yousif spied Zakiyeh, the daughter of Nimreen's headman, with a group of other village girls drawing water from the village spring. It was love at first sight. When he went to her father to ask for her hand in marriage, he was refused—as who would not refuse a young man coming alone with his gun and no one to speak for him. On the spot, Hajj Yousif swore never to marry another girl, a promise that sealed his fate as a bachelor forever. Some villagers speculate that the story was invented to account for his staying single, or worse yet, for his impotence.

In 1948, with the Nakba and establishment of Israel, Hajj Yousif went underground and became a smuggler of goods and people across the border with Lebanon. He must have developed good contacts with the various Palestinian factions in Lebanon's refugee camps. It is also generally assumed that he was active with the PLO, traveling back and forth on foot between Lebanon and Arrabeh to gather information for the resistance.

I learned these last details firsthand by virtue of my profession, his relatives sharing them with me as I tended to him on his deathbed. That wintry night I was called to see him at the home of his nephew, Mansour, the young assistant butcher in the mental picture I keep straying from. He had been dumped out of a taxi at the gas station across from his nephew's home by two unidentified armed men in civilian clothes. The men who delivered him reported that he had fallen out of bed in his sleep while in prison. He was intermittently conscious enough to recognize me by name and to tell me that he had been arrested and repeatedly beaten unconscious by his interrogators in jail. As he would open his eyes during brief lucid moments, he would say to me: "Those dogs killed me!" He had severe head injuries and multiple bruises over the rest of his body. I referred him to a hospital in Nazareth where I was sure he would at least be admitted, even if not guaranteed the most expert care for his injuries. He died there a few days later. Pressure was put on his family not to demand a post-mortem, despite my advice to the contrary.

The hospital too kept quiet, presumably to comply with the wishes of the threatened family. I wrote the nephews a detailed medical letter and encouraged them to take it to a good lawyer in the city. They went to Hanna Naqqara, the most competent Arab lawyer prepared to deal with such a sensitive case, and a Communist old-timer better known for defending Arab land cases. Nothing came of my advice, however. Apparently, using Hajj Yousif's renown as a smuggler and possible PLO agent as a pretext, the Israeli police and secret services violently threatened and harassed his nephews and the rest of his family until they agreed to drop the case. The nephews were repeatedly detained for questioning, accused of harboring their uncle. They were in and out of jail so frequently they lost all confidence to pursue the matter. At some level, I think they also lost their sense of belonging to the community. The system's repeated assaults on them managed to turn the young men into political and social pariahs, pushed to the very edge of village society by their tainted reputation and murky status as both security risks and/or collaborators. Also, it is likely that the elopement of their sister a while back with a Bedouin cattle trader had helped to besmirch the family's good name. In more recent times, they have been slowly rehabilitated and are regaining some social acceptance.

Back to Mansour, the junior butcher standing there, the exact picture of his late father, down to the details of a lit cigarette hanging from the corner of his mouth and the occasional grunting nervous cough. He looks stout and muscular, his shirt sleeves rolled up and the front of his shirt unbuttoned. He struts around as if challenging the cow and eventually holds it forcefully by the horns and tries to wrestle it down while its legs are tied to a peg in the shop wall. Around him and Musa Hailak, I count exactly 56 child spectators, including Musa's own half-dozen children, some no doubt waiting for the fresh meat, but the majority just onlookers from the neighborhood excited to witness the cow's slaughter. Fresh meat is no longer such a rarity as it used to be during my childhood.

There is also a retarded teenager standing in the circle of young children, his mouth gaping and emitting the occasional scream of irritation at the taunting and poking of those around him. Standing next to him and trying to comfort him is an old man, Mohammad al-Sin, the older of the Sin brothers, who is married to a distant relative of mine. He stands there leaning on his cane with his thick features, a week's worth of facial stubble, and a huge hand-rolled cigarette hanging from his fleshy lips, with the same empty amazed excitement and blank-eyed look of the retarded boy, both peering over the heads of the children to see the killing of the cow.

But where am I in this scene? I know, like all of my sanitary inspectors, that nobody in rural Galilee kills animals under veterinary supervision as required by law. It is customary in official circles to look the other way and blame it all on extenuating circumstances. Indeed, our entire existence as a mistrusted and neglected, out-of-sight and out-of-mind minority has become enveloped by one continuous mess of extenuating circumstances. At least, the blood does not flow in the streets, either in terms of sanitation or as a figure of speech. In some very minor and indirect way, I may have had something to do with that.

June 25, 1981

I am driving to the hospital in Haifa. On the way I will drop off my children at school, before making a brief detour to check on an old lady who has fallen and injured her back. The streets are full of blue-clad children, dressed in their uniforms. I stop at a clearing at the side of the road near the school and the children kiss me goodbye. They look and smell like beautiful fresh flowers. Everyone sees their children as beautiful flowers but, looking around, mine seem definitely more like flowers, fresher and brighter, than the other children.

The clearing is used as a disorganized open market, where traders simply park their cars and set out their goods. Women are streaming in from all directions, carrying their younger children in their arms while older children carry plastic bags, old woven baskets and younger siblings. All are flocking to the market: a few old men, old women, young women, children and more children. A flood of children from every direction: children who are going to school, and others who are not going to school, boys who are hanging around doing nothing and girls sauntering in imitation of their mothers' gait. Children with runny eyes and impetigo sores over their exposed skin, on the back of their necks, behind their ears, over their foreheads, and on their skinny arms and legs. Children with thick yellow snot running down their faces that they lick with their tongues and wipe on their shirt sleeves. The flies swarm over their heads. The hot gusty air blows dust in their eyes.

I am riding in my air-conditioned VW Kombi, fit to head for the beaches of Hawaii, where the idea of buying a pop-top camper that can sleep a family of four was first conceived. The contrast between the immaculate interior of my car and the squalor of the street scene provokes a sudden feeling of guilt and shame that strikes me like a thunderbolt. It is unbearable. I have my doctor's bag with all the standard equipment and emergency medications intended for the treatment of the sick. I know how to treat all of these conditions before me, and am tempted to grab a few of those children and wipe the snot off of their faces, take them home and give them a bath, and dress their open sores. I could physically do that for one, or two or even three, but not for all of them. It is so overwhelming that I have to drive away fast, relieved only that I manage to drive through the crowd without running anyone over.

What makes the encounter more painful is the realization that there, but for the grace of God, go "my" children. These are faces I recognize; I can tell from their features who their parents and grandparents are, some of them my friends and relatives. I cannot but identify with this crowd. I am one of them. I am reminded of the emotional panic I experienced on seeing my nephews and nieces the first day I came back from the United States. Several of them, I reassure myself, are now married, in college, or abroad studying medicine. I have become more hardened since that first day back as the village doctor. Yet, on this occasion, I could have pulled to the side of the road, put up the pop-top, lain down and cried for an hour or two. But I don't dare cry anymore. It would be admitting defeat, and I am not ready for that. I still aspire to bring about change, to have an influence, and to give those children the same chances my own children have, in body and mind.

But how many of them can I help directly and with how many courses of antibiotics? I have given Ty no less than four courses this summer. Impetigo scares and irks me; it carries the risk of serious complications, including damage to the heart and kidneys. But also it is so damn visible and hideous to look at. Those sores on the children's skin stare me straight in the eye. They mock me and make light of my medical know-how all summer long—every time I walk to my clinic, or the store for milk, or the baker to pick up fresh bread for the children's lunch. I would pretty much need to put every child on prophylactic therapy all summer to prevent skin infections, and then all winter to treat bacterial respiratory infections. It is simply the wrong approach to rely on medications as the only means in the struggle against disease; they have far more diseases than I can deal with. How many have tapeworms in their intestines, how many runny ears, diarrhea, stress, maladjustment or birth defects? In my clinic I see only the tip of the iceberg.

As I drive away, it is the children's turn to challenge and taunt me. They flaunt their intelligence and potential in their innocent tricks, their street games and their handmade toys. Realizing their hidden promise is the real challenge.

Eventually I make it through the impromptu market and make my detour up the hill to see the old lady, Umm Ahmad, who has fallen and hurt her back. Her son, Ahmad, is another childhood friend. She is blind, diabetic and has a list of other chronic health problems. The visit is more for her psychological well-being than to relieve her pain.

Her husband too has problems: a couple of his fingers are missing; the remaining fingernails are thickened and quite mangled up; one eye is missing and the other is of limited sight. These are the legacies both of growing up under Turkish rule and surviving smallpox. He is officially blind but he sees enough to move around the familiar surroundings of his home. He still looks after his old wife, feeding her and moving her from her bed to the window to enjoy the cool afternoon breeze. He does not ask for any medical intervention for himself. It is his wife who has to be treated for her chronic aches and pains, compounded by her recent fall. I satisfy myself that there are no fractures, reassure her, dispense some medications I brought with me, and promise to visit her again in a week's time.

And then, just as I am leaving: "But, won't you please see our neighbor, Umm Ahmad, across the street?" The other Umm Ahmad also has lot of pains and aches, and is also blind and bedridden. So, since I am in the neighborhood, why don't I, please, drop in and see what can be done for her? On the spot, I have to come up with an excuse. I am about to blurt out "I have to get to the hospital" when I get an acute attack of honesty. True, I am on my way to Rambam Hospital in Haifa and will be late if I stop to see her now. But I am going there for my own personal advantage. No one else will benefit from my trip to the hospital; I am not treating anyone, only to log in another day's worth of attendance that will count towards recognition of my public health specialty in Israel, not an insignificant matter in and of itself. Someday someone may benefit from my specialty, but in the here-and-now my going to the hospital will not do anyone any good except myself. And here I am trying to run away from these women's immediate problems, from the aches and pains of an elderly woman who once reminded me that a number of times in my infancy she breastfed me along with her own son, Ahmad. How can I get in my car and drive away?

While I am still weighing my options, Ahmad himself pitches in and puts an end to my vacillating:

"But you have to see my wife upstairs first. She is a stupid woman. I can't ever make her understand that when she is pregnant she shouldn't carry heavy loads. She is two months pregnant and lifted a sack of flour up the stairs all by herself. By the time she made it to the kitchen she started bleeding."

I cannot handle all of this and still make it to the hospital, so the decision is made for me. But still I am upset.

"Listen here," I say brusquely, "I came to see your mother and do not have the equipment and medications your wife may need. All I can do is refer her to the ER." So I write a short, cryptic and unprofessional referral: "Mother of twelve; aged 33; two months pregnant; heavy vaginal bleeding; for admission." Ahmad is happy to have the referral and tells his wife to get ready. For her part, she objects to the idea of being hospitalized. She wants to abort at home. Even if she goes to the hospital, I should see her and make sure she is not in shock or something.

She is in bed but vocal and argumentative.

"I don't want to go there; I don't want any treatment; I don't want to see other doctors. It is enough that our neighbor sees me."

We grew up in adjacent homes in the village, not far from the mosque. In those days everybody in the village was a neighbor. She is lying flat on her back with her two youngest children on the bed, the baby in a sitting position in her right arm leaning face down suckling at her breast, while a tiny toddler hangs on to her bent knee with one arm and holds her extended left hand with the other. Two children totally dependent on her care who will be left at home as she goes to abort their unborn sibling at hospital, or who will share her love and suffering in the same bed if she does it her way at home. I make sure she is in no immediate danger and insist that the husband call on other female relatives for help with the children before he finds a car to take her to the hospital. I leave him exchanging blame and curses with his wife and make for the house across the street.

"Oh, doctor, won't you wrap my hand for me?" On the way, another unexpected patient delays me, this one a diabetic with paronychia, an infected fingernail bed.

"Of course, I will!" And as I do, I proceed to explain to her the need for daily change of dressing, for antibiotic pills, and for dealing with her diabetes. I can see that she is worried about the cost and perhaps even suspicious of my motives. So I volunteer the reassuring information that there will be no charge for the change of dressing.

"Couldn't you prescribe something for my burning urine?" another pleasant old neighbor asks. I cannot possibly resist her solicitous, shy smile.

Again I prepare to head for the second Umm Ahmad. But someone else is in greater distress. It is the younger of the two old refugee widows next door. They used to be the two wives of the respectable Hajj Abu-Hasan from the destroyed village of Lubyeh. Times were when Lubyeh lorded it over much of the Lower Galilee, including Tiberias, thanks to its fertile valley and the generosity and valor of its residents. The villagers even made claims to have hosted and aided Salah-eddin (Saladin) in defeating Richard the Lion Heart and his Crusader armies at the neighboring Horn of Hittin. Young men from Arrabeh often used to seek seasonal employment there, reaping the plentiful wheat crops for Lubyeh's landowners. But in 1948 Lubyeh was demolished by the Jewish forces and its residents driven out across the border to southern Lebanon as refugees. A few found refuge in the neighboring villages that survived. Hajj Abu-Hasan made it to Arrabeh with his two wives, one young daughter and a disabled son. The more able-bodied members of his family fled to Lebanon.

The two old ladies are now all alone. They manage somehow to take care of each other physically and, more importantly, socially and psychologically. One, the younger of the two, is bedridden because of rheumatoid arthritis. She has a problem with peptic ulcers because of the massive doses of aspirin she is unable to manage without. The two women used to be regular patients of mine until the local sick fund took over responsibility for their health care. They both collect an old-age pension from the National Insurance and with that comes health insurance through the General Sick Fund. Inadequate as such care is in Arab villages, at least it is affordable. The older of the two takes care of the disabled younger one, washes and feeds her, combs her hair, gives her regular medications and scouts out for the occasional stray doctor making his rounds to beg him to come and visit her.

The last time I visited them was over a year ago, but I saw the healthier of the two in my clinic some four or five months ago for some transient acute problem. I always enjoy calling at their immaculately clean and tidy, thatched-roof, single-room residence. Although not entirely destitute, they fit very well the stereotype of the lonely, helpless, widowed, poor souls that they actually are. Still, they retain a large measure of self-respect, social graces, and the demeanor of Palestine's landed aristocracy. What they lack in material goods, they make up for with their welcoming remarks as one enters their humble abode, and constant cajoling and smiling, especially from the older of the two, with her deeply furrowed tattooed open face and fully alert clear black eyes. Is it my mother's face I see in hers? Mother died without ever having had a photo taken of her and her image has faded from my memory with the passage of years. But she did have big black eyes and an open smiling face. The two widows always insist on paying for my services and, when I refuse, they send me eggs from their free-range chickens, a present much valued by Didi.

The bedridden half of this charming pair of "sisters in suffering" tells how she has used self-hypnosis to overcome her insomnia: "I close my eyes and think of the days when I was young and in full health. I start at the edge of Lubyeh and walk up the village road slowly, greeting all the people I meet in the warm early summer morning. On occasion I even smile to a young man on his way to the fields. I stop by relatives and friends, asking for a drink of cold water here, a sip of coffee there, and accept a ripe fruit from a good friend back from her orchard. Sometimes I even join a relative's family eating breakfast of freshly baked bread, olive oil and zaa'tar, or watermelon and labeneh. I chat with everyone I meet and am reassured of their good health and welfare. By the time I reach my home and see my family, I am tired out and fall fast asleep."

The older "twin sister" shuffles over to the neighbor's yard, as I am struggling to escape from my temporary incarceration there, and insists that I see thourti, the colloquial term used in Palestine to refer to the wife of one's husband, literally meaning "my harm" or "the one who does me harm." Having personally witnessed the loving bond between the two old women in the past, and pondering for the first time the linguistic derivation of *thourti*, I have no choice but to comply with her request.

"What's wrong with her?" I ask.

"Oh, she is vomiting and crying, and she wants to see you." Not the other way round, you notice! She just wants to feast her eyes on the good doctor's face, or so the older *thourti* makes it sound. How can I resist such sweetness?

"Is she vomiting a lot?"

"Oh, no. But she is always like that. She vomits all the time."

"Since when?"

"Since she had her last stomach operation less than a year ago."

"Has anything changed today?"

"No. She vomited just once today. She saw your car from her window and asked for you to come in so she can see you."

"When was she last seen by a doctor?"

"Oh, I always go to Kupat Holim [the sick fund] and bring her medications. She hasn't been seen by a doctor since you last saw her, about a year ago."

No wonder she longs so much to see me! So I go in and do what I can. I encourage them to send for me if things get worse, eggs or no eggs.

Finally I reach the second Umm Ahmad. Her daughter-in-law, a mildly retarded, hyperthyroid mother of ten, has a sore throat and is truly anxious to do something about it before it worsens her recent affliction with facial palsy. On top of her neglected hyperthyroidism, for which she refuses to be referred to an endocrinologist because of the cost, she now has to worry about seeing a neurologist. On this one, I am forced to manage through regular guesstimates of her thyroid functions and medications. I reassure her that palsy is often a passing thing and that she is sure to look more normal again—or as normal as she did before, which is not much. Her husband is also borderline mentally disabled and epileptic. He is not able to hold a job regularly but can dig ditches and earn some income from menial work. To a large degree they depend on social security and on child support payments. And the little one who is two years old has an upper respiratory infection. I handle that on the spot as well.

What would they all have done had I not happened to come by? Here, in just three adjacent households, was so much pathology and need! Knowing the socio-political situation, I wonder if even a miracle can pull us out of the sea of malignant neglect in which we exist. Perhaps it is time I tried walking on water!

10
Genocide, Here and There

My two refugee cousins, Fatmeh and Amineh Rustom, in black, visit brother Ahmad and his wife. A third cousin, standing, is their formal host in Arrabeh.

September 25, 1982

This is our third week back in Arrabeh after a holiday in Hawaii. It was a great blessing to be away from the immediate vicinity of the war, Israel's invasion of Lebanon. We live directly in the path of the invading Israeli forces and a short aerial distance from the battleground, being constantly reminded of Israel's awful bullying capacity by the continual blast of its jets streaking overhead on their way to strafe Beirut.

"*Allah yiqtuss minhin! Allah yiqta'ahin!*—May God punish them! May He terminate them," my dozen sisters and sisters-in-law intone in unison with my visiting two cousins, Fatmeh and Amineh. Teenage girls shush their little sisters' and brothers' screams and wipe their own tears. The women's dirge cries of "*Yee! Azaa', azaa'! Batil, batil!*"* fill the air in brother Ahmad's crowded living room while we, the men of the family, sipping our after meal coffee in the adjoining foyer watch the same scenes of the Sabra and Shatilla massacre on TV.† As one picture after another of women screaming over piles of distended human corpses and ruined homes are shown, Ahmad repeats his mantra: "And they tell me there is a merciful God!"

Among the women folk only Fatmeh and Amineh, my two refugee cousins, whose family, the Rustoms, was driven out of their coastal village, Dannon, close to Naharya, in 1948, shed no tears.‡ In the last couple of days we have heard first-person accounts of war atrocities from them. Both are married now and live with their families in Sidon. Their stories are simply horrific. They are visiting us in Arrabeh for the first time since they left it in 1948. On their way to Lebanon, they had stopped here first and stayed with us for several months after they fled their village. I remember them well, especially their brother Faisal, my playmate. They first settled in el-Buss camp, but left it years ago. This

---

* These are typical cries of village women at funerals that express extreme distress and loss, approximately meaning: "Oh! What calamity! Tell me it is untrue!"

† *Sabra and Shatilla massacre:* In the summer of 1982 Israel launched what it dubbed "Operation Peace for Galilee," sweeping through southern Lebanon and heavily shelling Beirut from land, air and sea. Eventually Palestinian fighters evacuated the area under American mediation and guarantee of the security of Palestinian civilians. Then Israel announced its intention to cleanse Palestinian refugee camps of remaining "terrorists" and, in a "mopping operation," "encircled and sealed" the two camps, Sabra and Shatilla. On September 16, 1982 it sent its armed allies, the Phalangist militia, into the two camps to slaughter an estimated 3,500 unarmed civilians. Israel admits only to 700 killed. Though the UN Security Council termed it a "criminal massacre" and the UN General Assembly called it "an act of genocide," it never received a formal independent investigation.

‡ *Palestinian refugees:* The Palestinian Nakba—Arabic for catastrophe—of 1948 resulted in the establishment of Israel on 78 percent of historical Palestine with the violent displacement of 750,000 of its residents to neighboring countries as refugees. They lost their homes and livelihood and were mostly settled in camps under the auspices of the UN Relief and Works Agency (UNRWA). Despite the UN affirmation of their right of return Israel has denied them such an option. By 2005, Palestinian refugees numbered over 6 million.

time around they are visiting us under Israel's "Good Fence" policy.
Since 1978, when the Israeli army began occupying Lebanon, it has
permitted some of its residents, including Palestinian refugees, to cross
into Israel to visit relatives. This "magnanimous" policy, originally
meant to facilitate the importation of cheap labor from south Lebanon,
has turned into an effective propaganda ploy.

They have witnessed the destructive and lethal power of Israel's
modern weaponry raining down on their neighborhoods, destroying
their homes and dismembering the bodies of friends and relatives.
They spoke of their shock and fear at hearing the never-ending Israeli
air raids, which finally drove them out of the city to an area on the
Mediterranean shore for four days and nights with no food or drink
except for the polluted waters of a nearby river.

"We were separated from our families and later had to search for each
other amid the mayhem and destruction," the younger one, Amineh,
says. "I went to the hospital to search among the maimed and injured
for my fourteen-year-old son, Jalal. The sights there were enough to
make your hair turn white. I lived through what you are seeing in
Sabra and Shatilla except that those bodies still breathed. I refused
to go to the morgue to look for Jalal's body. For a whole week I was
certain that I had lost him. Then I received word that he had found
shelter in another part of the city. I tracked him down to a Christian
neighborhood. When I arrived at the home where he was staying he
rushed to hug me and whisper in my ear the new Christian name he
had assumed in order to be granted asylum. Your friend Faisal, who
is also a doctor, was smuggled out of his hospital in a full body cast
by the foreign staff. The trick worked and he got out alive, but the
improvised cast was too tight; it nearly suffocated him to death."

"*Shoo ahkilak ya ibin khali, ya Habibi; elhaki mish mithl eshshouf*,"
my older cousin, Fatmeh, says in an amazing monotonous and resigned
tone of voice, "—witnessing is different from hearing, oh beloved
cousin of mine. I saw with those two eyes, may they lose their sight,
through my kitchen window, my two sons, *muhjit qalbi*—the flames of
my heart—shot dead at point-blank range at the impromptu checkpoint
set up by a militia group yards away from the house. My third son
escaped and is now in a mental hospital. We had to wait till dark before
we could bring the two bodies in."

Fatmeh and her husband have been estranged ever since the trauma. The most awful part of listening to their various ordeals was seeing the vacant look on my cousins' emotionless, frozen faces as they spoke, and their ability still to smile for our benefit as their next of kin, injured, pathetic and melancholy as such a smile can only be. Looking into their tired, empty faces at such a moment forced me to confront my inner feelings of guilt, shame and betrayal that at those devastating moments for them I was with my family basking on the beach and partying with friends in Hawaii. I tried to explain. "*Allah yhanniku dayman*—may God always grant you pleasure" was their only response, a wistful wish far from understanding or forgiving.

I had another confession to make to my dear cousins:

"An added burden of emotional turmoil waited for me when I returned to my office after my summer vacation. I was truly happy to hear that none of my Jewish colleagues or any of their next of kin fighting in Lebanon has been killed or injured. The stark incongruity did not sink in at the time; only later, as I experienced the horror of listening to your stories again and again, did it dawn on me. I cannot possibly wish any harm to my close friends, my decent Jewish colleagues. And yet they and their husbands, brothers and children are the very same people collectively inflicting death and destruction on you, my childhood friends and cousins, and on your families. This is the emotional schizophrenia of our daily lives: we have to dissociate the individuals we work with from the collective actions of their state. We seek a scapegoat for the war crimes, such as Ariel Sharon, especially when his past and present acts should be enough to indict him as a war criminal. It is the system and its ideological underpinnings, not individuals, that fail us all here in Israel, Arab and Jew alike."

It is only a shame that my cousins never heard this confession; I made it in my inner thoughts looking at the two of them staring blankly at the televised pictures of the Sabra and Shatilla massacre. I couldn't bring myself to utter such thoughts.

"Despite all the explanations given over the past week by Israeli officials, high and low, of what happened at Sabra and Shatilla, this is nothing short of genocide," Sharif, my politically attuned anthropologist brother declares.

"Responsibility for the massacre rests squarely with Prime Minister Menachem Begin and his war minister, Sharon," I offer in agreement.

"They and other members of their government try to market their dastardly aggression to the world as 'Operation Peace for the Galilee.' Much as they try to hide it, the world is waking up to the criminal nature of their misadventure."

"The West, of course, refrains from blaming the Israeli leadership," Sharif objects. "It dares not countenance the thought that Israel regularly bombards civilians in Beirut and in refugee camps; it refuses to believe that Israel, cold-bloodedly weeds out a specific group of 'undesirable' people, Lebanon's Palestinians. That is Israel's bottom line: the physical elimination of Palestinians, period. They use the Maronite goons to do some of their dirty work for them. They even try to whitewash their horrific aggression by shifting the blame to their victims. Refugee camps are 'terrorist hideaways' in need of 'cleansing,' they explain. And the West is ready to listen to such poisoned logic. The stark facts pass unnoticed because they are too painful, too reminiscent of the West's own past genocides."

"Whether or not the Christian Phalanges carried out the actual killing in Sabra and Shatilla, the massacre was committed with the full knowledge of that fat SOB, Sharon," Ahmad offers. "He planned it and oversaw it, I am convinced."

"That is the most awful realization to live with," I declare in astonishment. "I am living in a country where my government, the system I am employed by, initiates, sponsors and promotes genocide against my people."

"And the conflict is rooted in an argument over land," Sharif goes on. "That puts demography at the heart of the conflict, and justifies for Zionism any tactic as legitimate. By Israel's current nationalist logic, Palestinians are the ones illegally occupying the land of Israel. Old, twisted and illogical as this claim may be, it provides a goal, redeeming the land from its occupiers, that legitimizes all means of dislodging such intruders from 'our land,' including genocide. An outrageous fact has just emerged as the numbers of civilian casualties in Beirut were reported by Israel and by the International Red Cross and other international agencies. There is a vast discrepancy in the two sets of figures which, it was discovered, results from the fact that Israel, in counting the casualties of its air raids and sea and land bombardments, counts only the Lebanese dead and injured. Israel does not record Palestinian casualties. The line separating the physical elimination of Palestinian refugees in Lebanon through systematic blanket bombardment of their camps and their slaughter in proxy massacres like Sabra and Shatilla is difficult for me to discern. In both cases Palestinians are clearly perceived as dispensable. A life form has to rise to a certain level of humanity to qualify as victim of genocide. And in Israel's eyes Palestinians are disqualified by definition, simply by virtue of who they are. They are not human enough to count as casualties; their elimination is not genocide, not a war crime."

"Your logic is painfully clear, Sharif," I argue in protest. "It is a fact that I am Palestinian. It is a fact that Palestinians, even when they die, do not count. It is a fact that the world has abandoned Palestinians as a direct consequence of its history of abandoning the Jews before them. Therefore, you and I should panic, should cut and run. We should take our American wives and children on the next plane to the glorious US of A. But war has rules. How can Israel get by with these crimes?"

"No one dares compare Zionism to Fascist or Nazi ideology, for to do that would be to commit the crime of anti-Semitism. World opinion has it thoroughly hammered into its subconscious that Israel, Zionism and the Jewish people are one and the same, three identical and coterminous entities. The current war-mongering leadership of Israel manages to project itself as representing all three entities."

"Well, it certainly feels like that at the gut level," I relent, "even if you understand its fallacy intellectually. I find it impossible to make sense of it to my children. How am I expected to explain to a nine-year-old that not all Jews are at war with all Arabs? Or that leaders like Begin or Sharon can be world-class war criminals and still be supported by the clear majority of their nation, one that lays claim to innocence and to a higher standard of morality than we, the Palestinians, can ever aspire to? The children's sense of hostility and alienation from their state is difficult to isolate and focus specifically at the real culprits. Jewish associates at work tell me that their children hold the same generalized enmity to all Arabs and all things Arabic."

"If the government plans and executes massive aggression," Sharif continues, "and if the general population of Israel approves of that government and does not bring it down, and if world Jewry continues to defend the actions of that government, then why should a child not reasonably reach the conclusion that all three are his enemies? When democracy gets misused to achieve such ends, one cannot blame children, or adults for that matter, for holding negative feelings against an entire population that acted in a 'democratic way' to make it possible for a an elected bunch of criminals to do 'legally' what 'our' government has done to the Palestinians in Lebanon. And yet there is one widely-held assumption that underpins the arguments of most Israelis. It boils down to the view, taken as self-evident, that this type of violence and cold-blooded killing is the common language of Arabs in dealing with each other and that the Jewish people, by definition, are above this. The assumption, in some fashion and to varying degrees, is made by every Jewish person, inside and outside Israel, that I have conversed with on the subject. I can hardly argue with my Palestinian colleagues in Ramallah who conclude: 'Anybody who holds that kind of concept about me is my enemy. If everybody who is French holds that view of me, then I hate all French people.' But Western civilization, with its hegemony over world opinion, has sinned so violently against the Jewish people that it dares not see the actions of Israel for what they are: genocide."

"There is only one hitch: blaming all Frenchmen is not anti-Semitic, and blaming all Jews is, even when it comes from a Semite. Even pointing out the near total solidarity of the Jewish people with Israel is a thought beyond the pale in polite Western society. It is a blood libel. Also, in my own heart I reject this conclusion. I seem to be rationalizing to myself a view I never thought I was capable of holding, a view that assigns total guilt to a whole race. God forgive me, but I seem to be reaching that point. There must be something wrong somewhere in that nice constellation of logical arguments that we have laid out here starting with the fact of Israel's leaders' physical elimination of Palestinians and ending with blame for all Jews. There must be some false assumption or faulty analysis in that logical sequence. Because I still refuse to accept my conclusion. Yet, so far, I am not capable of finding where the fault in the logic lies."

"Perhaps you simply dare not accept such conclusion," both of my older brothers chide.

Now, as I sit to record my thoughts, I realize that my current near-panic state stems from the knowledge that I am dispensable simply by virtue of who I am, a Palestinian. I now realize that, at a deeper level, this is where my feeling of constant physical danger comes from. But how afraid am I for my own life? At this very moment: no, I am not afraid that if I step out on the street somebody will kill me. My paranoia has not taken such firm hold of me yet. But I can imagine a scenario, within years, months or even weeks, in which the circumstances are manipulated in such a way that I find myself living in a place mad enough with violence, from forces that are beyond my control, to drive me from my piece of land. I am not alone. Sane people on the streets of Arrabeh speak of it as quite possible.

Another realization dawned on me recently. Subconsciously, at times like these, as a Palestinian occupying a responsible position in the system with a level of legal authority, I find myself becoming scared in the office for no apparent reason. I sat down with pencil and paper and tried to ferret out the cause; of what exactly am I afraid? Confronting it squarely, my fear turns out to be more logical than sheer paranoia, though paranoia has its own infallible internal logic too. I am afraid that somebody, say the Acre police chief or a Shin Bet agent, may see fit to pick some angry drug addict deprived of his usual fix or an outraged soldier on home leave, to settle a score with me. It could come on the heels of my issuing a citation to a violator of public health regulations. God knows there are many minor underworld figures in Acre who get in trouble with the law through the actions of my office. Were it to become necessary, from the point of view of the security services in the area, might they let one of their henchmen do me harm? He could slash my tires, or it could be much worse. Someone could just walk in and shoot the place up. It happened before to a predecessor who took on the city's drug dealers. There are so many armed people everywhere that it verges on anarchy as far as the use of firearms goes. In a fair anarchic state, everyone has an equal chance to be an anarchist. Here, I am at a disadvantage. Only Arabs are not allowed to practice their anarchy fully, to carry arms.

Pragmatism dictates that I should continue bearing the stigma of being an Israeli government employee. Still, for the past two weeks, apparently, I have blown in and out of the office obviously angry and distressed. Eventually, my behavior led a Jewish colleague and friend to speak to me about it. She expressed her personal objection to the government's actions and told me how much she and others in the office shared my sense of revulsion and sadness. She hoped that I did not hold any personal grudge against her and her family. I told her exactly how I felt: I hold the Israeli public at large responsible for their government's actions and for electing criminals to lead them.

One morning, Israel Oppenheim, my environmental engineer, came in with a question on which he needed my opinion. He clearly didn't like what I told him. But I am his superior and have the final say. He argued back forcefully and stuck to his guns, so to speak. The analogy crossed my mind and suddenly, right in front of my eyes, he was transformed into the real enemy I imagine he could be. Suddenly, as if by magic, his head was covered with a woven skullcap, long curly sideburns framed his face, a low-slung Uzi gun dangled from his shoulder, and his eyes sparkled with the fire of hatred. My mind went blank as to what we were arguing about. He stormed out of my room. A moment later my secretary rushed in with a glass of cold water.

It now occurs to me that there is a different form of genocide practiced against us, a chronic and hidden genocide. The biggest and most detrimental health issue in our towns and villages is, of course, sewage disposal. Since I am already in the mood to condemn the Israeli establishment, let me level one more accusation: Israel's intentional neglect of the health and well-being of its Arab citizens amounts to the intentional liquidation of many people, especially children. Infant mortality rates among Arabs in Israel have been twice the levels of Jews in Israel since the establishment of the state. This is not due to "natural causes" or some inborn deficiency. Early after the establishment of Israel in 1948, the infant mortality rate among Oriental Jewish immigrants, such as Yemenites, Iraqis and Moroccans, was even higher than that among the Palestinians who remained and became citizens of the new state. Through concerted efforts, specific policies, focused research, visionary plans and appropriate budgets, infant mortality among these immigrant populations was reduced to near the same level as that of Western Jews. In contrast, the Palestinian community in Israel was "left to stew in its own juice." Not even that. In fact, it was cordoned off by a military government, its lands were confiscated, its means of livelihood were truncated, its educational system was undercut and corrupted, and its leaders were persecuted or co-opted. To put it bluntly, the intention to exclude a group strictly on racial grounds from the state's development plans and willfully neglect its health needs amounts to another form of genocide. I realize how serious that allegation is. But, as I said, the facts are there and I am in an ugly mood.

Yesterday, I had a chance to hear directly how our leaders are abused and harassed when the heads of Arrabeh and Sakhnin's councils took a ride with me back from Acre. They had both been there to lodge a complaint against the local chief of the special police unit in charge of "public order," which specializes in quelling disturbances in Arab communities. He had called them into his office the night before a scheduled one-day strike declared in Arab towns and villages to protest against Israel's role in the Sabra and Shatilla massacres and to mourn the dead. The police chief spoke to each separately in his office, a ploy to avoid any risk of a joint response or the possibility of one testifying on behalf of the other. They both say he threatened them with deportation from the country and with physical elimination: "If anything happens in your village, you will be held personally responsible and will pay for it with your life. You know how in Gaza and the West Bank we shoot in the air and people get accidentally killed."

The strike took place on Wednesday. Our mayor showed every sign that he was scared stiff by the threats. All through the strike, every half hour, he went up and used the mosque's loudspeaker and beseeched all parents to keep their children off the streets, and not to incite any violence or trouble with the armed forces. We all, Didi, the children and I, participated in the mourning procession. Later I walked around the village for a while. There was not a single home that had not planted a black flag on its roof. Everybody expressed their sadness in that way. And everybody kept it at that level of peaceful expression of sadness and anger. I have not seen Arrabeh in such collective sadness since the death of Jamal Abdul Nasser.

11
Out of the Closet

Dino, the village plumber and a present absentee, arriving to connect our newly built home to the water network, 1979. Sewage disposal, on the other hand, requires sophisticated and futuristic technology.

November 1, 1982

Some half a dozen young physicians, residents of Arrabeh, have now established their own private clinics here. The motives, qualifications, skills and knowledge of each are another issue. But all in all, I could now close my clinic without much harmful effect on the general health of Arrabeh. I would like to encourage the young doctors to think about specializing and about joining forces in establishing a polyclinic with someone on duty 24 hours a day for the region. But it is too early in the game and specialty training is a tough nut to crack for Arab physicians in this country.

To salvage some of my professional dreams and advance my vision of better health and further development for my community, I have been working for the past three years on establishing an NGO, the Galilee Society for Health Research and Services, that attempts to promote public health initiatives from and for the Arab community itself. To assess the idea's potential, I initially enlisted the help of three colleagues, Dr. Runa MacKay, Dr. Anwar Awad and Dr. Shukri Atallah, all of whom work in the Ministry of Health's Department of Public Health and share my discomfort at implementing policies we neither decide on nor are always pleased with. As the one in the most senior position in the Ministry, I have often listened to their muted complaints and confidential expressions of disdain. Finally, after mulling over our options for the best part of a year, we decided to take the plunge and commit the faintly promiscuous act of creating a forum for professional activism on behalf of our community.

The envisioned role of the new forum is to conduct basic public health research and to raise funds in support of much-needed community health programs in our communities. We also aim to encourage, indirectly, general community development initiatives. All four of us share in the effort and have contributed significantly to the organization's expansion and rooting in its constituency, though I am the one fortunate enough to best afford the time and effort needed for the daily running of its affairs. Other health professionals from among the Palestinian minority have joined the Galilee Society but the four founders still make up its backbone.

This inspirational involvement has kept me busy for the past few years, physically, mentally and even emotionally; I seem to have fallen in love with the promise the Galilee Society offers of practicing public health from a genuine rural Arab community base free of the controls and impediments of the central authorities. It is born out of necessity and its timing is right. Policy makers at head office are intent on dismantling the public health services and transferring them piecemeal to other agencies.

I can imagine what will happen to environmental health in Arab rural communities under the Ministry of the Interior with its conservative Zionist religious functionaries. For them, impeding the progress of Arab communities takes on the force of a Biblical commandment. One such official is the deputy to Israel Koenig, the Commissioner of the Northern District, with whom I recently shared a ride back from Jerusalem. He has a crystal-clear understanding of his assignment in the Galilee: to Judaize its space and spirit. Anything that is seen as contrary to that goal, or does not positively reinforce it, is to be ignored, condemned and forcefully discouraged. And you cannot blame him as a person; the principle is approved by his state and consecrated by his religion as he understands it.

November 26, 1982

I am home today, the first day of a strike by the administrative staff at the Ministry of Health. Medical staff are not on strike but I stayed home anyway. Villagers here tell the story of a not-so-devout Muslim who found the door of the mosque half shut and decided that, had Allah intended for him to pray, the door would have been fully open. I guess it was not meant to be that I should go to work today. Fate has decreed that I stay at home and get a bit of sunshine working in my garden.

My enthusiasm for the Ministry job is extremely limited at this stage. To put it frankly, my principles stand between me and my ambitions. Had I wanted to move up the promotional ladder, then I should have compromised more. I should have become a full-fledged Uncle Tom and not a closet one.

With the Likud in power, I have lost even the illusion of being able to force some of my plans through the wavering liberal facade of a Labor government. The Labor party's style is to offer excuses: shortages of budget, ignorance of planners, faulty priorities, and so on. At least you can respond to that and try to think of ways to get around it, even if not fully. With the Likud it is a frank and open denial of any intention of dealing with the needs of the entire Arab community. The only rationale for staying on is the continued professional contact with the public health system, for what that is worth, and to have a steady, if meager, salary.

The other option is to surrender and narrow down your goal to advancing your own position in the system. From there the slope is very slippery indeed. The sky is the limit, so long as you forget who you are and start serving the system with full acceptance, if not full commitment, to its overall purpose and character as the "state of the Jews." Then the Shin Bet tests your true mettle with demands for proof of your commitment: Stand and fight for the cause; turn around and face your community over its lack of allegiance to Zionism; lead us to where the violators are.

Even at the level of District Physician, one is required to align one's purpose and vision with that of the state. When I was asked to replace Dr. Frank-Blume in that position, I declined because it was clear to me that at that level I would be getting involved with state politics and with considerations of the overall purpose of the state, for which I have no great feeling. I am not a Zionist, pure and simple. At the sub-district level, on the other hand, I still deal with people in the field, with my own people. I do not have to get involved with the setting of state policy and goals, such as how to deal with health needs of the residents of the occupied Golan Heights, for example. That way I truly avoid dealing with the deeper issues. I do the dirty work without getting the credit and, hopefully, without getting the blame either. I can hide from public accountability behind the formality of an official title. And the only one I am deceiving is myself; I am playing tricks with my own conscience. That is what I call a closet Uncle Tom.

On occasion, however, I do stand up and say "No more!" By virtue of my formal position, I should be sitting on three different committees for guiding and implementing local Neighborhood Renovation Projects. The projects are financed by donations from Jewish communities abroad matched by funds from the government. Arab communities are, of course, excluded from such schemes, and no parallel state schemes exist for them. For that reason, I have refused to represent the Ministry of Health on these committees and I have made my objections known to my superiors. No one seems to mind too much. My new District Physician has appointed Jewish staff from my office to sit on those neighborhood committees instead, appearing to regard it as a quid pro quo for her tolerating my continued active involvement in running the Galilee Society.

Gradually but definitely, I am coming to the inescapable conclusion that the only option left to me, if I want to practice the professional public health theory that all those world-class professors taught us at Harvard, is to go it alone and commit to the Galilee Society. You need a certain level of arrogance, or should I say "chutzpah," for that! From the very beginning, Anwar, my colleague and partner in mischief, called it "narcissism."

To my mind, environmental health issues, especially the lack of proper sewage disposal in our communities, and not medical services should be the overriding public health concern—for mayors and for central government agencies.

We, at the Galilee Society, have presented the problem in a nutshell: Tap water has been brought to most houses in most Arab towns and villages—a blessing, a convenience and a major health benefit. Arab housewives have learnt to "waste water," though not to the same extent as Jewish housewives. But while the drinking water supply network in each village has been planned and constructed collectively, no central planning or supervision exists for the other side of this ecological equation: the disposal of wastewater. In Arab communities, unlike Jewish ones, the wastewater usually drains into individually constructed cesspools or absorption pits that get clogged, fill up, and overflow. The shallow top layer of earth throughout the residential area gets drenched with sewage water. In that same earth lies the drinking water network. Frequently drinking water and sewage get mixed.

In recent years, this has led to three documented outbreaks of waterborne disease in Arab villages. Our village's typhoid outbreak, on which I am still reporting at national health conferences, is one of these. I am convinced that sewage contamination of the water supply occurs in every Arab village quite frequently, especially when there is a water stoppage, whether for repairs or during the summer when the water supply to Arab communities is intermittent.

Why do our mayors and other local leaders responsible for the health and well-being of our communities not build central sewage networks in their villages? The service is needed and desired; residents can afford to pay for it; the leaders are aware of its importance. Also, there is a government office that is supposed to provide earmarked loans to local authorities covering half the total cost of such a project. It is part of the legacy of a major World Bank-supported project that has benefited a large number of Jewish communities in the past. Even ignoring the planning failures made when running water was brought to Arab communities in the 1960s, the wastewater problem should have been solved years ago. Why the inaction?

To find the answer, we started by questioning the village mayors who had tried to tackle such projects and the private engineers they contracted to handle the planning. How did thcy go about this? How far did they get? And why did they stop?

Here is how it should work theoretically: Each community needs to plan, finance, (albeit with government support) and construct a two-stage project with four components: The first stage is the pipe network within the community to collect the wastewater from individual homes and a carrier pipeline to take it out of the village. The second stage consists of a sewage treatment plant to render the water clean enough for reuse in agriculture and an irrigation system for such reuse, normally by a collective farm such as a kibbutz.

In essence, a Third World rural community, with all the financial and cultural impediments that the term implies, is required to grope its way through a maze of intransigent bureaucracies rigged to impede its every move; to avail itself at its own expense of the services of greedy professional technocrats; to formulate, finance and promote a first-rate technical solution exceeding in its sophistication anything yet achieved in practice anywhere in rural Israel; and to prove to the satisfaction of deeply distrustful and misinformed officials that the entire scheme will function more to serve the overall interests of their envisioned Judaized Galilee than those of the village's own local residents.

For an Arab village facing Israel's hardened bureaucracy, its scheme for a solution to its sewage problem is destined to fail very early on, at the stage of financial planning. As soon as a village starts thinking about the project, long before it takes the first practical step on the ground, it needs a detailed plan that needs to be "approved," as in "reviewed-and-repeatedly-rejected-by-any-one-of-a-dozen-separate-government-offices." But while the impediments appear at first glance to be financial, on closer inspection it turns out that they are in fact administrative. It is hard to imagine a more cynically configured trap designed by the Jewish state for its Arab citizens.

Here is the catch-22 that took us such a long time to figure out. An average Arab village needs to find about $20,000 to cover the cost of the required initial detailed construction plan for a sewage network, and submit it to over a dozen government offices, each with an absolute veto power that can be exercised arbitrarily by any mid-level bureaucrat. The sum of $20,000 has to be incorporated into the village's proposed annual budget, which is reviewed, balanced and adjusted by the District Commissioner's office (yes, that's right, Israel Koenig again!). An amount equivalent to this expense has to be accounted for in terms of income from the village's own resources. To permit the levying of a tax for this purpose, the local authority has to pass a special municipal bylaw distributing the cost fairly among residents, to secure the approval of the District Commissioner for the bylaw, and to have it published in the government's official gazette. For this to occur, the village needs to base the tax on a detailed engineering plan which has to be submitted along with the proposed bylaw. And, for this you need ... yes, you guessed right, $20,000, the sum you began the whole process to raise in the first place.

Our communities, and no others, have to go through this process. The reason is that Jewish communities, by and large, are built in accordance with pre-approved plans that incorporate the whole range of modern infrastructure and public utilities, thanks to the zeal and generosity of the Jewish Agency and other international Zionist organizations in charge of settlement projects. In other words, Jewish communities do not have to plan and graft an entire modern infrastructure on an existing ancient village or town.

Here is an example I recently discovered of the double standard with which the whole system is imbued. Like other Jewish communities, Ma'alot, close to the border with Lebanon, was built with the standard community infrastructure. The planning was undertaken jointly by government agencies and the para-statal Zionist organizations of world Jewry. Sewage collection networks were installed before the homes were built. When the inhabitants moved into their subsidized housing, they were already connected to the electricity, telephone, water and sewage networks. In addition, an approved plan also existed for a facility outside the community to treat the sewage water and reuse it for agriculture, the formally required second stage of any sewage disposal scheme.

However, actual implementation of the second stage had been postponed because of its high cost. Instead Ma'alot's untreated liquid waste has been polluting an adjacent valley, one of the most beautiful in the Galilee.

The neighboring Arab community of Mei'lya pre-existed the state of Israel by many centuries, if not millennia. It announced its intention to move into the twentieth century by installing a central sewage collection network for its residents and completed all the required plans. Mei'lya is a Christian Arab community and, as such, benefited under the British Mandate from the partiality of the British rulers and the attention of the various church missions to Christians in the Holy Land. Unlike many other Arab villages, it has a smattering of leaders educated enough to guide their community's affairs through the intricacies of the Israeli administrative maze.

Given that Mei'lya has had a new Jewish development town, Ma'alot, built on its expropriated lands, it also has a simple and ready-made solution to the second stage of a sewage disposal scheme. Mei'lya drew up plans for its carrier pipeline to feed into the adjacent Ma'alot carrier pipeline, which in turn would lead to a joint treatment plant and onwards to a water reuse agricultural facility.

But now comes the rub. In order for the state to authorize the construction of a sewage collection network for Mei'lya's households, the village council had to guarantee that Ma'alot's sewage treatment facility, the one that had never been implemented, would actually be implemented. Even though Ma'alot is ten times the size of Mei'lya, it appeared to be in no hurry itself to address this issue. And the party that was responsible for building the external facility for Ma'alot's sewage, and which failed to carry out its obligations, was none other than the state of Israel, represented by the Interior Ministry, Housing Ministry, Finance Ministry, and so on. They have been unable to come up with the budget needed to stop Ma'alot's wastewater polluting the valley downstream. And so, say the bureaucrats, they cannot, under any circumstances, allow Mei'lya to add its untreated liquid waste to the existing environmental disaster.

Unlike Ma'alot, Mei'lya has no industry and would not pollute the water table with heavy metal waste products. All it has is its excrement, which will continue to flow in its streets while the Prime Minister's Advisor on Arab Affairs continues to issue reassuring promises, and Jerusalem's recalcitrant officials continue to weigh the pros and cons of whether to help an Arab border community, one in a sensitive "security" location and whose residents' allegiance to the state is seen as questionable. Franz Kafka surely would have pounced on a tale like this were he still around.

January 25, 1983

Finally the Galilee Society is up and running. We received a start-up grant from a church group in Belgium and have an office in Rama with adequate furnishing and equipment. We also have a part-time secretary on a trial basis. Wafa'a, my newly-wed niece residing in Majd al-Kroum, near Rama, does not have any previous secretarial experience but is prepared to work on a voluntary basis. She is on the pill, so her husband's family is allowing her to work. They would prefer that she delivers the goods: "A couple of babies now, and then you can rest and have the others later." So far she has resisted the social pressures. The stand of her mother-in-law is: "So what if you work? Who is asking you to raise children? You have no experience. You just deliver them. I've had twelve already and it won't be a problem to raise a couple more!"

I can now better visualize the role the Galilee Society can play: offering practical solutions to public health problems faced by the Palestinian minority. As a proper community-based organization we have the authority to speak on the health and development of our constituency. Funding is already assured for a prototype health education project in the village of Kufr Manda. The next step should be to establish a professional office with an expert engineer who will act as an advisor, a promoter and a lobbyist on behalf of local authorities on sewage system planning. In parallel, we will establish a revolving loan fund to empower village councils to move ahead with their projects. From our contacts with European funders, it looks like we are getting to the point where we may well find them competing over our projects. Hallelujah! *Alhamdu lillah!*

March 3, 1983

I am preparing for a fundraising trip and am busy preparing information about the Galilee Society and its target population. I wonder how my New York audience would appreciate the following story my old cousin and neighbor, Mustafa al-Ibrahim, aka Abu-Ahmad, is telling to fellow villagers with much gusto and a mix of admiration and disbelief. Abu-Ahmad is a burly and rough-hewn old-timer with a limited circle of village social contacts, almost a recluse. He sports a massive moustache merging into the stubble of his weekly shaven beard. His piercing jet black eyes are half hidden by the single arch of his thick eyebrows. Normally Abu-Ahmad maintains an air of contented independence and scowling self-respect that shroud him in an air of mystery and render him threatening to neighborhood children. Lately he has waxed sociable and started making the circle of evening village gatherings, clean-shaven and dressed in his best traditional *qumbaz*, all apparently to sing the praises of his honorable former employer, now a refugee in Kuwait.

I heard Abu-Ahmad's story one sunny morning last week when he accosted me on my way to work, suddenly interrupting his incessant digging in his land with a firm "*tfaddal*—please drop in" and a shout to his wife to make us coffee. Then with little introduction, as we leaned on opposite sides of the stone wall surrounding his yard, he proceeded to tell me his well-rehearsed account of his recent strange encounter. I couldn't help but stand still and listen:

"Have you heard of my recent visitors from Kuwait?" he started with the biggest smile I ever saw spread across his thick-featured face.

"*Kheir inshallah?*—Good tidings I hope?" I feigned ignorance.

"Well, let us start at the beginning. As you of course know, in my younger days I used to work as a *hassad*—a crop reaper. I used to be much stronger than the *shabah*—the ghost—you see now."

I imagined him as a young man with a scythe in hand let loose on a field of ripe wheat on a hot summer day and I shuddered in awe.

"They didn't have combines in those days. I swear to you, as a young man I worked better than a combine. Back in '48 I worked in Lubyeh harvesting wheat for Yahya el-Said, *zalami maysoor*—a God-favored man—with much fertile land. Every summer as we finished the harvesting and thrashing of the wheat I would bring my share home and it would be enough for my family for the year. You know I had only my wife and two little sons to feed. We had no doctors then and God claimed all of our other children to his mercy in their infancy. To cut a long story short, that summer as we were busy thrashing the wheat the Jews invaded and we were lucky to escape alive. The people of Lubyeh were brave and defended their village like the heroes they really were. Still they lost and we were separated from our landlord and crops never to meet again. At the time I thought that maybe I could go back in a week or two and finish thrashing and sifting the wheat. But it all went to waste and Lubyeh's residents fled to Lebanon as part of the unending stream of refugees. I came home to my family empty-handed. Somehow we managed to survive on God-only-knows-what from relatives and friends. I never saw nor heard from Yahya el-Said again. Until this winter.

A couple of weeks back, one cold and rainy night, at about midnight I woke to loud knocking at the door. I was sure it was the police. They used to come often looking for my brother Salim because he was a Communist as you know. But they haven't bothered us in recent years. I rushed out expecting the worst. There were three young men that I didn't recognize. I invited them in out of the cold and was about to have Umm-Ahmad start a fire and put on a kettle of tea. But they were in a hurry and needed to finish their honorable mission. They asked for my full name and told me that their father al-Hajj Yahya, on his deathbed, had entrusted them with the task of paying me the debt he owed me from the Nakba days for harvesting his wheat. They said they were sorry it took them this long to pay me. He had performed his religious duty of hajj to the holy sites in Mecca and kept my pay for me in a bag since that day. With that he slept better and felt ready to meet his maker, they told me. And now they too can sleep better. I tried to convince them to take back the money. After all, he is a refugee and I live in my home, humble as it is. But they wouldn't hear of it. I looked around for something to give them as a present to remember me with. The only thing I could find was my headset, my *hatta-wi-iqal*, which they accepted."

At that tears were streaming down Abu-Ahmad's cheeks wetting his bushy moustache. And as he sipped his coffee you could hear his slurping noise clear across the neighborhood.

As I told the story to Didi I had to add an explanation: The pilgrimage to Mecca, though a highly valued pillar of Islam, is not acceptable if it brings any kind of duress on the person or his family. This restriction specifically mandates that a person preparing to perform hajj has to clear all his debts first, both financial and social.

It is a peculiar thought, but would this tale of honesty and justice impress the people I need to win over in Europe and the US? Would they understand it as a testimony to the humanity and honor of my people or would Bernard Lewis, the current super-orientalist, somehow manage to squeeze it into his readymade mold of "blind Islamic fanaticism"?

January 21, 1984

Things are getting harder for the family financially, as the economic downturn affects everybody. Still, I do lots of things that don't make economic sense. For example, I still spend two afternoons a week chairing a three-physician panel that decides on the degree of mobility limitation of physically disabled applicants for tax relief on their cars. Our decision carries much financial weight for the disabled. The pay I collect for one of these sessions hardly covers the cost of the round-trip from my office in Acre to Afula, where the committee meets. But if I were to opt out of the panel many disabled Oriental Jews and Arabs would be unjustly denied formal recognition of their disability, that magic dispensation that the committee is empowered to issue. Many such disabled people are judged to be imposters because they show too much dependency. An attitude of excessive self-pity and acceptance of help from others is still standard behavior for the disabled in Middle Eastern society. My two colleagues on the committee are new Russian immigrants whose qualifications in orthopedics and neurology fail to impress me. They fail to understand such behavior and take most oriental applicants, whether Arabs or Sephardic Jews, to be imposters. They often make a snap judgment about the disabled person as he or she enters the examining room and then they perform the required physical examination and fill in the forms with their foregone conclusion. As the chairman, I have the prerogative to request a repeat detailed physical examination to be conducted under my direct supervision, a process always leading to the assignment of a higher degree of disability.

The committee chairmanship also carries with it the added bother of having the occasional disgruntled applicant visit my house for a cup of coffee and a chat about his or her disability status. The last one was a below-the-knee amputee who lost his leg while collecting *a'kkoub*, a delicious thistle, from the fields to feed his family. He wandered off the fenced road in the Golan Heights and stepped on a landmine.

Brother Ahmad errs in the opposite direction with his disability. As a child he fell and broke his arm. This has left him with an atrophied and paralyzed left upper extremity, apparently a result of the manipulation of the local bonesetter. It was always my late father's contention that in overcoming his physical disability Ahmad had overcompensated for it thus becoming the overachiever he has always been. To this day he is in total denial, taking any offer of help in any daily function as a personal insult. For a long time he made a living by driving a regular van. He did well, especially after he helped circulate a rumor that village women in labor using his van to go to hospital delivered boys. People are often spellbound by his casual habit of rolling cigarettes while driving full speed on narrow curvy Galilee roads.

12
Tribal Politics

A scene from Land Day commemoration, 1984.

March 31, 1984

I am feeling gloomy. It is a spring morning, no different from most others: cool breeze, beautiful flowers, and birds singing in my garden. Obviously, the gloom is in my heart, not out there.

It is the Saturday after the annual Land Day commemoration, marking the killing by the security forces of six of our number, all unarmed protesters, eight years ago. Maybe that is the reason for my gloom, but I suspect not. The Land Day processions went off uneventfully: Arrabeh was the site of the Galilee's gathering, and there was another in the Little Triangle. Because the security forces kept their distance from Arab villages, there were no clashes. The only problems in Arrabeh were scuffles between factions of Arab youth, with supporters of the nationalist Abna'a al-Balad on one side and supporters of the Democratic Front for Peace and Equality, allied to the Communist party, on the other. The Front is in power in most of our village councils. As the official marshals of the procession, the Front's young members attacked the Abna'a al-Balad youths, who were engaged in "disruptive behavior" such as raising the Palestinian flag. It is very difficult for any Palestinian to object to someone raising the Palestinian flag or to physically force offenders to take it down. But the Front's elders behaved "responsibly" and showed "restraint and maturity" by doing exactly that.

The previous day there was a study day at Haifa University on relations between Arabs and Jews in the Galilee. It was organized by Professor Sami Smooha, an Oriental Jewish researcher in political science who is making a name for himself by studying the Arab minority in Israel. Haifa University, which has a large number of Arab students, has an Institute for Middle Eastern Studies and a Center for Jewish-Arab Coexistence. Smooha is involved with both and organized the study day in anticipation of Land Day. The study day had two parts, one scientific and the other open to public debate. In the one he likes to sell as science, Smooha presented some of his research findings, which suggest that assumptions long held by officials and the general public that the Galilee's Arabs are hostile and a threat to the state need to be revised and should not form the basis of state policy towards them. The rehashing, repackaging and offering of such trivia as the focus of academic research and debate seems to me to serve the purpose of according a degree of respectability and formal legitimacy to the very view Smooha is supposedly questioning, as well as to the state's oppression of us and its systematic racial discrimination. The most disturbing part is that we, Arab intellectuals, play along with such nonsense. We sit there and listen to this garbage, and even debate it and contribute to its acceptability as legitimate discourse.

A local young man presented a summary of his PhD thesis on employment in the Galilee. He endeavored to show that there are many reasons why the Arabs are disadvantaged, including lack of capital for industry and a shortage of land for agriculture. An Israeli demographer presented his demographic statistics and sounded a warning bell about the threat posed by the growth of the Arab population. Then the Rev. Shahada, head of the National Committee for Defense of Arab Land, gave a less than convincing lecture on the topic of land confiscation from Arab communities, quoting old figures from 1970 and 1972.

Next, a planner discussed a future plan of the Galilee that the Jewish Agency had contracted him to draw up, but which was rejected because his starting point had been that the interests of all the Galilee's residents, including the Arab half, should be considered equally. He took the needs of the Arab population into consideration in the positive sense, and not only as a stumbling block to be avoided or a hindrance to be planned around. He proposed, for example, to concentrate the new Jewish settlements in the eastern part of the Galilee, which is less populated. Later on, in the discussion period, a representative of the Jewish Agency replied on behalf of his organization. He stated that the Jewish Agency respected the planner's concept and accepted the plan as excellent, containing everything that one would want—except, he added, that the time was not yet ripe for it. Or rather, the government and the national policy makers were not ready for it. His statements were tantamount to an admission that official bodies still consider the Arab citizens to be an enemy, one that has to be subdued and overcome, not planned for.

As if to confirm my conclusions, Raa'nan Weiss, a charismatic, independent-minded, colorful and outspoken old-guard Zionist, spoke next. To my great surprise, he obviously still believes he is fighting the 1948 war. I have been operating under the assumption that the war finished long ago, and that perhaps enlightened Arabs and Jews might even be struggling together against injustice. I even thought by now it might be feasible for me to commit openly to working for the benefit of my Palestinian community in the Galilee without fear of reprisal. Raa'nan Weiss, and the level of respect accorded him by everyone, proved to me how naive and falsely optimistic I have been. Certainly I did not expect to find people like him still running around all this time after the war. Perhaps it is that discovery that is making me feel so gloomy.

October 14, 1984

Recently Didi, the children and I went on a two-week tour of Egypt, an eye-opener in more ways than one.* When walking around, and without speaking a word ourselves, the street hawkers would greet us in Hebrew. I asked a couple how they knew we were from Israel. They said it was our appearance. Our clothes and behavior gave us away. That says something about our identity in the eyes of the other. There we were trying to approach Egyptians as Arab brothers and sisters and they responded to us as foreign tourists or, even worse, as the enemy.

At work, I find myself walking an emotional tightrope between my desire to improve the health and development status of the Palestinian minority and my equally strong desire to empower us and preserve our dignity. In a normal world, the two wishes would not be contradictory, but we live in the "Jewish and democratic state," and here they most definitely are.

In truth, Israel excludes from its consciousness and worldview nearly a fifth of its citizens. Is it possible that Israel could ever attune itself to the health and development needs of its Arab citizens and start according them the same level of benevolent attention it does to newly arrived Jewish immigrants? Of course not—as long as it is committed to its identity and character as "the state of the Jews." With that as its founding idea, no room is left for true empowerment of the Palestinian minority; not in the minds of Zionist decision-makers. Experience teaches that we must pay an exorbitant price before Israel will lift its oppressive policies or ease the physical and developmental "boycott" imposed on our towns and villages: we must part with our land and identity; that is the asking price!

"Would you then prefer that the state maintains its distance from us," my friend, Toufiq, argues with me, just for the sake of arguing, when I raise this familiar dilemma with him one evening. "Do you prefer that Israel continues to avert its eyes and attention from our needs?"

"Yes, when it continues to pursue its 'Jews first' policies, which in practice really mean 'Jews only.' It makes sense for us, the Arab

---

* On the heels of Egyptian President Anwar Sadat's visit to Israel and the Camp David agreements, a peace treaty was signed between Egypt and Israel. Though the treaty proposed a linkage to Palestinian autonomy, this was never implemented and Israeli-Egyptian relations at the public level have remained cold and strained.

minority, to choose to suffer such neglect and remain out of sight and out of mind if only in the hope that that may be enough to prevent the authorities from continuing their slow and relentless land grab."

"Biding our time in the shadows, as practice shows, simply emboldens the state to confiscate more of our land."

"So, we are damned if we do and damned if we don't! In Israel if an individual wants to make material progress then he must first subordinate himself socially and psychologically to the state's own narrow tribal definition of itself. It is designed to force you and me to abandon one or other of the integral parts of a community's healthy existence, two components that are normally intimately connected: empowerment and progress," I conclude as if telling Toufiq something he didn't know.

This summer, for one month, I attended a course at Stanford University on Microcomputers and Development. With such new technology, we, at the Galilee Society, dream of effectively addressing our concerns to the world community from our current humble one-room office in Dr. Awad's clinic in little Rama. Our strategy at the Galilee Society is to bring political attention to our community's valid concerns through being heard at international conferences, publishing in research journals and developing our limited contacts with the foreign embassies. We hope to make the Israeli government become more sensitive, or even embarrassed, about its neglect of the Arab minority. If we can bring enough pressure to bear, Israel may feel compelled to come forth with a more equitable share of the budget for our towns and villages to address outstanding problems with our communities' infrastructure.

Another problem that we need to draw attention to is the fact that we lack our own cadre of health professionals in Arab towns and villages. No community dreaming of taking charge of its own health affairs can do so without the right number and quality of trained professionals. To achieve this end we will almost certainly need to seek help from international organizations; I now despair of getting any positive responses from national decision-makers or those in academia. From my seat at the Ministry of Health I have repeatedly tried to intervene personally with medical and nursing schools, and with the only school in the country for speech therapists, to change the rules of admission that seem designed to disqualify the best Arab youth. Even my cogent argument to university officials that it is necessary to have speech therapists who can speak the language of the child they are helping has failed to persuade them to admit a single Arab student to their program.

January 6, 1985

On New Year's Eve we hosted a party for our friends, including Dr. Toufiq Karakara and his wife. This young psychiatrist's career is an eye-opener for the uninitiated. As a youth, he was a card-carrying member of the Israeli Communist party. That, and his ambition, were enough to secure him a scholarship to study medicine in Romania. While there he roomed with my nephew, also an aspiring psychiatrist. Toufiq married a quiet and pretty classmate and, on returning to Israel, did an internship and qualified to practice medicine. I had known the young man, named after no other than my close friend, Toufiq, who is his maternal uncle, before he left to study. I saw the younger Toufiq for the first time after his return when he and his wife came to my office to collect their licenses to practice medicine and she completed her application for Israeli residence status. As part of my duties as Sub-District Physician, I am required to interview any non-Jewish immigrant to assess their mental stability and health condition. Jewish immigrants, on the other hand, have their own separate process—under the supervision of the Jewish Agency, I believe—which is pretty much automatic. My own wife had to go through this minor inconvenience as well. What is more significant is that she had to opt between her American citizenship and that of Israel. Had she been Jewish she could have both.

Toufiq was interested in psychiatry from the start. He consulted with me about his career options and I encouraged him to pursue psychiatry, interceding on his behalf with a colleague, the head of the psychiatry department at the regional hospital. As far as I know, Toufiq is the first Arab in Israel to train in psychiatry. He had an offer to do surgery but I advised him against it because it is a hospital-based specialty and, in the long run, Arrabeh would lose him to some big-name central hospital.

The problems with specialty training for our young graduates who attend foreign medical schools are complex and numerous indeed.

Hospitals regularly and openly give preference to locally trained graduates, among whom Arabs are a tiny fraction because of discrimination in university admittance policy. Then there is the competition from, and priority given to, new Jewish immigrants with medical degrees, both authentic and otherwise. And beyond that, there is an added hurdle: most Arab professionals have graduated from an East European school, very likely on a Communist party scholarship, which constitutes an *a priori* transgression against the political sensitivities of the state, as Toufiq soon discovered.

Three months after he started his residency training, he was called to the office of the director of the hospital and given a letter of dismissal on security grounds. Trying to find out who was behind his dismissal, Toufiq was referred down the hierarchy of security agents till he reached a lowly teacher from Arrabeh, who told him he would arrange a meeting with the security agent for the area. A taxi driver from the neighboring village of Dier Hanna showed up for the meeting and promised in turn to arrange another meeting with a higher security agent.

Later I was drawn into this web of secret agents. It turned out that the Ministry of Health's top security officer, to whom all hospitals in Israel report on security matters, once worked as the security officer at my office in Acre. I knew him by name but had never had dealings with him. I did not like him either, because I knew he was bugging my phone. My secretary, however, was on good terms with him, even though she was the one to alert me to the bugging business. A relative of Toufiq's asked me if I would get my secretary to introduce Toufiq to my former phone-tapping coworker. I agreed and advised him, for his own sake, against mentioning my name. That was the last I heard of it. A short time later Toufiq was given back his position as resident in the psychiatry department at the regional hospital.

A revealing detail is that Toufiq was required to dissociate himself from the Communist party, and announce the termination of his membership in it in a signed statement published in the press. He must have had an intimation of what was coming. Soon after his dismissal, he protested loudly that he would never disavow his loyalty to the party, which had arranged for his medical education with no strings attached. Toufiq is an honorable person and a serious and committed member of our community. He joined the party less out of ideological devotion than the fact that it was a precondition for high school graduates who wanted to join the waiting list for free higher education in a Communist country.

But it seems "the system" wanted to teach Toufiq a lesson from his own medical specialty, psychiatry. In denouncing the party, his name has been forever tarnished in the eyes of his associates, family and friends. Psychologically, the scar in his psyche must be deep and permanent, enough to undercut his self-confidence, self-respect, and earlier enthusiasm to serve his people.

This carefully thought-out practice of undermining people's integrity as the price they must pay to earn a living is so pervasive that it affects even simple workers, as happened not long ago to a member of my extended family. This man had to take the same demeaning step of renouncing his former affiliation to the Communist party before being allowed to return to his job as a night watchman at a sewing factory in a Jewish town.

One interesting document passed to me at the Ministry of Health lately deals with a new group of immigrants from Ethiopia. For the last few years a trickle of these immigrants has been arriving in Israel. Commonly known as *Falashas*, apparently a term they find derogatory, these Ethiopians are supposedly the descendants of Jews that migrated from here 2,500 years ago, after the destruction of the I-don't-know-which temple.* (Believe me, I used to know all of that in my high school days, but the moment I got an A in Jewish history exams, I managed to block it all out. That, I suppose, is another weapon of the weak: the system removes all traces of my people's history from my school curriculum, and then I wipe from my memory all of their history that I was forced to learn.) At any rate, these people look Ethiopian, they sound Ethiopian, they behave like Ethiopians, and they have suffered whatever famine and war atrocities Ethiopians have suffered. But as luck would have it, Israel has decided to latch on to them for its nation-building and demographic purposes, claiming them as its own and actively bringing them over to Israel en masse. Let us not forget,

---

* *Falasha:* Meaning wanderer or exile, the term is applied to a group of Ethiopians assumed to be Jewish. Between 1980 and 1992, some 45,000 Falasha were brought to Israel and their number now stands at over 70,000. Of late they have voiced much objection to their discriminatory treatment by the state.

however, that the state justifies dispossessing me and my folks of our land based on the same historic claim. So this is not an entirely neutral issue from my point of view.

Apparently a clandestine operation was planned in 1975 to implement this "homecoming," but Moshe Dayan leaked the information, through a slip of the tongue, angered the Ethiopian government and the plan had to be aborted. Since then there have been repeated clandestine attempts to bring over the Ethiopians. The recent war and famine there have been a boon to Israel's plans.

Details of the current campaign have just been released. Falashas, with Israeli guides, trekked to the Sudanese borders by foot and from there they were moved by bus to Khartoum. A Belgian charter company supplied the planes to fly them from Khartoum to European airports, and from there on to Israel. Though this has been happening over the last few weeks, it has been kept secret, even here. Suddenly we noticed that all the hotels, the youth institutions, and the army barracks in Acre and Naharya were filling up with Ethiopians of all ages.

Locally, the General Sick Fund was tipped off about the Ethiopians' arrival before we at the Ministry of Health were. Because of the initial secrecy, coordination between the various health providers has gone out of the window. So to make amends, a meeting was arranged between the local offices of the Ministry of Health and the sick fund, together with representatives of the hospital and the health departments of the two cities of Acre and Naharya. I went along with my epidemiological nurse.

An ambitious and very manipulative young physician heading the sick fund team—fresh out of the army and full of the locally nurtured brand of impudence, aka "chutzpah"—began by picking on my nurse. Then, when she proved to be his equal in arrogance and showed herself to be better informed on the health issues under consideration than he was, he decided to try having a go at me. He questioned the appropriateness of my participation in the meeting since it dealt with a "Jewish problem." I had to assert my authority, telling him and the group that I believed he was not alone in seeing things from a narrowly racial angle. I began a speech about the massive effort invested in caring for the Ethiopian immigrants in comparison to the chronic neglect of the health care of the Arab minority. "Given a couple of decades from now, the Ethiopians will fare better socio-economically and health-wise than my own village people, and I am expected to close my eyes and follow instructions from above despite their racially motivated logic. Since I started working in a government office, there has never been money for any project specifically addressing a single need of the Arab minority except perhaps for family planning." It was clear that I was confirming his doubts. Still, I must have come on too strong for him. He has not shown up to any of the follow-up meetings.

But still his point is well taken. It has always been my contention that the conclusions of ultra-rightwing Jewish nationalists such as Rabbi Meir Kahane that Arabs have to be expelled from their homes in all of Greater Israel are perfectly logical.* I totally agree with their conclusion, given the basic racist tribal exclusionary premises. It is with those basic premises that I beg to differ.

Some aspects of this tribal ingathering enterprise border on the absurd. There are serious internal arguments among the chief rabbis in Israel as to the authenticity of the Falasha's Jewish identity. Some do not accept them as Jews because apparently they are not circumcised in the correct way, not deeply cut enough, or the tip is too long, or whatever. If this sounds sacrilegious, let me for a moment tell you about my own circumcision. I must have been three or four years old at the time. I don't remember the surgical procedure itself, but I do remember its aftermath. For weeks I would wake up at night crying with the pain, physical and mental. The only relief that I could obtain was from devouring some of that delicious home-made grape molasses that my mother offered me. It was only after I finished the entire family supply of the stuff that the late-night pain attacks stopped and I was fully healed, perhaps even psychologically.

From a health point of view, the Ethiopians have been arriving with exotic diseases including malaria, schistosomiasis, hook worm, and various other parasitic diseases. There is a routine for how we deal with members of the group once they arrive to prevent the spread of

---

* *Meir Kahane:* An American-Israeli Orthodox Rabbi and Knesset member, founder of an ultra-rightist movement that advocated the forced expulsion of Arabs from all of Greater Israel. He was assassinated in New York in 1990. Though his movement was termed racist and terroristic in Israel and the US and his political party was banned in Israel, his views have recently gained wide acceptance in Jewish circles in Israel under the now politically correct term "transfer," and the even more politically correct "Judiazing Israel's space."

disease to the rest of the population. In Western Galilee I am the official
responsible for that, though the actual implementation is delegated to
the sick fund, acting as the field contractor for providing preventive
health services to the Jewish population in my area. Preventive health
services for the Arab population, on the other hand, are handled
directly by my office at the Ministry of Health. Officials explain this
as a consequence of "historical developments." In fact, the real reason
is that for several decades the General Sick Fund defined its mandate as
caring exclusively for its Jewish members, arguing that it was assuming
"national responsibilities"—another example of the state's patently
tribal focus, to the detriment of the Palestinian minority. The Ministry
of Health's direct involvement in preventive health services only to
Arabs in the Galilee was originally why I decided to take on the duties
of medical officer for the sub-district of Acre, where Arabs made up
two-thirds of the population. If that is not tribalism on my part, I
don't know what is.

13
Tales from Area Nine

The ruins of the mill that my father formerly
owned in Wadi Salameh.
(Photo by Makbula Nassar.)

January 15, 1985

On my way from Arrabeh to nearby Rama, the village where the
Galilee Society's offices are located, I take the road north, the first part
of which was paved in the 1940s by the British Mandate rulers. It is in
total disrepair, with garbage strewn on both sides. This section of road

once led to an army camp, known to this day as *al-Kam*—The Camp, and an artillery target practice area called *al-Marjam*—Bombardment Hill. The surrounding area, including fertile valleys much farmed by the three neighboring villages of Arrabeh, Sakhnin and Dier Hanna, used to be periodically and briefly closed to civilians, including farmers, by the British army. The practice was that a senior officer would come to each village and announce, through the village crier, that on such and such a day there would be target practice and the area would be off-limits.

When Israel took over, it permanently closed the area, designating it a military zone renamed "Area Nine." Civilians now could not enter and it was only possible for farmers to till their land, graze their flocks, or tend their crops for specified periods and with a special permit from the Israeli army. Then in 1976 it became clear that the government was going to confiscate this land and much more to build a series of Jewish agricultural settlements to further Judaize this part of the Galilee. The three villages, backed by the Arab minority, stood up as one man and said NO! They led the protests known as Land Day; the security forces responded by shooting dead six unarmed demonstrators. In the end the government did not confiscate the land but established new Jewish settlements mainly on state forest lands, on the area's hilltops. They became essentially bedroom communities for people making their living in the nearby cities and not the agricultural settlements planned by Ariel Sharon and his pack of land-grabbing right wingers.

With the establishment of the Jewish settlements, known as *mitzpim* or "lookout" communities (the word is meant to suggest to those of us being looked out on that we are also being spied on), the area was finally demilitarized. Arab farmers started reclaiming their fields from years of neglect and overgrowth and planting them with olive trees to re-establish their de facto ownership.* Because of this long-drawn-out struggle against both the British and Israel, land has acquired symbolic and sentimental value much in excess of its actual worth in terms of real estate or productivity value.

---

* Fallow Land Regulations of 1948 made it possible for the Israeli government to confiscate Arab land that was judged uncultivated by the Minister of Agriculture. These regulations applied retroactively and were used in conjunction with the legal powers of military commanders to close an area for security reasons.

The first section of road to Rama has not been repaired since the Mandate days. People using it are either farmers on their way to their lands or Bedouin women from another local community, Wadi Salameh, carrying milk to sell door to door in Rama. There is little traffic on this road and I make a habit of stopping for anybody I find on it. I stop instinctively, perhaps to avoid boredom and maybe also because I derive some pleasure from helping those farmers reach their land and work it. After all, I enjoy digging around and planting trees in my own garden. And there are nationalist undertones in working the land too.

Another thing I appreciate are the quaint ways of the old Bedouin women who ride with me: their accents and the way they pronounce certain words in Arabic, and their attempts to strike up a conversation about my late father or mother, who were their friends, or about the time they brought their sick child to my house at night, or the time their legendary matriarch, Aunt Siniyeh, made a Bedouin bridal dress for my wife. In season, Rama's housewives expect their daily supply of fresh goats' yogurt to arrive in my car on time and seem to blame me on the rare occasions that I arrive without my Bedouin friends.

I have a family connection to Wadi Salameh. The old water-powered flour mill there was once owned by my father and it still stands as a ruin at the edge of the stream, now the destination of tour groups in summer. My father inherited it from his father but sold it to cover the expenses he incurred in marrying his second wife, my mother.

Wadi Salameh is now a thriving small Bedouin village. Over two centuries ago it was a Druze community and its residents held sway over much of this part of the Galilee. The story of the demise of its powerful and tyrannical Druze sheikh is connected to the oft-told story of the rise of Daher al-Omar al-Zidani, the founder of the first, and so far only, independent Palestinian state—or so Arrabeh's local historians would like to believe. I have heard several versions of this oral tradition from village elders and never felt the urge to check any historical text to verify or refute the facts. The story stands on its own, as part of local Palestinian folklore, and I would hate to discover something that might challenge any part of it. The various versions differ mainly in the degree of exaggeration of some of the details. A particularly spicy version, not suitable for this innocent recording, was told to me many times by my old brother-in-law, Abu-Salih, who hosted me for the first couple of years after I returned from the United States.

According to the most common version, the elderly Druze sheikh, head of the grand old Salameh clan and ruler under the Turks of the entire Lower Galilee, spotted a beautiful girl from Arrabeh one day on her way to the flour mill. He inquired about her, identified her family and then asked her father for her hand in marriage. That was a major violation of the honor and sensibilities of the people of Arrabeh, as he was a Druze and she a Sunni Muslim, but no one had the courage or the means to object to the merciless local ruler's dictates. Daher al-Omar, a small time Bedouin chieftain, happened to be camping on the outskirts of Arrabeh, one of many grudgingly tolerated guests of the village. The local farmers preferred to accommodate the Bedouin's flocks grazing in the fields after the harvest rather than face up to the threat of their marauding horsemen. Someone in the village had the presence of mind to consult with the wily al-Omar about the offense of the Druze sheikh's proposal. The Bedouin chieftain devised a scheme that everyone in the village accepted.

The Druze sheikh was told that the proposed wedding would go ahead and he was invited to the guesthouse, or *diwan*, of the girl's clan to conduct the formalities of the marriage contract. They set the time for the next evening, as the old lecher was in a hurry to get his prey. When he arrived with his men just after sundown, they found an extravagant dinner waiting for them. Much expensive rice and many a roasted lamb were devoured by the jubilant guests. That was when Daher al-Omar's men jumped from their hiding places and slaughtered every last one of the guests, including the tyrant sheikh. The same night al-Omar led a raid by the men of Arrabeh, Sakhnin and Dier Hanna, that destroyed Wadi Salameh, the stronghold of the dead sheikh. The village's lands were distributed among the victorious raiders, especially ones from the landless smaller clans. The descendants of those who defended Arrabeh's honor own these lands to this very day. That is how Daher al-Omar first made his mark and started his climb to power, eventually seceding much of Greater Syria from the Turkish Empire. More significantly to me, that is how the flour mill came into the possession of my family.

This morning, as I arrived at the edge of Arrabeh, at the junction with the potholed, garbage-filled road to Wadi Salameh, I saw a young man with a pick axe and a large sledgehammer standing on the wrong side of the road. I knew he was going to work his land, so I picked him up.

He greeted me: "Hello, doctor. How are you?"

"I am fine. Where are you heading to, *inshallah*?"

"With Allah's permission, we will be clearing our land. You can see it from here. The Caterpillar has already moved the big rocks to the edges. Now we need to clear the smaller stones. Some stones need breaking up and that is what this pickaxe is for. All of our family is there today to help out. We are planting olives there."

I looked to the left of the road and, sure enough, in the distance there were over two dozen children, women and men at work spread out over the freshly scratched land.

"And since when have you been able to enter this area and work your land?"

"We started slowly. For a few years we worked with our bare hands. Finally we saved enough money to pay for a Caterpillar to really clean the land of boulders and of the wild brush that has grown in it."

"What kind of olive trees are you planting in it?" I asked.

"Souri, of course," meaning the traditional local variety deriving its name from Sour, Arabic for the Lebanese coastal city of Tyre.

"I thought Menzalino olives, this new European variety that thrives on irrigation, was better," I said.

"No! Of course, not!" he protested. "You know that our fathers and grandfathers have tried to raise olives here for centuries and obviously they hit on the best kind of olives for the area. Souri olives are the most suitable for our climate, do not need irrigation, and give the best-tasting oil and the highest yield." His language belied his disheveled looks. "Menzalino olives," he continued, "may be larger and better for pickling but that is not what Allah created olives for. When He, praised be His name, spoke of 'figs and olives' in his holy Koran, He meant Souri olives. Those are the right olives for us to continue planting on our land."

"That's all very well, but how come you are allowed to work the land now? At one point nobody was allowed in." I have rehearsed this question so many times before that I know how to give it the right nuance in Arabic to elicit an outraged and indignant response.

"It's true, the area was demilitarized only for the benefit of the Jewish settlers. But we take advantage of that fact and access our own land. Who is to stop us? We have *kooshan* and *tabu* papers [the title deeds]. But not long ago, before Land Day, none of us could object to our exclusion. It is not wise for a bare hand to slam against a cobbler's needle, as the saying goes." He then launched into another local proclamation of the uselessness of fighting the authorities if the people are weak and divided: "*In kan hakmak thalmak?*" "If your ruler selects you for his injustice, whom can you complain to? If the bosses come down hard on you, what can you do but bide your time?"

Next, he cussed those who had sold their land, those who did not stand up to the system when the time was right, and those who did not act the minute it was possible to clear the land and plant it.

"You know, land is priceless. There is nothing healthier than working on your own land. You are a doctor and you surely know that. As a farmer I can tell you that nothing is more beautiful than seeing your land cleared of brush and planted with olive seedlings and seeing those Souri seedlings grow."

It may not be much of a story, but it sums up the sentiments of many people here, including my own.

Yesterday I picked up a man from Sakhnin, a very quiet type, on his way to his land.

"Where are you going?"

"To my land."

"What will you do there?"

"Work. Toil is the only thing that joins a man and his land."

Again, I tried to elicit his views on the politics concerning this area of land and on the fact that it had recently been in the news. But he continued to respond with factual one-liners, speaking about the need for self-respect and his conviction that there was an inescapable bond between himself and his land and its toils.

Recently the positions of the Jewish mainstream and more liberal Jewish groups allied to cabinet minister Ezer Weitzman have clashed. On late-night TV last week, one of Weitzman's advisors triggered the noisy debate. He argued both that the Arabs' ownership of the land had never been contested and that they had worked it all these years despite the military regulations that prohibited them entering it. Now that the area had been effectively opened to civilians because several new Jewish settlements were being built within it, there was no sense in maintaining the defunct military closure regulations. Opposing him was Mr. Milo, a deputy minister of some government department or other. Mr. Milo explained that such an approach went against the grain of Zionism. "Our mission is to redeem the land from its Arab occupiers. Nobody in this country has the right to give an inch of land to Arabs." Weitzman's advisor replied that no one was giving anybody any land; it was simply being recognized that this military area had been opened to civilians—all civilians, and not just Jews. The debate went back and forth for the better part of an hour.

What has been most surprising is that as a result Weitzman, a former super-hawk and Israeli air-force commander whose name is forever tied to the early days of aggressive Zionist conquest and more recently to the destruction of the air forces of Israel's Arab neighbors, is suddenly the darling of the Arab minority in Israel.

I was hoping to get my hitchhiker to comment on this and relate to the media furor around the fate of the very piece of land he was heading to. But he sat there as firm and unperturbed as the rocks in his land. All that mattered to him was to get there and start digging and planting. That was all that mattered between a man and his land. His silent comment was eloquent enough for me.

About three weeks ago, driving the same road, I picked up a man who looked much older than me. Actually, he turned out to be about my age. He was with his wife and they were carrying several empty buckets and some food provisions and water. I said "Ya msahel?" a combined inquiry about their destination and a wish of God's speed for them. Before answering, the man made sure to thank me for stopping to pick them up and to spice that up with recollections of the many times I had cured their sick children and how lucky and thankful they all were to have me around—the villager's usual humble expressions of appreciation for any small favor.

"Our children never get better except in your hands," the wife concurred.

"Ya msahel?" I inquired again.

"We are going to clear stones from our land."

"What do you mean 'to clear stones from our land'? In that area there are a lot of boulders. How can you clear them with your bare hands?" I teased.

"Of course, it has been cleared already with a Caterpillar. You know, it took us so long to save enough money ..." The same refrain.

"And how many *dunams** do you own there?"

He quoted an impressively large figure, such as 100 dunams that he, his brothers and his cousins own.

"You have official title to all of that land? You own it?"

"Yes, of course. Before we couldn't enter because of the military regulations, but now it is usable again. We went to court and sorted out the issue of ownership. We have established our title to it in court. Actually it was my cousin, old man Abu-Hussain, who did it. You know my cousin Abu-Hussain, don't you?"

"Yeah, yeah, I do." I said this to prevent a long digression. In fact, I didn't know him.

The man started chuckling and his wife joined him with a wild fit of laughter. That was her only contribution to the conversation, and it came as a surprise given that otherwise she was so reserved in the presence of a stranger.

"Well, when Abu-Hussain was fighting for this land in court he made fun of the judge and his laws and got away with it. But toward the end of the hearing, it looked like the case was going against him. His lawyer told him that he would probably lose his land. The Jewish Agency representative showed an aerial photo that showed the land to be overgrown with brush."

This refers to a law in Israel, one of three dozen laws enacted by the Israeli parliament to legalize the confiscation of private Arab land. It states that land that lies fallow for three years reverts to state ownership. Often the army declares an area closed for military purposes so that no one can enter it for the three-year period and it lies fallow. Then in coordination with the army, the Jewish Agency goes to court to claim its ownership on behalf of the state. Some obstinate farmers have endangered their lives and violated the ban of the armed forces by entering their fields and tilling them at least once every three years.

---

* *Dunam:* Local area measurement equal to 1,000 square meters or a quarter of an acre.

Some farmers have been hurt or killed doing that, either from being shot at by the army or from stepping on a landmine they have laid.

"Old man Abu-Hussain," continued my passenger, "realized he was about to lose his case. So, before the final court session, he dismissed his lawyer, shaved his thick old beard, and spoke in court on his own behalf."

Another round of wild laughter rang in the car.

"When the judge asked him if he had anything to say for himself, he said: 'Yes, I do, your honor. You may have noticed that I had a beard before and now I am clean shaven.' The judge said: 'Now that you mention it, I did notice that for the first time you appear in my court properly dressed and clean shaven.' And my clever cousin replied: 'Your honor, I am afraid for my own beard' [the Arabic equivalent of being afraid for one's own neck or one's own soul]. It has dawned on me that anything with natural growth on it is likely to be confiscated by this court. I have decided at least to escape with my own head on my shoulders.' And he won his case!"

Another round of applause for old man Abu-Hussain, the cousin who saved his land with a gimmick straight out of Arabian Nights. I laughed heartily as well.

"What exactly are you going to do on the land on a cold December day like this, and especially one with bitterly cold easterly winds. You will freeze out there," I asked, hunting for some added statement of commitment.

He picked up my drift:

"Our land is the only thing left for us Palestinians in this country. What do we have left? Palestine is gone; we have no flag and no leaders. But we must not despair. The only future my little ones have is on their land. My oldest knows how to drive a tractor. He loaded all eight of his brothers and sisters in the trolley and went ahead of us. If each clears a couple of bucketfuls of stones the land will look better by the end of the day."

I imagined what it was like for this man to hold on to his land. He had been clinging on to it for dear life, literally fighting for it with his bare hands. I had noticed that three of his fingers were missing on his right hand and now asked about their loss. And, lo and behold, they too were part of his struggle for the same piece of land. In the early 1950s, when he was a boy working illegally on the land, he accidentally picked up an unexploded mine. It blew up killing his cousin and maiming himself.

"I lost a very dear friend in the accident, my good cousin. You know, several people have been killed and maimed with unexploded munitions. That is what the British Mandate left us to remember them by. And the Israelis added some of their own."

When we reached the land, as he and his wife got out, I said my regular parting words of encouragement. He responded by sticking his head through the window and letting out a tirade of cussing of his few relatives who had sold land to the Israeli government. His wife, speaking to me for only the second time, ran around to my side window and joined in the vocal condemnation, until the cussing reached a crescendo that rang in my ears for hours that day.

An eighty-year-old man from Sakhnin who caught a ride with me to his land one morning began with a social observation:

"It is so surprising and pleasant to have someone from our own stop to pick up an old man like me. You know, nowadays, if you are not a young woman with a short skirt, nobody stops to pick you up. I have been standing here since dawn. If my legs were a little stronger I could have reached my land by now."

I responded with the standard phrase in Arabic that it is our duty to respect and help our elders. I added that his land was sure to welcome his visit now that the sun was up and the weather a little warmer. I quoted to him a saying I heard from my late father many times: that the land smiles when visited by its owner. He concurred that trees are happy to see their planter; they flower more and give better fruit.

"Of course, there is good reason for that. After all, the farmer does not just go to look at his land and trees; he goes to do a little clearing here and a little weeding there. Even with his feet as he walks he may kick aside a stone or a thorn-bush. It is a true and reasonable saying that your father taught you. How old is he?"

I told him my father's name and that if he had been alive he would be about his age.

"*Allah Yirhamu!* May God rest his soul! You must be Dr. Kanaaneh then. I have visited your clinic but failed to recognize you in this car. I thought you were a door-to-door salesman. No wonder you are such a decent fellow. Your father was a good *fallah*—a proper villager. I knew him well. On the occasion of his death I came and paid my respects to your brothers. You were in America when he died. Your father was a man of principle. He was straight as an arrow, honest and frank to a fault. Many an old widow in the village would trust him to keep her meager savings for her. People from other clans in your village and even from outside Arrabeh would come to him to arbitrate between them on serious disagreements. In the long drawn blood feud between the Kanaaneh and the Naamneh clans of Arrabeh, yours was the only household exempted from the random violence and attacks. Your father gained that status because of his stand on principle, may his soul rest in peace."

I remember the social consequences of that stand well. My father rejected the blanket assumption of responsibility for the actions of nephews and distant relatives as traditionally expected from him as an elder of the clan. He refused to testify blindly on behalf of all the young men in his clan without having personally assessed their culpability in the murder of which they were accused. All the other elders in our clan, including his own senior brother Salih, the formidable boss of the clan, went to the mosque and swore on the Koran before God and the whole village that none of the Kanaanehs had anything to do with the murder of the young merchant who was found dead and buried in the Kanaaneh fields. My father took the oath very seriously and believed a false oath would likely result in the illness and death of one of his children. He broke rank and would swear on the holy book only to the fact that he had no knowledge of who committed the murder. For that, of course, for quite a while, we gained the enmity of our own next of kin.

I asked the man about his land.

"We have about 120 dunams. My God, it took us so long to get title to it." And he started showing me where it was, what a good piece of land it was, and how well it had been cleared of brush and rocks.

"Look at that other piece. It is my cousin's. He sold his to the government. May God damn his soul to everlasting hell fire! Do you know my cousin Mohammad? He is the one. You know, he owned much land in this area, in the Battouf valley, and within the borders of our village as well. One day he came to me and asked if I wanted to exchange my land here with some of his land in the village, where I can build on it for my children. I had already heard the news that he had sold all of his lands in the Battouf valley and that he was working as an agent buying land from unsuspecting farmers for the government. I decided to teach him a lesson. I wanted to shame him. I set a condition that he could never meet. I said: 'Listen Mohammad, I'll exchange my land that you want for a similar area of land in the Battouf valley, provided it is from your own land, because it is right next to mine.' He understood exactly what I meant and has never spoken to me again. You should have seen the way he dragged himself out of my house with his head down and his tail between his legs. The Battouf valley is not for sale, is it?

"Your good father must have told you about how the farmers of Arrabeh and Sakhnin worked the land of Eilaboun in the Battouf when its Christian residents were driven out to Lebanon [in 1948 by the Jewish forces]. Their priest, al-Khouri Murqus al-Mualem, may his soul rest in peace, an honorable man if there ever was one in these parts, sent out an SOS message asking for help. Every farmer in your and my village took their work animals and equipment to the abandoned land of Eilaboun in the valley and in no time had it plowed and planted with wheat. By the time al-Khouri Murqus managed to use his influence with the Pope to bring his people back, they returned to find their crops ready for harvest. We helped them bring it in as well. That is how honorable neighbors care for each other, not by selling the land to the Jews for paper money."

We reached his destination but he delayed me on the side of the road.

"You see Jabal Abu-Qarad, that mountain over there. From a distance it looks rocky and steep. But the top of that mountain is an area of about 200 dunams that is as clean and flat as the palm of your hand. It is perfect land for wheat and barley. And we just received news that my cousin Mohammad has sold it all. May God shorten his days! I'll have you know, my life was threatened. My house was threatened with demolition. They said they would never employ my oldest son as a teacher, and that they would not give my other son a license as a taxi driver. But none of that ever raised a pimple on my ass. I told my cousin my land is for my children to inherit, and your children will have to sell the honor of their own wives to buy the produce from it, for they will have none of their own. I will never accept any price for it. Look at this piece of land and the olive seedlings we put in it. Look how beautiful! What does he have to feast his eyes on every morning? A stack of paper money is all he has!"

He thanked me, praised my medical know-how above that of all other doctors he knew, asked God for mercy on my late father's soul and walked toward his beloved patch of olive seedlings.

Suddenly I missed my father and the times I used to spend working with him in our olive fields, and earlier, sitting in his lap in the *diwan*. A telling story of his came to my mind, one he repeated many a time to his men age-mates from the village gathered to sip black coffee and to while their free time together. It told of the time when, as a single teenager, he tried to live from subsistence farming like everybody else in the village. It happened during the drought years at the very end of the Turkish rule in the area, the period everyone in the Middle East knows by the Turkish name of *Seferberlick*. Those were times of terrible deprivation when southern Lebanon was hit hard enough to send its men seeking livelihoods across the oceans and its women into neighboring Galilee as migrant laborers in exchange for their daily meals. In Arrabeh several dozen such women took refuge in the church where villagers who needed their help and could afford to feed another mouth at their table came and hired them. Father drew up a scheme that combined economic benefit with romance. One morning he went to the church and selected a tall, green-eyed, fair-skinned beauty as hired help. As he walked ahead of her back to his house, he would narrate to his fellow villagers, his heart was pounding hard and fast, so much so that he was on the verge of fainting with excitement. Alas, that lasted only for few short moments; the beautiful creature behind him spoke one single sentence that put an end to all his rapturous thoughts: "Brother," he reported she called to him, "how far is your field?"

"That sealed the honor relationship between us," my father had told me. "I never could bring myself to feast my eyes on her beautiful face or enjoy looking at her graceful figure again. She was my sister till the day we collected the wheat we planted together and she headed north with all the wheat she could carry on her head. With one single word that angel of a woman cleansed all of my evil thoughts and won me as a brother. I never saw or heard from her again. My brother Salih has traveled as far as Beirut and Damascus on horseback; I have often considered traveling to Bent-Jbail to check on my sister there. But I never managed to do it. Who knows? One day I may see her again!"

January 26, 1985

Spring is in the air, a two-week stretch of unseasonably warm summer weather preceded by good rains. That is enough to bring out the Bedouin yogurt sellers and the Sakhnin farmers.

Traveling the Wadi Salameh road the other day on a pleasant, warm and clear morning, with the ground so rich and fertile-looking where it had been tilled and so flowery where it had not, I experienced that old sentimental urge to start looking for hitchhikers again. At the junction, three people got off the bus and ran towards my car: a couple I did not recognize and a man with a familiar face. As the single man stepped into my VW camper with his work tools, I remembered giving him rides to his land before. He has a malformed thin red face with badly crossed green eyes and straight platinum blond hair. I had often wondered how his genes had been pooled over the centuries and what claim he had to his identity as a Palestinian Arab. After all three had said "Good morning" and "How are you, doctor?" and as soon as they had arranged their pick axes, hoes, rakes, buckets, and water and food supplies for the day on the floor and were seated, they began tossing the standard Arabic platitudes back and forth. I already knew what the first would say and how the second and third would respond.

"Oh, it is a blessing to have such kind people around."

"The world abounds with kind-hearted people."

"And we are lucky to find one of them right here."

"You can't judge people by their looks or money. Some with more expensive cars would pass us by, even some who know us. It is into their hearts that Allah, praised be His name, looks. Each gets his due reward."

"*In khilyat bilyat*—It takes all kinds. If the rotten ones went missing, the world would not be complete."

And then predictably, and with the most natural immediacy and casualness, the topic shifted to the land. They were all going to their fields in the newly demilitarized "Area Nine." They spoke with a sense of victory, pride and elation that they had finally gained access to their land.

"Look how well everybody is taking care of his land. Everybody is planting olive tree seedlings. It is the blessed tree that Allah has chosen for our land and mentioned in His holy book."

I was particularly impressed by the middle-aged woman's enthusiasm for her land. She was rightly proud of the sacrifice made by her family to reclaim the land, and bragged about it.

"We own fourteen dunams in al-Marjam. They were half rocky, half cultivable. Before our land was liberated we could not get to it to plant the good parts. The last time Allah blessed me with working on that land was when I was pregnant with my firstborn son. Because of the landmines and the military closure, we only managed to set foot in it again a couple of years ago. But we had title to it and we kept it. Lo and behold, one day recently my firstborn son—he is in his twenties now—surprises us all by announcing that he is going to sell his car, the most dear thing to his heart, so that he can pay for a Caterpillar to come and clear the rocks from the land, now that it is accessible. We all thought he was kidding because we know how much his car means to him and to his friends. But that is exactly what he did. Within a week, he woke the family up one morning shouting excitedly for all of us to come to al-Marjam because the bulldozer was coming to clear the rocks. He had already paid the operator from the money he collected from selling the car."

The husband enriched the story with his role in it:

"Almighty God forgets no one from his blessings. Allah gives when the need arises and He gives again and again. I know my own son and told him that he was doing the right thing although it was the last thing I expected him to do. I told him I would pitch in and make sure that all the cleared land would be *mnassabeh*—properly planted with olive seedlings. Allah, praised be His name, had ordained that we would succeed in our effort. Right then and there, when we needed the money most, I received my disability compensation pay. I had retired early because of my illness and the National Insurance official in Nazareth was dragging my claim out forever. But God inspired him to reach his decision at just the right time. With that money I bought enough olive seedlings for the fourteen dunams."

By now we had arrived at the edge of their field and I reached over and unlatched the side door for them to get out. The man slid the door open and the couple stepped out. The wife, as if emboldened by her husband's withdrawal from the car's physical and social space, continued to hold us captive, leaning into the car with her boney torso jammed in the doorway and ignoring her husband's hurried attempts to close the door and end her conversation with a stranger.

"I have never seen land more beautiful than this land in spring," she continued, as if unaware of being repeatedly nudged by the half-shut sliding door. "*Hatha tithkar lalwalad aw-lawalad alwalad*—This will be a present kept for generations to come, in memory of their grandpa investing his disability pay and of his firstborn investing the price of his car so that they will enjoy the blessed taste of *Souri* olive oil."

The man finally pulled his wife away and slid the door shut. We were on our way again, my blond friend and I. He cannot afford the price of a bulldozer for land reclamation, he told me, and has been doing it with his bare hands and with the help of a pick axe and a tiny hoe. He had a water jug as well.

"Oh, there is nothing to it. It may take me a few years, but I am enjoying it. This is the life, indeed! Last spring, when the rains stopped and it got a little warmer, I came here just like this with my own bare hands and I worked two and a half months straight. I slept in the field. I went home only on Fridays. I never spent a more beautiful two and a half months in my life."

As I stopped for him to disembark, it was my turn to dilly-dally for a while. I asked him about some totally insignificant topic just so that I could continue contemplating him and pondering the significance of his life as an act of faith. He was dressed in a tattered, wildly mismatched colorful shirt and pants outfit and a relatively well-preserved pair of laced white leather shoes that he apparently had purchased at some secondhand store. He cut a comic figure, standing there in front of massive boulders and wild shrubs, spitting and blowing into the cupped palms of his rough hands to warm and lubricate them in preparation for the serious task ahead.

"I'll show those pigs. *Ana deebak, dactorna*—You can count on me, my doctor!"

I didn't know if to laugh or to cry. This scrawny shriveled-up miscreant, this cross-eyed weakling was not only preparing to reclaim his land from massive rocks and years of neglect, but also congratulating himself on having halfway defeated the Israeli military establishment and the political and financial clout of world Zionism. Doubtless that was not quite his meaning, but he clearly sensed that "those pigs" were out to grab his land and he was prepared to resist. That is something you cannot but admire and respect.

"*Allah yqawweek*!—May God grant you strength!" I said in response and encouragement.

One morning at Wadi Salameh I found three Bedouin women waiting with their jerry cans of yogurt and their fenestrated plastic handbags for carrying back the household items they would buy in Rama's stores. This has become a regular stop where I pick up Bedouin hitchhikers on my way to the Galilee Society office. All three are regular customers by now. They said "Good morning, doctor" and "How are you, doctor?" in their pleasant accent. They thanked me for stopping and cussed all the other drivers that had not, including one from their own village whose car tires they jokingly threatened to slash with the sharp knives they would buy in Rama.

The two older women sat in the back with their containers of liquid merchandise on their knees while the younger, rather bulky woman sat up front. I asked her to use the seatbelt and both old women chuckled together about what a lot of seatbelt she needed to go around those hips. It was very light-hearted and pleasant till they closed the windows because it was a little cool outside. The very distinctive smell of the goat herder, a sort of mixture of body odor and goat cheese aroma, is not all that offensive to me, even familiar, but it became a bit suffocating in the closed space. I asked if there was not a bus service to the village now that the road to Rama has been widened and paved. They said that there was a bus that came by at six in the morning to take residents of the area's Jewish communities to work in the city and again in the afternoon to bring them back. By six they were not ready. "We don't have enough time between the morning call for prayer and six o'clock to get our act together, to take the herds out for morning grazing, to do the milking, and to get the kids on their way to school."

Somehow, for me, it did not add up. There they were, paying the fees to send their children to school by selling yogurt door to door in

Rama. True, yogurt from Bedouin goats brings a special price: it is much desired for cooking, perhaps because of its appeal to the trendy palates of uppity Rama housewives or of its sentimental value for them. It has a value much beyond its biological or nutritional worth. Still, it is extremely difficult to make a living from the door-to-door sale of goat yogurt. It is hard to see what these women have in their lives to be so jovial about so early in the morning. Theirs is an impressive and apparently happy struggle for survival.

14
Donkeys with Neckties

Abu-Sliman, the jovial village elder, dancing at a grandson's wedding.

May 15, 1985

I have already served notice to Dr. A'daya Barka'i, my immediate superior at the Ministry of Health, that I will be taking a year's leave of absence without pay with the understanding that I have the option to extend that for a second year. Hopefully, by the end of this month I will start working full-time for the Galilee Society on a salaried basis. This coincides with my plan for a tour of European capitals in search of funding for various projects.

We, at the Galilee Society, are planning to bring primary health care to inaccessible Bedouin communities in the Galilee through a mobile clinic.* These villages are inaccessible by governmental design, not by accident or fault of the Bedouin. During the Ottoman era these Bedouin made the transition from a nomadic lifestyle to settled pastoral living; they hold title to their land and have permanent structures for homes. Yet the state says they cannot live where they have done for generations, that their homes will be demolished and they must relocate to new "planned settlements," to Bedouin reservations. To put pressure on them to relocate so the same hilltops can accommodate new Jewish settlements, the state then withholds all services from these villages, including electricity and water. The legal Jewish settlements being built next door are not allowed to share their amenities with the "natives," even if they are willing to do so. Raise your voice in complaint and the typical responses are: "This is a democracy. You have an equal vote. If you don't like the law that made you and your kind criminals, you have recourse to the courts and parliament."

Our intended activity of providing primary health care to the Bedouin in these unrecognized villages and raising awareness of their plight has immediate political implications. Our plan will make the Bedouin's lives more tolerable. It therefore means we are helping these "criminals" stay where they are and continue their crime of living on their land. By implication, we will become party to the crime.

The available statistics show that the health status of this Bedouin group compares very poorly to the rest of the country and even to the

---

* *Bedouin:* In its persistent attempt to divide the Arab minority, Israel assigns the Bedouin, a traditionally nomadic group now semi-settled, a separate identity from those of Muslim, Christian, and Druze, and targets it specifically for recruitment into its defense forces as trackers. The Bedouin reside in two areas in Israel: the Galilee in the north and the Negev in the south. The Negev Bedouin, the poorest of the poor in Israel comprising some 150,000, have been banned from using their extensive tribal lands, long consecrated by tradition and the sword. Israel created a special unit, the Green Patrol, known for its aggressive and violent tactics, to enforce its policy of concentrating them into urban reservations. It is ironic that despite its name, the Green Petrol pursues a policy of Bedouin house demolition, animal slaughter, and, especially, crop destruction.

rest of the Palestinian minority in Israel. Currently, a mother who wants her child immunized has to carry it, walking or riding a donkey down from her hilltop village for an hour or more to a recognized community and then return to her village the same way. A ride in the trolley of a tractor is considered a luxury. And clinic hours in neighboring villages are usually anybody's guess. Our plan will provide a mobile clinic that visits each unrecognized village at regular intervals, at least once weekly, providing preventive care to pregnant mothers and their children, and providing limited curative care for the sick.

This requires a modest investment initially and some continuing subsidy even though we plan to use volunteer physicians and nurses. We obviously do not expect to obtain financial assistance from any governmental or charitable agency in Israel. In fact, government agencies are known to object to anyone interfering on behalf of the Bedouin, the enmity between the two unequal contenders for the Galilean hilltops is so great. Bedouin villagers who try to widen the steep narrow footpaths to their communities find the armed forces arriving soon afterwards with heavy machinery to make them unusable again. And schools that already exist in the Bedouin villages have been forced to close in compliance with the planning law that declared the villages illegal retroactively. But we are intentionally disregarding all these considerations and focusing on the villagers' need for and right to primary health care. We are going to give them medical care where they are. All the rest is none of our business.

On several occasions on initial scouting missions for this project, Dr. Anwar Awad and I had to leave our car in the fenced-off new Jewish settlements and trek across the countryside to meet the Bedouin natives to find out what they need and win their support for our plan. Our standard questionnaire included asking the Bedouin to identify the one health service they wanted most for their village if we could guarantee only one such request. One leader of a Sawaid tribe wistfully asked for an ambulance service to be provided to the neighboring Jewish settlement. "A woman in labor could walk there in less than an hour and be transported to the hospital," he explained. His vision of the future excluded any possibility of a paved access road to his own village.

Another Bedouin leader was impressively astute in his response to the same question. "You are physicians and you write prescriptions for your patients that they take down to Musa, the pharmacist in Acre, and Musa fills your prescriptions by weighing the different chemicals exactly and mixing them in the right way. My prescription for the health of the whole Na'im tribe is simple, and needs no pharmacist to prepare it. It has one single component that is sufficient to cure all of our ills: water!"

I was dumbfounded. Where did this guy learn his public health? He understood its principles better than all of my Ministry of Health colleagues.

As the Acting Northern District Physician, I found myself compelled recently to accompany the Deputy Minister of Health on a field visit to three Arab villages in my area. She was interested in paying a visit to her political allies there. On my side, I tried to make her aware of the health concerns of these villages. The day before, I called on all three mayors and encouraged them to confront her about the subject of the sewage flowing in their streets. One, a crude and pompous party associate of hers, assured me that he would show me how to deal with "that Zionist bitch." As she was eating lunch at his house, he opened up the subject of sewage:

"I am putting responsibility for the sewage on your shoulders. If you don't do something about it, I promise you that I will turn all the shit of my village downhill towards your city of Karmiel. I will have it flooding the highway and splashing you every time you visit the Galilee."

It was a hard act to follow and the visit ended on that note.

On the way back to my office I caught a ride with two other Arabs, both servile party functionaries of the Deputy Minister: one an administrator in the Ministry of Health who is a former military officer; and another associate who is known contemptuously by a comical nickname referring to a food preference of his, a nickname equivalent to "banana head." I suddenly became aware of being in the company of two Zionist functionaries, both having a public profile as disloyal and suspicious to their fellow Arab citizens as can be imagined. I noticed the way all three of us spoke as concerned Palestinians when we were together, and how different our tone, terminology and shared assumptions were now from the way we had spoken earlier in the presence of our Jewish visitors. For a moment, I could feel that the image I project to the outside observer and, more significantly, to my own alter ego is indistinguishable from that of my two companions: a sheep in wolf's skin. My function that day had been to provide a thin veil of health professionalism to a political party event.

Earlier that day, following the mayor's sewage outburst, Mr. Banana Head commented apologetically to the Deputy Minister "You would think the mayor wasn't one of ours!" and gave me a clear conspiratorial wink, as if to say "We are all in this together." He clearly assumed that I am another political appointee—his professional counterpart. And he had every reason to assume he was right, because it is well known that Arabs can infiltrate the government system only through party connections.

I could not help but compare my operational style with theirs. We all are involved in the same type of maneuvering to gain favor for our villages in any way we think appropriate. We all are aligning ourselves with the powers that be to secure a scrap from the banquet at which we all are undesired guests. They use political channels, and I use professional ones. They have as valid a reason to lay claim to serving their community, or even to nationalism, as I do. These are people I despise, and their tactics are below my dignity. Yet, here I felt like one of them. It was enough to make me very uncomfortable and invite suicidal thoughts, professionally if not physically.

I have approached a couple of organizations in Europe about funding a special kindergarten for mildly mentally handicapped Arab children. A year or two of intensive stimulation and an individualized program of therapy may be sufficient to bring such a child to the level where he or she can be mainstreamed and attend a regular school. Such programs exist in Jewish communities but there is not one in an Arab town and Arabic is never the teaching language. We intend to initiate two such special rehabilitation kindergartens.

There are now plans for the School of Civil Engineering at the Technion, the Israeli Institute of Technology in Haifa, and the Galilee Society to hold a scientific conference on the topic of Rural Environmental Health. Although our new connections with the Technion smack of colluding with the system, they also reflect positively on the Galilee Society's growing seriousness of purpose. Our village councils are unable to start work on desperately needed sanitary projects because of an artificial financial bottleneck, and the Galilee Society is offering interest-free loans to enable these councils to bypass the bottleneck. The Interior Ministry, through Mr. Koenig, is prohibiting them from using the loans. The whole fiasco of sanitation in Arab communities is a damning confirmation of apartheid in this country. Still, the fact is that we need help from such a special godfather as the dean of the Technion to convince the authorities of our legitimacy.

It is also a shocking indictment of Israel that its Arab communities are still underdeveloped at a time when the country is exporting, with much fanfare, its own experiments in community development to all corners of the earth through international training courses and training manuals—such as the Institute for International Development in Haifa—and the various kibbutz volunteer programs. Israel sees financial and political incentives in promoting these successes internationally, while ignoring its own underdeveloped minority. I judge that to be short-sighted and likely to have far-reaching consequences, including growing polarization and alienation between Israel's two ethnic groups.

It seems, however, that very few people in our own community understand the significance of what we at the Galilee Society are doing in terms of community health development and awareness-raising. At the local level, people are simply not used to this kind of language or to this way of doing things.

Only two people in our circle of leadership have really been involved in community development. Father Chacour in Ibillin, and Dr. Sami Geraisy, better known to his fellow Nazarenes as Abu-Farah, who has worked through the World Council of Churches.* In recent years, for example, he has helped the people of Eilaboun to mount a land

---

* Elias Chacour was born in Biram, a demolished Palestinian village whose residents have been prevented from going back to it despite repeated Supreme Court rulings ordering their return. Prior to his 2006 election as the Malkite Catholic Church's Archbishop of Galilee he contributed significantly to the welfare of the Palestinian minority in Israel, with several successful educational projects especially in his adopted village of Ibillin. He holds many international honors including three nominations for the Nobel Peace Prize. He has written two widely-read books that reverberate with his family's struggle as "Present Absentees" or internal refugees and with his efforts at peaceful coexistence.

reclamation project, clearing out rocks to form soil-retaining walls and borders.

A large boulder just east of the village of Eilaboun, by the road to Nazareth, with a small square-shaped area etched into its rough surface, stands as testimony in stone to how much his actions have defied the country's Zionist ethos. The site of the memorial is very scenic, overlooking a hilly expanse that abuts the Horn of Hittin before falling away to the Sea of Galilee. To the right are the massive military installations that have been built over the destroyed village of Nimreen, and to the left, in the distance, can be seen the city of Safad perched on Mount Kana'an—a mountain to which my vain uncle Salih once tried to lay legal claim on the strength of its name alone. On a clear summer day, you can almost see, with your mind's eye, the armies of Saladin and Richard the Lion Heart poised to do battle here. The land is dusty, gray and rocky except in spring when it seethes with a carpet of flowers. The harsh and unforgiving summer scene belies the land's grain-productive potential.

In recognition of his contribution to Eilaboun's successful efforts to hold on to its land, the village affixed a copper plaque to the boulder, a symbolic gesture common in thousands of locations in Israel, usually in recognition of Jewish donors from abroad who have supported the establishment of settlements or the planting of forests in the Holy Land. The plaque had not only Dr. Geraisy's name on it but also that of the local branch of the World Council of Churches, as well as the date of the project. It was probably the only sign in open fields in Israel bearing an Arab name. Three times, I am told, the plaque was removed from the boulder and Eilaboun's local authority would replace it before giving up. Eyewitnesses say members of the Israeli army have repeatedly vandalized the simple memorial.

March 8, 1986

The Galilee Society and the Nazareth Arab Academic Union are planning the first ever Arab Health Conference in Israel. One day I led a delegation of the organizers to the Negev.

The Bedouin population of the Negev has the worst health conditions of any group in Israel. We were well received by the small number of young Bedouin academics, including a few doctors, and by a group of

Bedouin notables. Dr. Yunis Abu-Rabia'a was there, the first Bedouin to graduate from the Hadassah Medical School in Jerusalem, where I was refused admission. Did I feel a twinge of jealousy? He is a pleasant, mild-mannered and benign gentleman who fits the physical image of the average Ethiopian man: very thin, on the tall side, handsome, with slightly hunched shoulders, large black eyes, and an unthreatening fatherly demeanor. The elders of various tribes in Rahat, an artificial town of over 20,000 Bedouin settled in tribally based neighborhoods, also attended.* Rahat has a local council, comprising seven well-behaved "representatives" of the major tribes who have been appointed by the state, as well as four outsiders, all Jews. The head of the council, and the person who makes all the decisions, is from a neighboring Jewish community. Superficially, all seemed to be peaceful and orderly in Rahat, as might be expected in a good Bedouin reservation. Yet, in one day it was easy to detect the strain.

The infighting in the group that received us was interesting to observe. The Communist party was represented by one young man who used obstructive tactics, shouting and arguing against the status quo. He was problematic procedurally but, of course, perfectly right to want to concentrate on getting rid of the appointed sham council rather than on health matters. A local elder declared us "unwanted intruders," adding: "We can handle our own situation. We don't need anybody's help. After all, it's only right to have the decision-making in the hands of the Jewish gentleman who is the appointed mayor. He is well connected to the system and the Jews understand each other, and they know what's best for us."

The majority, however, were simply non-committal, prepared to settle for what they had. Dr. Abu-Rabia'a appeared neutral and stuck religiously to his medical field, dutifully serving his community, his profession and his pocketbook. Not unlike what I would look like if I let down my guard or abandoned my role at the Galilee Society. We did

---

*   Rahat is the largest of seven Arab towns established in the Negev, the arid southern two-thirds of Israel's land area, as part of the state's efforts to sedentarize and concentrate the area's Bedouins away from their traditional lands and way of life. The experiment has failed badly with all seven towns being at the lowest rung of the socio-economic scale in Israel and with about half of the total Negev Bedouin population refusing to reside in them. Rahat in particular, with 40,000 residents by the year 2006, has become an overcrowded den of poverty, unemployment, and crime.

our best to keep politics out of the discussion and to talk health only. It did not work too well, of course. Health is as much politics in the Negev as it is in the corridors of the World Health Organization. There were several shouting matches, but it ended with promises from Dr. Abu-Rabia'a and another physician to present papers at the conference.

I also saw an old acquaintance of mine, Sheikh Musa al-Atawni. About eight years ago, I took my family for a visit to his in the Negev and on to the Sinai. For a few days we lived hippy-style with "the nomads." I had not seen him or heard from him since, and yet when we met he asked about my children and wife by name. He is a man of obvious intelligence, very well-spoken and well-mannered, and respected by his people. He had flirted briefly with one of the leftist Zionist parties, a move that may have helped him stay on his ancestral tribal lands, but is now apparently out of politics. One of his daughters is a nurse working in a clinic we visited, one headed by a colleague and friend of mine. The inhabited part of the Negev is a small place, but a complete universe of intrigue, factionalism, poverty, ill-health, superficial submissiveness, deep-seated mistrust and much pent-up anger.

Subsequently, we held more meetings in Nazareth about the conference. To avoid political factionalism, we hid behind the Higher Monitoring Committee on Arab Affairs, a body supposedly inclusive of all the political streams in the Arab community. A proposal to invite Ezer Weitzman to the opening session of the conference was defeated. People objected on the grounds that it implied an acceptance that we need an "Arab minister," or "godfather" as his current position is being called. The majority view among members was that he has shown himself to be amenable to "conciliatory steps" and "lenient" toward the Arabs. We hoped Weitzman's participation might help to deflate the authorities' opposition towards the conference and those behind it, especially those who are employees of the Ministry of Health, myself included. We have it on good authority that the Ministry is boycotting the conference and may punish any Arab employees who participate.

April 26, 1986

About 420 people, nearly all Arabs, came and paid the equivalent of $10 each to attend our First Arab Health Conference. The largest group was the physicians, about 170 of them.

It turns out that despite all our Hebrew-language press releases and the press conference we held in Tel Aviv in advance of the conference, only one newspaper, *Haaretz*, included a very small news item. Press coverage was limited to the Arabic press. Sadly, it dawned on me that the conference will not in truth impinge on the consciousness of the top decision-makers at the Ministry of Health. The average official there never reads the Arabic press. Our conference was not even cited in the mimeographed press review sheet circulated daily among managerial and professional staff by the spokesperson's office at the Ministry. Although Arabic is the state's second official language, the office scans only Hebrew and English papers. Two separate communities live, think, and communicate here, but the state seems to be aware of only one.

It is not a coincidence that our conference was covered in the other news clippings sheet, this one circulated to all main government offices, originates with the security services and is full of quotations from the Arab press. The system's awareness of our existence is limited to its permanent conception of us as a threat to the state. Officials do not speak our language, not only literally but figuratively as well. We are speaking in two different voices, and neither is hearing the other. Or at best communication is one way: we hear what the officials say, even if we do not necessarily agree or comply with it. They do not hear anything we say, except when it is conceived of as proof of the threat we pose. The impossible task for us at the Galilee Society is to bridge that gap and to make "them" aware of "our" existence, needs, and positive potential.

The first Arab Health Conference, at one level, was an attempt to do this: we thought that if we spoke in a professional voice we had a better chance of breaking down racial and political barriers. In practice, we did not even manage to break down the linguistic or cultural barriers. The *Jerusalem Post* for example took no notice of the conference at all, even though its correspondent was there and asked relevant questions. She even considered what I said significant enough to record it and check it with me afterwards.

April 27, 1986

Sunday morning, and I am in the garden. I have planted an oak tree, the big kind that grows wild in this country, carries big acorns, and lives anything from a hundred to a thousand years. I think it is called Atlantic oak. The two olive trees near the gate have even greater longevity. Olives, oaks, the hawthorn and mastic bushes in the rock garden are all very much part of the Galilee. At the same time Didi has succeeded in growing some Hawaiian decorative trees from seeds we had smuggled in. That is the geographic and time perspective in our garden. Admittedly it is self-aggrandizing and self-congratulatory, but the thought crosses my mind to ascribe such dimensions to my real hobby, the Galilee Society.

A disaster has befallen a family we know, leaving my daughter Rhoda extremely disturbed by the death of her classmate. The father is among the wealthy landed aristocracy of a neighboring village, known for currying influence with the authorities and carrying a gun, a clear stigma of all collaborators. Yesterday the son shot himself dead while playing with one of his father's handguns. The village rumor mill offers an alternative interpretation: The boy committed suicide in shame and disgust with the father's tarnished name. The general view is that the boy would have done better to turn the gun against its owner.

It just so happened that, the day before, Rhoda had gone with this classmate collecting donations for heart units in the country's hospitals. The fact that the list included the Nazareth Hospital made us feel obliged to assist in the effort. She came back upset because somebody accused her of collecting money for the Israeli armed forces, a mistake probably prompted by the name given to this campaign, "*Liv-el-liv*" or "Heart to heart" in Hebrew. The campaign for donations to the armed forces is called "Libi," an abbreviation which also means "my heart." I reassured Rhoda that the two are close enough for somebody who does not know Hebrew well to get them confused. Still she was upset by the accusation. She added: "And I had to be with none other than the son of Yousif al-Ali, which gave people every reason to be suspicious."

Yesterday I had to hospitalize Abu-Sliman, the cutest old man in the village, who is critically ill seemingly through self-neglect. Perhaps he just wanted to die. A sufferer from severe Parkinson's disease, he

recently stopped taking his medications and his muscles essentially
froze with rigidity. He lay in bed till he developed sepsis. I checked on
him yesterday partly because I had not seen him for a while and partly
because I wanted to have a sip of his most special black Arabic coffee.
Perhaps, unconsciously, I was also sniffing around for more village
talk about the shooting incident. I was met at the door by his youngest
grandchild, a friend and classmate of my son, who announced:

"My grandfather is dying! Come and see him."

"How long has he been that bad?"

"Three or four days."

I found Abu-Sliman still conscious. He even recognized me by my
voice without opening his eyes. He had a high fever and was dehydrated.
His lungs sounded like hell with pneumonia. I insisted on sending him
to the hospital. The family agreed when I explained that they could not
just give up hope on him because of his age and his limited ability to
move. We asked his opinion and he nodded faintly in agreement.

Abu-Sliman's illness saddens me because he is the last living childhood
friend of my father who has also become my friend. I have always
derived great pleasure from visiting him and his always-pleasant wife
in their home of two *a'aqids*, the thick stone-walled and cross-arched
structures that once served both as a residence and a symbol of wealth
and social status. His father was the village priest and his maternal
uncle the *mukhtar*, or appointed head, of the village's Christian
neighborhood. He had sufficient status and wealth in his younger days
to warrant the British Mandate authorities issuing him a permit for a
hunting gun. He has managed to keep the permit and the gun till now,
without his name being besmirched in the village by his ownership of
a firearm. On occasion he would stop at my house on his way back
from the hills, his shotgun slung over his shoulder and the loose ends
of his black *qumbaz* tucked to the sides under his belt revealing his
funky-looking loose *sirwal*, and deliver a quail or two and a pocket-full
of green almonds he had picked from the fields. That occasional visit
would make Didi's day even more than mine, and she would insist on
making fresh coffee for him.

All of Arrabeh knows Abu-Sliman as a light-hearted and jovial
villager who likes to tell jokes, including about himself, and to recount
the pranks he pulled on his friends in his younger days. He always starts
his stories with a loud chuckle, sometimes laughing till his eyes fill with

tears, before he commences the story. He claims that, when my father married his first wife, they were both still children. It was an arranged marriage, sealing a pact between two respectable clans: two Kanaaneh brothers from Arrabeh marrying two Abu-Raya sisters from Sakhnin. Apparently my father was much younger than his bride. On the night of the wedding, Abu-Sliman tells me, he went with another friend and peeked through the cracks in the old door of the matrimonial room. The bride had my father lying on the ground with his head in her lap as she searched his hair for lice. "They were both fully clad," he hastens to add so as to exonerate himself of any indecency in spying on them.

Another favorite story of Abu-Sliman's concerns the time he managed to get a cousin of mine, a close friend of his in their younger years, to do some amazingly fast leg work. Early one morning, Abu-Sliman was on his way to the fields when he met a new bride only two days after she had been brought to the neighborhood from another distant village. She was on her way back from the village spring carrying a jug of water on her head, apparently intent on showing how industrious she was and how well she had adjusted to her new surroundings. She was a pretty young thing and in the light of the rising sun her flushed cheeks were irresistible. On a sudden urge, Abu-Sliman rushed over and planted a kiss on her cheek. She smiled pleasantly and each of them went their own way. Minutes later Abu-Sliman was having breakfast with his closest friend, my cousin, and told him of his experience with the friendly new girl in the neighborhood. By early afternoon my cousin had contacted the newly wed groom, entered with him into a business partnership, brought him a donkey and two jerry cans of olive oil, and sent him to the city of Nazareth to sell the oil door to door. With the new partner gone, my cousin then went knocking at his door to inquire from his bride about the way the olive oil business was faring. Abu-Sliman could barely finish the story, he chuckled and laughed so much. My knowing the two protagonists as the old and wilted specimens they are today and whom I treat regularly makes the story even funnier.

In 1950 Abu-Sliman attained the status of a living legend for another of his practical jokes. At that time his half-brother, the village priest, was entrusted with distributing donations received through a church organization to the villagers. The donations were originally meant for the refugees in our village but in fact everyone in Arrabeh and elsewhere in the Galilee benefited from such gifts. I recall the priest standing at the balcony of his second-story house throwing down armfuls of clothes at the gathered children in the alley. No adult would allow himself to compete for such donations, though they were much appreciated. I also remember coming home with a red and blue striped shirt that I managed to catch on such an occasion. I lost it to my older brother, Sharif, who at the time was attending eighth grade in Sakhnin and so was in greater need of decent garments than I was. Still, I was allowed to wear the brightly colored shirt on weekends and holidays.

One bagful of clothing received by this route from Belgium turned out to contain neckties and nothing more. No one knew exactly what the item was for, much less had any use for them. Abu-Sliman volunteered to dispose of them, claiming that he could use the strips of cloth for grafting trees in his orchard. Shortly thereafter donkeys in the village fields were seen grazing with Belgian-made neckties adorning their necks and tails. Abu-Sliman's mocking of our European colonial masters in this fashion was not lost on the villagers. "The way they seek to befriend us by sending their surplus food and clothing while aiding our Zionist enemy to steal our land showed what stupid asses they were," he later explained.

15
Different Resistance

The author on the day he left for the US in 1960, taking leave of his fellow and former teacher, Sheikh Kaid. (Some other teachers didn't dare be photographed with someone abandoning the system.)

December 16, 1986

A while back the most popular host on Arabic-language TV in Israel asked me to participate in a panel discussion on his new show, *"Itarat"* or "Frameworks," that dealt with health care in Israel. In the studio, he was determined to provoke a public confrontation across the racial divide between the six participants, three Arab and three Jewish physicians. He wanted to discuss "medical issues that have practical application," as he phrased it. His assumption was that it must be difficult for an Arab physician to treat Jewish patients, and vice versa. I was unable to relate to the subject in any meaningful way except to disregard it as trivial on point of principle.

The young host touched lightly on various aspects of modern medicine, but was particularly interested in trans-racial organ transplantation. He failed to trigger the desired row, however, mainly because the Arab doctors could not find it in their hearts to argue with the accepted precepts of their Jewish counterparts. They were anxious to prove that "Of course, we are not against the state. We treat Jewish people, and we do not even refuse to treat army personnel." Similarly, the three Jewish physicians asserted that they even treat patients from Gaza and the West Bank. They condescendingly told us how much they personally respected the Arabs' historical contribution to the medical field before concentrating on the contributions made by the famous Jewish sages to Arab medicine and culture in general.

It all rang hollow in light of Israel's continuing occupation of Palestine and the never-contested two-tier health care system within Israel proper. My suggestion that Jewish physicians could protest against the immoral occupation by refusing to do military service in the occupied territories was rejected out of hand by the participants and edited out of the final program. I then tried to shift the discussion to the issue of health manpower training and the system's blindness to the Arab community's needs. Also I spoke about the glass ceiling that Arab physicians quickly come up against. Somehow I could not get any of my points across.

On the trip in a shared taxi to and from Jerusalem for the show, I had the chance to chat at some length with the TV show's host and with a couple of the other participants including an Islamic judge.

The other participant, the medical director of a missionary hospital in Nazareth, is an ambitious young Israeli-trained Arab physician who projects the image of a business-like professional. I find him too aggressive in a shallow Israeli manner. He plans to start a medical library at his hospital and offer health education courses for key lay members of the community, such as school teachers and policemen. But he seems not to know how to relate to his specific local setting. He assumes he will fail to make a dent in "the mentality of the ignorant masses" he serves, as he put it. In that sense, he is typical of the new generation of locally trained and marginally integrated Arab physicians who are unable to see things in any light except that offered them during training by their Zionist mentors. They have a myopic, unkindly vision; they see the Arab community through the eyes of a superior, scornful and hostile outsider. Anxious to please their bosses, they relate to their fellow Palestinians with arrogance and contempt.

In short, this doctor shares the same perception of the Arab as servile and inferior as the Jewish majority in Israel or the colonial missionaries who run his hospital. In his case, it results in a clear conflict between his ambitious plans and his near-zero expectations from what he conceives of as a group of uneducated, unresponsive, "worthless Arabs." Somehow he is unable to see through the curtain of public prejudice that he has learned to accept over the years.

I am about to rejoin the Ministry of Health after two years of leave without pay. This time it will be under a different job description, as the deputy to the District Physician in Nazareth, a woman who seems to be very liberal. On a visit to my expected new office I meet few staff members there. Since it happens to be on a Saturday only Arabs are working and I join a few of them for coffee. I have worked here off and on in the past but always on a temporary basis and was always shown the customary courtesy accorded to a guest. This time it is for real and that adds to the frank and trusting spirit of the discussion I initiate.

"She might be liberal," one old-timer warns me, "but only within the confines of the Israeli establishment's Zionist view of the Arabs in general as the enemy and the Arab minority in Israel as a problem and an accursed fact of life that one has to work around and to make the best of."

"She seems to think I can be of assistance to her by spearheading an effort to improve the health services to the Arab half of the district's population," I argue back.

"That probably means she is setting you up as the 'fall guy,' the one to blame when the impossible task of changing the status quo from within fails."

"Don't start dreaming the impossible," my former classmate, now the district treasurer, concurs; "money is the bottom line; to set out to patch up the deficiencies of their long years of neglect is self-defeating. You will be swimming against the current and none of us has the strength for it as long as a decision at the highest political level has not been taken to deal with the situation."

"What remains is slogans and a grandiose title that they will offer you." This from a young sanitary inspector.

"No Director-General of the Ministry of Health is about to appoint me to a national level job or to a post representing Israel abroad without my first professing commitment to Zionist ideology, even if only as lip service," I protest.

"What is left then for you, like the rest of us, is to adopt a strategy of subversion," the most senior member of the group opines. "I do not mean overthrowing the government or inciting to armed struggle, not even to civil disobedience. Land Day is still fresh in our minds. Rather, I mean subversion in the sense of working within the system to serve a goal not included in the original overall Zionist scheme of things. Like several other Arab minority members that I have come to respect, I focus on my own community and try to address its basic needs."

I like his approach and start sizing him up for membership in the Galilee Society.

"You know that there is another track for our struggle that we, at the Galilee Society, have started following. We bring up our issues at major world forums. We have written papers about the sewage problems in our villages for example and presented them at international scientific conferences. That way we announce to the world the fact of our existence. In the long run, that reveals the reality of the bi-national nature of the state of Israel."

"By providing such information, we can point up—purely on factual grounds—the absurdity of Israel's proclamations of democracy and equality for all of its citizens under the law," my friend intones. "We can expose the built-in inequity and the racially-biased distribution of resources. In world forums we can question the credibility of the concept of a Jewish and democratic state with a sizeable Arab minority. And we can do it independent of the Israeli system; we can present our own set of data that does not start with the Jewishness of the state as given and *a priori* modifier of all data." He obviously is a shoo-in as a member of the Galilee Society.

Our meek and feeble form of resistance to the Zionist enterprise that seeks to obliterate our national identity reminds me of a secret that a fellow Ministry of Health employee once confided to me. He lives in the village of Tarshiha, the Arab part of the twinned communities of Maalot-Tarshiha near the Lebanese border and a much-vaunted experiment in Jewish-Arab communal coexistence. It was election time and my friend was complaining to me about the unequal access to resources for the Arab half of the experiment. He complained that the all-powerful local politician, Abu-Tbol, a Moroccan Jewish immigrant backed by the more numerical population of Maalot, had tipped the balance even further in favor of his own community, Maalot. Abu-Tbol justified this policy apparently on the grounds that the immigrants reaching Maalot had special needs while he totally neglected the parallel needs of the Palestinians of Tarshiha, many of whom are internally displaced. At that point, my friend dropped his bomb: not only was he intending to abstain from voting in the municipal elections, but also "for the past two months I have started writing my return address on all of my correspondence as 'Tarshiha' and not 'Maalot-Tarshiha.' I'll show those pigs!"

I relate this story to the group and we all have a good laugh. As each returns to his desk I accompany my wise senior co-worker to his room to continue our discussion. In the old days he was a firebrand and a student leader and had even served time in jail for his nationalist activism. But he has since gained redemption by joining the Mapam liberal Zionist party, and through this he found employment in the Ministry of Health, long held as the exclusive domain of Mapam.

"I guess resistance comes packaged in all kinds of forms, from the protest implied in a return address to addressing the issue of inadequate sanitation in Arab villages at an international conference, from the shouting of angry accusations of neglect from the podium of the Israeli parliament to throwing a Molotov cocktail at a passing military vehicle," my senior co-worker adds. "Your work at the Galilee Society sounds more meaningful than the job you will have here."

"Believe me, as the official in charge of protecting and promoting the health of the Western Galilee's population, I should have been fired a long time ago for failing my duty. I will not apologize, however, for cheating the state out of a relatively generous salary so that I can now, through the Galilee Society, try to achieve outside my office what I have been prevented by racist policies, attitudes and practices from doing inside it."

"How is it going for you guys there anyhow?" he inquires casually.

"Join us and you will find out. Actually several factors are hindering our work. One is the daunting task of persuading competent Arab health professionals to veer off of the standard career track in the formal Israeli health care institutions and commit to work with us at the Galilee Society for pay. Another is dealing with the across-the-board discriminatory practices of all four existing Health Maintenance Organizations—HMOs. Their managements harbor views and tolerate practices no less discriminatory than government offices."

"Well, of course. Unlike state institutions, they are under no obligation to be fair. If you don't like what they offer, you stop paying your dues and seek someone else to give you a better service. It is the same as of the standard public statement from politicians and government officials when Arab citizens of Israel complain: 'There are many Arab countries in the Middle East. If you don't like it here, you should pick up and move to one of them.' As if that were a real option!"

"Initiating our own prepaid medical insurance system as an alternative crosses my mind often enough; we have discussed it a few times at the Galilee Society."

"If we were to try to establish an Arab-based HMO it would be fought tooth and nail by every official in the Ministry of Health, from the lowliest driver to the Health Minister herself. Our current Minister's known distaste for Arabs and contempt for everything Arabic stands out even in the sea of Israeli anti-Arab officialdom."

"Aren't we intent on faulting the system regardless? Tell me your honest opinion."

"I think there is an element of truth in that too—in the sense that, to my thinking, Israel can never be a benevolent state as far as the Arab minority is concerned. No measure of improvements to health services or of cosmetic gestures can negate the deleterious health effects of the Zionist system on both of its victims: the advantaged majority and the disadvantaged minority. Israel has no intention of changing its Zionist, racially-based apartheid ideology. As long as the issue of land is not settled in a just way, as long as Israel denies me full equality under its laws, as long as a Jew has a birthright that is denied to me, as long as my state keeps my villages poor and underdeveloped, as long as it defines itself as not mine, as long as it portrays me as the enemy, as long as it continues to paint me out of its symbols and out of the image it is proud to project to the world, my health will not be wholesome. Health, to my understanding, is inclusive of all of the above. Apartheid is unhealthy, full stop," he concludes with a slam of his fist on the table.

And I thought I was uncomfortable serving in the Ministry of Health!

I concur with the analysis and give my oft-repeated simplistic explanation of the untenable basis of the Zionist enterprise as it has materialized in the state of Israel: "Imagine a three-piece puzzle with space in it for only two pieces. A democratic and Jewish state with close to 20 percent of its population Palestinian Arabs is illogical by definition. So far Israel has managed to secretly throw out the democratic piece of the puzzle; it has been a democracy for the Jews only. Now we are making sure to expose that to the world. Rightist Zionists would like to solve the conundrum by throwing out the Palestinian minority. I think that we have enough voice and international connections that we will not allow that to go through. What will have to go out is the exclusive Jewishness of Israel. It is my contention that, over time, our continued presence, basic decency and common sense will bring that about. Part of this vision of true liberal democracy will have to be the right of return for Palestinians."

"I have my doubts. Perhaps it will happen but it will not be in our lifetime. Perhaps with the passage of time Israel will lose its paranoia and feel secure enough to become part of the Middle East. It will cease to be a colonialist foreign body."

January 22, 1987

With my encouragement, Didi has embarked on a career change and commenced a one-year master's course in public health. We are vaguely expecting to break out on the international health scene as a team once the children are well on their way in college. Didi's thesis advisor is none other than my former colleague and mentor, Dr. Ted Tulchinsky. A conservative Director-General of the Ministry of Health found him too aggressively liberal and tried to fire him. When he could not do so legally, the whole public health service was reorganized in such a way that, even though Dr. Tulchinsky continued to hold the same title and collect the same salary, his position was emptied of all significant content and he lost authority. He turned to writing reports on field research projects, including a couple of papers I co-authored on the health of asbestos factory workers in Naharya.

Much later, this maverick public health activist's duties were downgraded to writing glowing annual reports about the health of the occupied Palestinian populations of Gaza and of Judea and Samaria, the official Israeli designation for the West Bank. Apparently he has not only mellowed down and lost his edge but also changed trenches. He lacks the traits that endeared him to me in the past—the old proactive stance, the verve and the sense of injured justice that is the *sine qua non* of all sincere public health advocates. What a shame! Perhaps he has lost a loved one in the violent enforcement of the Israeli occupation with which he seems so enamored of late.

May 1, 1988

Sheikh Kaid, Arrabeh's religious leader, has a habit of sounding off about all sorts of issues not to his liking, especially during Ramadan, when he has two occasions a day to express his opinion through his regular sermons broadcast live on the mosque's loudspeakers. The other day he got mixed up between the missionary high school that our children attend, the Galilee Christian Gymnasium, and the Galilee Society. He attacked the "Christian Galilee Society" for poisoning the minds of our youth and declared that there was no need for such a foreign institution. He added that, as a Muslim society, we should develop our own Islamic civic institutions, including a Young Men's Muslim Association instead of the imported YMCA. The trigger for his outburst was the attempt by a group of young professionals to establish a Rotary Club. Which, in the sheik's view, is the same as the Masonic movement whose central mission, he says, is to spread the Jewish faith and hence should not be allowed to function in Arrabeh. And somehow the Galilee Society was mixed in with this hodge-podge of foreign institutions.

Sheikh Kaid is the unsung hero of community development in Arrabeh prior to the era of an elected council. With the authority of the mosque and its considerable land holdings, especially before the loss of much of the land to the Israel Lands Authority, he single-handedly initiated many communal projects, such as repair and maintenance of water wells, agricultural roads and the village school. His special social skill, other than making good use of his religious standing, was to actively network with all the influential clan heads in the village. Eventually he joined forces with the younger members of the community in agitating for and pushing through such major modern community projects as the electricity and water supply. Both he and the Catholic priest taught me at the village school. Later, for a brief period in 1960, I joined them as a teacher in the village.

Considering the sheikh's central position in the community and his record of long service to it, in addition to the fact that he has the whole village as his captive audience, I decided very early in the game to avoid any confrontation with him. Shortly after my return from the United States he chose to focus one of his lessons over the loudspeaker on young men who err by bringing foreign wives from abroad. There was no avoiding the fact that he was including me since there were only a couple of such cases in Arrabeh in total. I simply did not respond and continued receiving him and his family whenever they needed any medical care and affording him his due respect as my former teacher.

The storm blew over quickly and no one ever said a word of criticism to me or to Didi on the basis of his sermon. Didi, however, never liked the guy and still holds a grudge against him, not only for this but also for committing the sin, in her view, of marrying three wives and for never looking her straight in the eye on the rare occasions that their paths cross. He obviously averts his eyes from all women as a matter of proper behavior for a good Muslim. She, on the other hand, cannot help but feel insulted by this interpretation of her mere existence as a temptation of sorts. She does not agree with the locally accepted interpretation of his behavior as innocent and pious. "I wonder who chose his three wives for him if he never looks at women!" she argues. The grudge she really holds against him is for how he looked away and dismissed her with a wave of his hand the one time she stopped her car and offered him a ride when he was hitchhiking at the edge of the village.

16
Suffering the Lashes

Celebrating the Galilee Society's first EC grant, the first to be made to an NGO in Israel. From left: Dr. Sami Geraisy speaking, the author with a waiter behind him, Ambassador Gwyn Morgan of the EU delegation, Mr. Ilias Kassis (mayor of Rama, the Galilee Society's host community), and Dr. Anwar Awad and Dr. Shukri Atallah (two founding members of the Galilee Society).

May 1, 1988

Since the outbreak of the Intifada, the Palestinian uprising against Israel's occupation of the West Bank and Gaza, I have been busy with my new role as head of the National Relief Committee, coordinating relief efforts by Israel's Palestinian minority in support of the Intifada. The task fell to me as the head of the Monitoring Committee on Arab

Health Issues in Israel, a national political and professional body established at the conclusion of the first Arab Health Conference two years ago. In every Arab village and town in Israel, as well as in the Arab neighborhoods of the mixed cities, popular local committees have sprung up, comprising active young men and women from the different clans and neighborhoods with a smattering of religious elders. They collect money, food, clothing, blankets, medications and other items of humanitarian aid for their brothers and sisters in the occupied territories. We at the Health Monitoring Committee have "cornered the drug market," so to speak, since we concentrate on handling donations of spare medications from homes, medical supplies from pharmacies and cash donations earmarked for the purchase of medical supplies for Palestinian medical institutions.

Early on, I revived contacts I had made previously with a group in Jerusalem, the Union of Palestinian Medical Relief Committees (UPMRC). We, at the Galilee Society, had invited the leaders of this group to attend the Arab Health Conference in Nazareth in 1986, long before the Intifada. Now, with this most significant development for Palestinians on both sides of the Green Line,* I found it appropriate to rekindle the spontaneously warm relationship that had developed between us. With the Intifada raging, I called at their headquarters in Jerusalem, where I met their chairman, Dr. Mustafa Bargouthi, and his aides. I offered to help in any professional and material way we could in providing medical relief to the Palestinian sick and injured in the Intifada. The offer was graciously and thankfully accepted. I came back and alerted my committee to the opportunity of helping our professional counterparts in the Palestinian occupied territories. We called for a public meeting of all interested Palestinian health professionals on this side of the Green Line and obtained a mandate to act at the national level to coordinate medically related humanitarian aid.

The Health Monitoring Committee has also offered assistance to other groups active in emergency health care. The United Nations Relief and Works Agency in Jerusalem—the UN body responsible

---

* *Green Line:* The 1949 Armistice line between Israel and Jordan. Israel has so far abstained from determining its permanent borders. Within this framework of lack of clarity, and after the occupation of the West Bank in 1967, the Green Line was erased from maps and Israeli political consciousness. The two Palestinian Intifadas (uprisings) served as desperate reminders.

for the welfare of Palestinian refugees—has asked us to supply them with spare oxygen tanks, as the clinics' standard one tank each is no longer adequate because of curfews, closures and roadblocks. At the Shifa government hospital in Gaza, where staff are under strict orders to report the admittance of all patients to the occupying Israeli military authorities, attendance is extremely limited. Intentionally, the Ahli hospital and active volunteer community medical facilities do not register patients in the emergency room. Everything is done clandestinely, and false names and addresses are provided if at all. As a result, Palestinian youth with Intifada-related injuries feel safe seeking help there. They are given first aid and immediately released to be followed up at home. The Ahli hospital management has issued an appeal for equipment and supplies; in response, we have provided them with 10,000 shekels worth of sutures, for example.

The Ahli management has also issued an appeal for financial assistance in installing an elevator for their surgical department, which is spread over three floors in a hospital built in 1920. Patients are carried by orderlies up and down to the operating theater on stretchers. Unfortunately, so far I have not been able to convince anyone on this side of the Green Line to donate the needed amount. All donors wanted their money spent on oxygen tanks for people exposed to tear gas and possibly poisonous agents used by the Israeli forces, or on needles and sutures to sew up Intifada wounds, or on first aid salves and bandages to dress injuries. The important thing for most donors is that their money is used to buy items—short of arms—that will directly assist participants in the Intifada.

What is striking is the eagerness of members of our public—men and women, old and young—to donate blood. And this enthusiasm comes from a group known in Israel to be particularly reluctant to donate blood. Health education campaigns have been launched in recent years targeting Arab schools on this very subject. Early on, the head of al-Maqasid hospital in Jerusalem allowed a few busloads from our side to arrive and donate blood, but merely as a token of solidarity. He was clearly doing us a favor when he instructed his blood bank staff to give us top priority in donating blood; they have enough from their own donors. We have managed to take a few groups to visit the hospital and see where monetary and blood donations go. That way, people feel assured that they have shared in bearing the blood burden of the uprising. People want to pay this blood tax and feel that they are actual participants in the Intifada, this "shaking off" of the Israeli occupation.

The Galilee Society recently gave a dinner party in honor of Hans Bernath, the dedicated Swiss missionary physician who is retiring from long service as the director of the Nazareth Hospital. When Hans was asked about where he felt he most belonged—Nazareth or Switzerland—he gave a very endearing answer. He told of the acacia trees in the Sinai desert, originally a tropical species that has adapted well with thin leaves and thorns to its new dry environment, so much so that it is hard to guess its origins. Yet, when the time comes, it flowers with its sister acacias in tropical Africa. "I am fully a Nazarene," he said, "but deep in my heart I flower with the Swiss."

Dr. Martin is his successor. We immediately tried to get him involved in the Galilee Society's attempts at coordinating the work and future development of Nazareth's three competing missionary hospitals—the only hospitals in the city. With the partial exception of the Nazareth Hospital, known locally as the English Hospital, all decisions at the other two—the French and Italian hospitals—are still made by the religious orders abroad, with little if any local input. To varying degrees, all three hospitals continue to function as hostels for pilgrims from their orders. They seem not to want to have anything to do with the coordination committee we have established, viewing it as interference by a "foreign element," though they have not dared to tell us that openly. They also have deeply rooted historical enmities between them, to such a degree that one threatened to go to court over the other using "Nazareth" in its official name.

As a committed missionary, Dr. Martin has his own vision of saving the world through prayer and good deeds. He wants to keep his independence from us in deciding what to do with his little private shop, the Nazareth Hospital.

September 23, 1988

Two weeks ago my daughter Rhoda left for the United States to begin her independent life as a student at Harvard-Radcliff. Geographically, socially, and psychologically she has crossed into another world.

But I was extremely upset by Rhoda's treatment at the airport. For sentimental reasons, we wanted my brother Ahmad to accompany us there. He is Rhoda's favorite uncle, the one who provided her and Ty with candy and ice cream in exchange for hugs and kisses, and we knew he would enjoy coming with us to the airport. Of course, he came in his traditional Arab headdress; he would not be the same "Ammo Ahmad" without it. He drove the way there but just before arriving at the checkpoint at the entrance to the airport he switched seats with Didi. At the checkpoint anybody who looks vaguely Arab is automatically stopped for extra security searches, and we gambled on Didi's presence at the steering wheel—few Arab women drive—possibly balancing Ahmad's appearance and getting us through. But it didn't. We have never before been stopped at the checkpoint with Didi driving; this time we were motioned to the side.

This was at three o'clock in the morning, all of us having spent the evening and the previous day with friends and extended family. Didi had used up her nervous energy by hosting the entire crowd of family and friends at a combined going-away and birthday party for Rhoda. Everybody had stayed till one o'clock to see Rhoda off. Arriving exhausted, we were greeted by a gruff and cantankerous Druze soldier, who seemed intent on proving his loyalty to his state by shouting orders in Hebrew for us to open various pieces of luggage, take out items and hold them up high. I did all I could to keep Ahmad from starting a shouting match with the guy, whom he was cussing under his breath with the foulest Arabic obscenities, while Didi was repeating at the top of her lungs in English: "Stupid, stupid, stupid!"

The soldier must have understood that much English. He got more abusive, pushy and threatening: "I am warning you. If I find any nationalistic songs on these tapes, you will miss your flight and I will confiscate all your luggage!" He then proceeded to look individually at every piece of clothing, every book, and every tape Rhoda had packed. Wrapped up as he clearly was in the Israeli army's confined culture of regimentation, he was not familiar with current Palestinian nationalistic music. He picked up an Arabic recording by a group from Rama, probably because he recognized the name of a village in the locality from which he comes. He listened to that and confiscated it, but left Rhoda the real hardcore Palestinian Intifada songs by

Mustafa Kurd and the even more inflammatory recordings by Marcel Khalife.

We then moved on to the departure hall. Before reaching the check-in counter, Rhoda had to go through another thorough search, and this time by professional security officials with sophisticated training that is designed to leave you feeling dirt cheap and sorrowfully guilty at being born an Arab. Rhoda had to show proof that she had been admitted to Harvard. (And why, they might have asked, did she have to study abroad in the first place?) Everything in the luggage had to be checked; every little item had to be opened, and every container shaken clean of its contents; all candy boxes had to be opened and fingers poked into them and a few candies crushed to see if they might explode.

Carry-on luggage and handbags have to be tagged with one of the many color-coded strips. Rhoda's were tagged red, the highest level of security threat, to alert the personnel at the next set of checks before the boarding gates. We had to leave her there. On the phone the next day she told us that she went through two successive body-searches before getting to the boarding gate. She cried her eyes out in anger and disgust.

Her treatment was so morally demeaning and mentally discomforting that, if Rhoda harbored any lingering feelings of belonging to this state, they must have vanished at this last stop, forever relinquished to those prying and insulting "experts." This treatment is not incidental; it is intended to alienate, distress and discomfort Arab youth in such a way that they will never want to come back. No real security consideration in the world could possibly justify the harassment; and harassment of the utmost ugliness is reserved for the bright-looking ones. The procedures involved are very familiar to us from our regular travels abroad. But even by those standards they went to extremes with the harassment, repeated body-searches and questioning they put Rhoda through. And all on the occasion of her leaving for university and us bubbling with pride, happiness and hope for her. It is the intentional callousness, the aggressive putdowns and the spiteful timing of the implied mistrust that is so insulting. Rhoda was made to feel that, somehow, she is suspected of base intentions and subhuman motives for no reason other than her race. And it is all wrapped up in and justified by that holiest of Israel's holy cows: security.

After they did all that to my sweet, innocent, loving child, the very same system expects me, thanks to my position as Deputy District Physician of the Galilee, to show up today as part of the entourage of the Health Minister, a super hawk who is coming to Kafr Kana, the Kana of wine-from-water fame, to open a new mother and child health clinic. My boss, Dr. Barka'i, who is on vacation for six weeks, has asked me to mind the store. I accepted on two conditions: that, except in the case of emergencies, I would continue showing up at the office only one day a week; and that when the Health Minister makes one of her frequent political visits to the area she would not find me there. I said I would play sick, and that is exactly what I did today.

Initially I had intended to go along. It would have given me the opportunity to stand up and say in public what is on my mind. Then I thought about it for about half a minute and reached the conclusion that it was not worth the effort. For one thing, it would not be news to her. I have said it all to her before, as well as to the Director-General, to the heads of the local authorities, and to whoever cares to hear about the discrimination, about the lack of services to the Arab population and about the terrible deficiencies in sanitation in our towns and villages, not to mention the awful intentional neglect of so many unrecognized villages. It would be all in vain, an exercise in futility. The glib woman, an entirely political creature, would make promises she has no intention of keeping and might even publicly instruct me to follow up on her false promises.

My imaginary contentious stand against my unwelcome guest reminds me of the empty gesture of a cousin of mine, now a retired school teacher. I recall him relating an incident to my late father, his uncle, sometime in the 1950s. He was then one of many unqualified school teachers whose livelihoods depended on steering clear of trouble and never crossing the path of the Shin Bet. He was in the company of another cousin of ours, a known collaborator, when a policeman and a presumed Shin Bet agent turned up. The teacher considered his options: he could get up and leave, arousing the ire of the guests; or stay and hear some unsavory comments about the pan-Arab hero of the time, Jamal Abdul Nasser. It was wiser to stick it out and keep silent, he decided. In relating the incident to my father he became quite agitated, shouting the vilest of curses against the Zionist system and making the most heroic of declarations of support for the Egyptian revolution. He prefaced every loud pronouncement with a softly whispered "I should have said." To this day, this tale of subdued and secret revolt is part of our family lore.

An outbreak of polio in the Hadera sub-district has briefly pushed environmental sanitation into the spotlight. The new head of the epidemiology department in the Ministry of Health does not have much experience. Like so many settlers, he is a religious Jew, freshly arrived from the United States with a blind messianic zeal and little understanding of local realities. With the first two diagnosed cases of polio in the Jewish town of Or-Akiva, he announced the isolation of the virus from the town's sewage. The media and local politicians latched on to his discovery. TV reports highlighted the deteriorating state of the central sewage network in Or-Akiva, making various unsubstantiated claims, including that the sewage had backed up and not been treated properly and hence the outbreak.

Any second-year medical student knows, of course, that if there is an outbreak of poliomyelitis in a community, you will find the causative virus in its sewage effluent. That does not prove that the sewage is the source. As a matter of fact wild polio virus is routinely found in sewage in Israel even without any clinical disease outbreaks. With his misunderstanding of the science, the Ministry's epidemiologist has put the poor maintenance of existing sewage disposal systems in Jewish communities on the national agenda. Yet, no one seems to remember that Arab communities in Israel lack sewage disposal systems altogether, that their sewage flows openly in the streets and that children walk in it and passing cars splash it on their clothes on the way to school. That is as it should be, it seems. The issue at hand is maintenance, not installation, of sewage systems. Such systems are a given in Jewish communities; no one there has to struggle with the task of installing a new sewage system from scratch.

"I should have said" something ugly and foul. Indeed, in this case I did—to the media, at the national meetings of experts and to my superiors at the Ministry of Health in Jerusalem. But no one was listening.

April 30, 1989

The Arab Knesset member for the Labor party, Nawaf Masalha, has initiated a meeting with the Director-General of the Ministry of Health in response to a new law that requires Arab graduates of foreign medical schools to pass a state exam before they can do their internship in Israel. Until now the state was automatically responsible for providing an internship for all medical graduates from recognized universities, here and abroad. This will no longer be true except for local graduates and certain immigrants. In other words, the law essentially singles out Arab students for the state exam. The first two rounds of this exam showed that 96 percent of Arab foreign medical graduates who took it failed. The resulting outcry forced Masalha to arrange the meeting, to which I was invited. Nothing much came of it, of course, apart from promises from the Director-General that those taking the exams would be offered a specially designed preparatory course, like the one given to new immigrant physicians, but at the participants' own expense. We were told that the law is the law and, as citizens, we should not expect to be above it.

Even more revealing was an incidental conversation with Masalha on the taxi journey to Jerusalem we took together, along with the head of the National Committee of Arab Mayors. All the way there and back, Masalha kept on about the timely need for setting up a national-level NGO that would incorporate Arab non-partisan leadership and attract and distribute the plentiful sources of money available from American Jewish donors. This was too much of a coincidence. There seems to have been a policy decision by Masalha's party, Labor, to try to co-opt and control those leading the Arab minority's recent successful organizing activity, whether by the Higher Monitoring Committee, the National Committee of Arab Mayors, and the plethora of nascent NGOs, including the Galilee Society. From various directions I am hearing the same message: "we would like you, the activists on behalf of the Arab minority, to work for us through a system that we set up and control. You will be handsomely rewarded." The pressure is on to draw us to the glitter of easy money. That is the clear message I get; and it is the traditional approach of the Labor party.

The Galilee Society's mobile clinic serves seven unrecognized villages in the Galilee, six of them Bedouin. At the time of its inception, it was intended more to call attention to the lack of health services in the villages than to make up for such a lack. And it has succeeded. We have been bringing visitors, such as the recent delegation from the World Council of Churches, to see what we are doing with their donations, and incidentally they learn who it is we serve and what a difficult life they lead because they are boycotted by their own state. My two favorite locations are Arab al-Naim and Kammaneh because of the stark physical evidence of the discrimination they suffer in comparison with the new Jewish settlements right next door to them.

More recently, a group from within the unrecognized villages, led by Mohammad Abu-al-Haija from Ein Hawd, has established an NGO to speak on their own behalf. It is called the Association of Forty and aims to bring about formal state recognition of the villages. They have started with a very convincing public relations campaign.

A while back Mohammad Abu-al-Haija brought a group of leftist political activists—including leaders of Jewish NGOs and several Knesset members—on a tour of unrecognized villages in our area. I waited for them in al-Naim at the single-room, corrugated-iron family home that we use as our clinic there one day a week, with the family of seven relocating temporarily to the shade of a carob tree. After the traditional round of black coffee, one resident made his pitch to the visitors about the degree of discrimination suffered by the community. "Aren't we human beings?" he asked. The politicians answered with their standard slogans and vacuous promises: "We are with you in your struggle." Some of them sounded unconvinced and others totally powerless—Toufik Touby, the grand old man of the Communist party, clearly speaking for the latter.

As they were leaving, a little old man who had kept silent throughout the whole tour, and walked behind us at a safe distance, saw me returning separately to my car and came over to greet me. Suddenly he raised his arms to the blue spring skies in a gesture of thanking God and hurried over to me. He dropped his walking stick by his side and gave me a warm hug declaring "Whoever heard of al-Naim before *al-dactour* Hatim came and visited us the first time?" I recognized him as the wise old man who some time earlier had prescribed clean water as the cure-all for his village's health problems. I was happy to see him still alive, for he had looked quite ill at the time.

Since the first day I visited al-Naim I have had a deep feeling of failing the villagers by not being one of them, not experiencing their actual pain and deprivation. My learned "knowledge by description," as Bertrand Russell puts it, can never be as real as their "knowledge by acquaintance." Or, as the local saying goes, "counting lashes is not like suffering them!"

December 10, 1989

Israel's government has recently mounted a serious attempt to quash the nascent Palestinian NGO movement in Israel and the occupied territories. An amendment to the Ordinance for the Prevention of Terrorism from the days of the British Mandate is under discussion in a committee of the Knesset. The ordinance, originally promulgated by the British Mandate administration to counter Jewish terrorism, was the legal basis for imposing arbitrary military rule on the entire group of Palestinians who became Israeli citizens from the state's establishment in 1948 until 1966. Now the government hopes to use it against the emergence of an Arab civil society that might demand its rights. I used my attendance in August at the annual United Nations NGO Conference on the Question of Palestine, held this year in Vienna, to bring this plan to the attention of the world's NGO representatives.

Under the new amendment, all of us, active leaders of the Palestinian civil society within Israel, could easily be labeled terrorists. That is not far from the view widely accepted by the majority population in Israel. Zionism leaves little maneuvering space for an Israeli citizen; if you do not serve its goals, you must be its enemy. There is no neutral ground.

Since my return from the trip to Vienna, the Health Monitoring Committee has refocused its activities on the most pressing issues for our communities, including the water supply to the unrecognized villages. We have lobbied the authorities to allow a "water point" for each unrecognized community. In most cases, this could be simply done as the water mains pass right by these communities on their way to new Jewish settlements nearby, to supply their swimming pools and water their lush front lawns. We are asking the authorities to allow a single tap for each village to drink from—evidence, indeed, of learned helplessness on our part. Even to this defeatist little request, the response of the relevant authorities, specifically the Agriculture Ministry,

the government water company, Mckorot, the Interior Ministry and
the Ministry of Health, has been for each to pass the buck on to the
other in a never-ending round-robin fashion. Mr. Diri'i, the Interior
Minister, turned out not to be the savior his Moroccan background
and election-day promises had led some Bedouin supporters to believe.
He has since found technical excuses for not supplying drinking water
to these waterless Arab villages.

A significant development for the Galilee Society in the international
arena is that one of our funders, ICCO, thanks to my friend there, Sjord
van Schoonefeld, has successfully submitted a proposal on our behalf
to the European Community arguing that we, the Palestinian citizens
of Israel, represent an underdeveloped enclave within the developed
country of Israel. Therefore, an exception should be made in our case
and we should be supported directly and not through bilateral aid to
Israel, since such aid hardly ever trickles down to our communities. I
suspect that the current level of world awareness about Palestinians,
and the Intifada, has somehow worked to our advantage. For the EC
to approve this grant on the basis of our unique and different needs
as a minority is a significant gain for us in strategic terms. It has taken
us nearly ten years to get this message across and we should build on
it for further reaching out to the international community. It gives a
glimpse of hope.

As part of a targeted campaign to internationalize our issues as a
national minority, I have also befriended the European Community's
ambassador, Gwyn Morgan, a fine Welsh diplomat with an open mind
and a good heart. I find chatting with him over a glass of fine Scotch in
his office delightful and informative. He warned me, not so diplomati-
cally, of the wrath that mentioning my name incurs in contacts with
Israeli government officials. He judges it to be second in severity only to
mentioning the topics that I always raise with him and that he, in turn,
raises with Israeli officials, including health services to the unrecognized
villages, the land rights of Bedouins in the Negev, and the inequitable
share of resources and budgets allocated to Arab communities all over
Israel. I have attempted to illustrate vividly my claims to him by taking
him on tours of the Galilee and the Negev.

On one such tour of Kammaneh and Arab al-Naim, his driver, an immigrant from Australia who plays the classic butler role, always appreciative of the master's jokes and laughing on cue, and his French Jewish secretary who always meets me with open arms and a peck on the cheek, went missing for a few minutes between the corrugated iron hovels that serve the locals as homes. My friend Rita McGaughey, the senior American volunteer who acts as my PR advisor and all-round assistant, and whom, at age sixty plus, Ambassador Morgan had identified as the one person at the Galilee Society that piques his curiosity most, accompanied us on the tour. The brief scare of the missing driver and secretary inspired Rita with the idea for a novel that she and Didi, my wife, should write. The plot revolves around the sporty American ambassador who one Saturday accidentally lands his hand-glider in an unrecognized village in the Galilee and is taken hostage by the locals in the hope of forcing the Israeli government to provide them with drinking water. The incident leads to a political impasse because no American government official would be so foolish as to negotiate with an Arab whose residence is not even recognized by his own government. Then "Rita of the Galilee" comes to the rescue. End of plot.

June 30, 1990

Under the ceaseless pressure of our situation paranoia is apt to set in, and my mind plays a near perfect trick on me in this respect. I am currently at a Health Emergencies in Large Populations course in Geneva. Another participant, a young blonde Dutch woman, recently invited me to supper at her hotel. I declined, seeing in that too strong a come-on and immediately suspecting her motives. Then a few days later she suggested supper at one of Geneva's Old Town romantic cafes. This time I accepted. Her attempts to befriend me piqued my paranoia; her behavior fits perfectly a Mossad plot,* in which I am entrapped and discredited after pictures are taken of me in a compromising position with her—if not worse (or rather, if not better).

---

* *The Mossad:* Literally "the Institute" and short for "the Institute for Intelligence and Special Operations," Mossad is the Israeli equivalent of America's CIA or Britain's MI6. It is credited with high efficiency and the frequent use of unorthodox tactics including sexual enticement, murder and kidnapping.

I went to dinner after taking the precaution of leaving exact information about my evening plans with several members of the study group. Over a plate of cold seafood specialties and a glass of wine, she divulged to me her secret. It totally deflated my paranoid, self-deluding ego. No agent 007 high adventure here. The woman is in charge of the Dutch National Red Cross Society's planned program in Gaza. She is apprehensive about her coming trip to the area and wants to get an idea of what to expect. She would even like to have the reassurance of having a contact and a family where she can stay if need be. No more and no less. Equality of the sexes makes it natural for a Dutch woman to invite a man to dinner to ask for a favor. My chauvinism automatically inserts a sexual motive into the plot. Why would a young blonde choose me over twenty younger men in the group? That is only a short imaginary leap to the paranoid scheme of discrediting me through the use of a honey trap. I am much relieved, and a little disappointed, to learn the truth.

17
Agonies of War

Toufiq's and my family practice donning gas masks, January 1992.

August 20, 1990

We are in Hawaii. We sit sunning ourselves in my mother-in-law's backyard. Birds and sailboats crisscross Kaneohe Bay and its gentle waves lap against the wall adding to the romantic setting. It is our annual family R and R vacation, intended this year also to give me and Ty a chance to bond as two men and to consider the future together. Ty can visit the University of Hawaii, Didi's and my old alma mater, to see what it is like to be a student there.

As we sit here, our peace is disturbed by the frequent deafeningly loud roar of jets landing and taking off as part of military practice at the Kaneohe Marine Base across the bay. The pilots are training for war in Iraq. Part of the military force based here has already sailed to the Persian Gulf. Didi and I talk of the impending war for the umpteenth time:

"War is inevitable," she starts. "Judging by the way Bush is betting his political career and prestige as President of the United States against the will of another madman the Iraqi president, Saddam Hussein al-Takriti, we are at war. What really makes for fascinating analysis is how the American media and government have gone about systematically dehumanizing this former ally, and how they had previously marketed and justified their support for such a merciless dictator."

We mull over our decision to return to our home in Israel against the advice of friends and exhortation of relatives. We try to dismiss doomsday predictions of Saddam targeting Israel with his missiles with their expected payload of poison gas or deadly germs.

"Still, why should sane people like us, sitting in their swimming shorts here at water's edge in Hawaii, turn away from the easy choice of continuing their vacation in paradise a while longer? Why go back to the eye of the storm?" Didi wonders.

"I try to tell myself that it is not sheer obstinacy or romantic attachment that is at the base of my insistence to go back home to Israel. There is a consideration that transcends my obligation to be there to offer my professional services should disaster strike my community. It is beyond our physical survival. It is the hope, conceited as it may sound, that my voice, and not only my profession, will count for something in such hour of need. My worst-case scenario is ethnic cleansing of Palestinians again. War breaks out and Israel takes the opportunity to throw us out of its still-undetermined borders as refugees. Regardless of who strikes first, a general war in the area directly involving Israel will provide its transfer strategists with the perfect cover to drive all Palestinians—including us, the near-million minority of its citizens—out of our homes and to deposit the survivors in the lap of UNRWA, as yet another batch of Palestinian refugees to deal with. Under the guise of war-time measures a news blackout can be imposed and the go-ahead given for the generals to activate their readymade contingency plans, or what Israelis call their 'drawer plans,' for driving us out. This is the crux of my argument in favor of returning immediately home and staying put in Arrabeh regardless of everything. In such a development my voice and international connections may count for something in informing the world."

We vacillate back and forth till Ty joins us and is welcomed as an equal partner in the discussion.

"Primarily," I apologetically explain, "I fear most for 'my family,' meaning Didi, Rhoda, Ty and me. But this way of framing the issue narrows my own conception of myself to the American 'me,' the Western definition of who 'I' am and who 'my' family is. This is really the crux of the matter. I never conceived of myself as just this physical entity that now sits with you here. The 'I' that I have internalized is inclusive of many significant others: it is the Dr. Hatim that the people of Arrabeh know and trust; the Dr. Kanaaneh who heads and inspires the Galilee Society; the brother to Ahmad and Jamileh, and the uncle to Eyad, Hiam, and their dozen siblings and cousins. It is that person whose survival is at risk if we remain here. The person who is defined and constituted by friends and relatives in Hawaii is different, is another person, almost of a different species altogether. The question then becomes: Which of the two is to survive? Faced with this quandary and in my hour of need, I have lulled myself into dreaming of a peaceful resolution to the conflict through the diplomatic efforts of the UN and the European Community. I am no longer arguing with people; I just have to convince myself. And I am scared stiff."

"Well, it's a real war, God damn it! And it is going to blow up in your face," Didi shouts in disgust. "The whole Middle East is about to go up in flames; chemical, biological and even nuclear weapons are bandied around as the default options—and you theorize about the nice development policies of the EC!"

"Shit! This is impotence and it simply stinks," Ty butts in.

"Well then can I, can we, can this bunch of dummies conclude this fruitless debate with a meaningful straightforward answer? Can we give a yes-or-no answer to the cruel and unrelenting question of whether this dummy ought to risk sacrificing himself and his family, you, for an egotistical and delusional ideal?"

"Are you going back or not? Just say it! Spit it out, for God's sake!" Ty begs.

"Well, here is a compromise. Let us draw a clear line beyond which we will not go: We go back, but if and when the US government issues a call for its citizens to get out of Israel, we cut and run."

Old habits die hard! While in Hawaii, despite my preoccupation with the war, I have contacted a few prospective participants for our planned Health for Minorities 2000 conference in April. Our friend and Galilee Society volunteer Rita McGaughey, who leads the team working on preparations for the conference, called from Israel to put me in touch with Haunani Trask, the head of the department of Hawaiian studies at the University of Hawaii. I arranged a meeting with Ms. Trask, who arrived in her usual native attire, the traditional lava-lava, a wrap-around piece of Hawaiian print. A fragrant flower *lei* adorning her neck and more flowers in her hair highlighted her lovely features. She looked to be in her mid-thirties, a star with nowhere to go but up. She greeted me with the customary hug and kiss on the cheek and proceeded to enlighten me regarding the reality and point of view of native Hawaiians: "There is a genocide plan for the Hawaiian people. We don't recognize the takeover of the Islands by the whites. America is a colonizing power. The basic issues for us are our physical survival as a people and the survival of the Hawaiian culture and language. For that the retrieval of our lost lands and sovereignty is the first fundamental step."

Wow! Was that *wahine*—Hawaiian for woman—speaking for the Hawaiians or for the Palestinians, I wondered.

You talk to any member of an indigenous minority anywhere in the world and you find yourself talking about land rights. It is the problem of problems, "the mother of all problems," as Saddam might put it, the common thread at the base of what befalls all native minority groups. It is encouraging to see how identical are the root causes of the health problems suffered by the indigenous Hawaiians here and the indigenous Palestinians in Israel. It is those commonalities that I am interested in bringing into focus at this conference.

January 13, 1991

Sitting alone in the quiet of my study in Arrabeh at this early hour of day with no one to argue with but me, I am scaring myself stiff. The most frightening thing is sensing that humanity is about to fail me. Humanity is proving to be not all that sane; in fact, the behavior of its representatives all around me is attesting to its insanity.

First, the Israeli public has been whipped into full preparedness for war in the next few days, and for chemical and biological warfare at that. Everybody has prepared sealed rooms inside their houses, preferably in the center of the house on the second floor, or higher if possible. Civil Defense instructions are for us to stockpile in our airtight rooms water for drinking and washing poison and germs off the skin, flour to soak up poison from the skin, canned food in case it is too poisonous outside to make it to the kitchen, a radio to listen to instructions about what to do with the poison and those poisoned, and a flashlight to see our way around the poison if the electricity goes out. And we must not forget to keep our gas masks with us in our sealed rooms.

Civil Defense has distributed gas masks to most city dwellers and is ready to distribute them to rural folks from today. Given that the expectation in this war is of a chemical attack rather than a conventional missile hitting our homes, we have been advised not to head for the shelters when we hear the sirens. Instead we should go to the sealed room, turn the radio on and listen to instructions. This has stirred up a frenzy of buying not only of sealant, masking tape, canned food and bottled water but also of everything at the store "because this is war and you don't want to be caught short on toilet paper or writing pens, God forbid." The buying frenzy has finally subsided. Now people are getting used to the idea of war and act like "Yeah, we are ready for it. Let it come." Everyone has been lulled into feeling personally secure.

In a way that is typical of what Jewish leaders proudly call the *Masada* mentality, of "die and not surrender."* The same heroic attitude of readiness to stand one's ground and perish is the standard battle cry in Iraq as well, though it lacks the historical romance it has in Israel. Iraq's crazed dictator readies his people for war with much less "airtight" preparedness. Instead he is preparing them with religious and nationalistic rhetoric: "A war is coming in which many of us, of

---

* *Masada:* From the Hebrew for "fortress," this is the name for the historical site of the last stand of Jewish rebels against the Roman Empire on top of an isolated mesa overlooking the Dead Sea. The siege of the fortress by Roman troops led to the mass suicide of the fortress's occupants when defeat became imminent.

you, soldiers and civilians, will be martyred. It is a big war but we will survive it as a nation and we will beat them and we will send them back to their families in body bags, those imperialist dogs." But then, he is a vile dictator and we are the only democracy in the Middle East, so you know whose people deserve support and sympathy.

It is now evening and I am back from Acre. In time of trouble you seek company, even if to do nothing exactly. Didi has left on a long-planned vacation in Egypt with our friend, Rita. This morning I had breakfast with Ty and we separated, each joining his village gang. Mine included Toufiq and his band of young Communist-educated professionals. I half sought them out, half chanced on them gathered in anticipation of a fish dinner in Acre with a bottle of the local aniseed spirit, *Araq*, apparently a betting debt owed by one of them to another.

The contempt for "Saddam the *maniac*"—and *maniac* is Arabic for "fucker"—was almost palpable; the contempt for Bush was open. Both leaders were rated by the group as morally sick and evil. There was no ambivalence in what the group envisioned as the outcome of the conflict:

"The game of chicken is due to culminate in two days in a modern, high-tech warfare, with the most unconventional of conventional wars. With the deafening drone of war rhetoric from both sides and with total inflexibility from the United States in its surrealist and colonialist paradigm that equates oil in Kuwait with 'our way of life,' even the best of minds and purest of hearts the world over have been hypnotized into accepting the unavoidability of a war in which hundreds of thousands, if not millions, will die. But who will come out the winner?" I start off.

"Saddam's threats are totally empty; he does not have beans in terms of nuclear, chemical or biological weapons; he is bluffing; he will be toppled in no time and deserves to be dragged with a rope around his neck in the streets of Baghdad like he did to his predecessors; war will be short and decisive," Toufiq responds emphatically.

We go on for hours with little finality in any of our views. Still, despite the doubtful credentials of these local pundits, it feels better to hear others state the obvious. Also, I was somewhat relieved when Ty approached me in the evening and asked in a beseeching tone: "Dad, shouldn't we take the protective precautions the Israeli Civil

Defense recommends? Shouldn't we seal a room in the house in case of a chemical attack?"

At first I displayed my incredulous reaction, my true disbelief. But he persevered.

"Wouldn't that be better for our psyche, dad?"

"That would be fine. Let us do it!" I quickly agreed.

I got the message he needed a psychological security blanket. And in truth, I found it reassuring as well. We air-sealed my study room with plastic sheeting over the windows, put in a few bottles of mineral water, masking tape, sodium bicarbonate, wheat flour, my doctor's bag, extra bandages and 4x4 gauze, a thick towel to block the air entering under the door, some sardine cans with a can opener, a flashlight and Ty's pocket radio. My trust in the sanity of humanity is not airtight, not 100 percent foolproof. Certainly not enough to prevent me from getting psychological relief from knowing that this step has been taken.

It is an open secret that psychological reassurance is the main idea behind the Israeli Civil Defense Authority's recommendations. Saving people's lives, even if a concern, is a less realistic goal. Civil defense precautions are intended to give people a feeling of individual security and to lull them into accepting the stand of the United States as unquestionably valid, accepting war as inevitable, and accepting the possibility of chemical and biological weapons being used without creating mass panic. I wonder how Saddam handles the psychological impact on the Iraqi public of Israel's threat of using nuclear weapons. I suspect he relies mainly on drowning out such threats with his own and with his constant strutting around on Iraqi TV.

Despite these two "maniacs," I am not ready to abandon my own sanity or to give up on my trust in the sanity of humanity. I am not giving up on the peacefulness of my Galilee; I think nothing will happen here. Even if the worst scenario is pursued, Iraqi missiles will target the city and little will happen to affect our tranquility in Arrabeh. But then, goddamn it, why did we buy the materials to seal my study?

That, I suppose, is the infinitely tortuous logic of the human subconscious. That is when it becomes handy to quote the Prophet's sayings and to call on his all-encompassing wisdom: "*I'iqil watawakkal*— Tie up your camel and then depend on the good lord," he is reported to have told a Bedouin who hoped to rely on Allah to watch over his camel for him. He bettered that one when he told another Bedouin who depended on his prayers to cure his camels of the mange: "Mix your prayers with a little tar." It is simply safer to err on the side of the Israeli interpretation of things. After all, isn't that what Bush is doing in the first place?

January 31, 1991

The war has come and not yet gone. My wife is back from her trip to Egypt with Rita in one piece, reporting that the Nile still flows peacefully by the Cairo Sheraton Hotel and that Egyptians are oblivious to the happenings in the Gulf area. I had finally to admit the inevitability of war when it did break out, though it hardly looked like a war. After all, it takes two to tangle. It looked more like a one-sided attack on a bunch of uniformed folks waiting to be wiped out—or so the coverage by the Western media makes it look.

At any rate, the technically and strategically superior forces of "the civilized world" are using their superior media and psychological warfare tactics to convince us that, miraculously, they are blowing the cowardly devil Saddam to bits without harming his people—as if by a magic wand, General Schwartzkopf is capable of devastating the entire military capacity of Iraq and its civilian infrastructure without hurting Iraqi civilians. Only a few cases of "collateral damage"! Good old Bush and his "new world order"! He has the gall even now, after the awful slaughter and destruction he has inflicted on Iraq and its people, to speak of "a kinder and gentler America."

It sounded depressingly familiar to any observer of Israeli doubletalk about the benevolent occupation and the "purity of Israel's arms," or about the terrorist Palestinian "occupiers" defiling Israel's historic holy land. Listen long enough and you forget which side is which. You start with the Israeli occupation and end with condemnation of all Palestinians for resisting it. You think it is strange that your average misinformed American, including your next-door neighbors and your own brother-in-law in Hawaii, swallows this twisted logic hook, line and sinker? Then try speaking to the average "well-informed" Israeli and, by Jove, you find they have come to believe it themselves, they have accepted their own lies. At the end, somehow, everyone creates the reality he can live with.

Slowly but surely, I have become aware, convinced and forced to accept the reality of war and the reality of Israel's involvement, even if at a distance through the silent absorbing of Scud missile hits from Iraq. So far, of course, no chemical or biological warheads have been delivered. Conventional warheads have been hitting Haifa and Tel Aviv areas daily or every other day. A rush of sympathy materialized instantaneously the world over for the innocent Israeli civilians targeted by the devil himself, and the US immediately shipped a consignment of Patriot antimissile batteries to Israel. One of those Patriots resulted in pieces of a busted Scud falling on the Arab town of Shafa'amr, blowing to smithereens my Galilee tranquility theory. As the physical danger moved closer, everybody, including me, stayed home. Life came to a complete standstill: no one went to school, no one shopped, there was no traffic, and no socializing except by phone.

A different sort of "tranquility" descended on the Galilee. It lasted for about four or five days and then, slowly, people emerged from their holes. Workers went back to work; children went back to school in stages, first high-schoolers and then intermediate pupils. The elementary school children are now attending for a few hours, picking up homework assignments that they follow up on by radio and TV.

The first time a Scud missile was detected heading our way from Iraq was on the night of January 18. We heard the explosions in the Haifa area and some missiles landed in Tel Aviv. When we detected the alarm signal on TV and heard the sirens on the radio, Didi, Ty and I rushed to our sealed room, put on our gas masks and sat there glued to the radio. Within minutes Rhoda called. The news of the attack was on CNN instantaneously. Rhoda was crying on the phone asking if we were hit and if we were all still alive. After the experience of crowding into my cold narrow study, we decided the next day to enlarge our hiding space and sealed the adjacent bedroom and the bathroom as well. Now with a full unit sealed, we can hide comfortably every night or two when we hear the sirens.

I stick to my view that we are out of danger here in the Galilee, though I am keeping quieter about it of late, after I was screamed at by a distraught secretary at my Ministry of Health office. I had been offering my standard reassurances to my underlings, my own version of "double talk," and half jokingly telling them that we were out of danger's way. "I personally guarantee it, and should anything happen you have me to answer to you for it." At that point, a pregnant young woman, Tami, jumped at me, screaming her head off, and almost attacked me physically: "Where will you be if we are hit? You will be under the rubble together with us. How can I hold you responsible for it then?" I do not know if it is her pregnancy, a case of rebelling against the boss, or anger at an Arab telling a bunch of Jews he is braver than them. It took her colleagues nearly half an hour to calm her down. Later she came into my office and apologized tearfully. It reminded me not to parade my machismo around and not to make any more bets on war events. I have already lost several whisky bottles to friends.

At least in the house, my views about the war still hold some credibility. But the strain is most visible on Ty, who is not sleeping well. One is constantly reminded of the threat of physical danger by the media. War is the only topic of conversation between people on the street and in the family circle. People have their masks hanging from their shoulders wherever they go, as if physically tethered to the likelihood of personal harm. Everybody takes pictures of themselves wearing the mask; we did the same. Everybody cracks jokes about it, and so do we. Ty goes around with it like everyone else, despite the display of macho indifference appropriate to his age.

He shows the effects of stress most clearly by constantly asking questions about the war and arguing about who is stronger and who we should side with. His logic is clear: We cannot abandon Saddam Hussein because he is the only one carrying the banner of the Palestinian cause. It is the unanimous stand of Palestinian youth, with the clear understanding that it is not Saddam's personal traits or his humane qualities that is being talked about; it is simply his declared policy that concerns us. For his own reasons, Saddam has focused attention on the Palestinian question. For that gesture, he deserves the support of the Palestinian community, even if limited to vocal support and no more. After all, the Palestinian community has no other strategies. Since the start of the war, the Intifada has completely quieted down. The entire Palestinian population of the occupied territories has been placed under a total curfew, lifted selectively on a rotational basis to allow residents to go out and buy food items.

I am being called on again to organize the much-needed relief effort for our brethren in the occupied territories by my community—the "48 Arabs" or "Inside Arabs" as so many other Palestinians call us,

or "Israel's Arabs" as Jewish Israelis insist on referring to us. I have
been asked to reactivate the National Relief Committee I headed at the
start of the Intifada. A Ministry of Health Arab employee who assisted
me in the earlier relief efforts, admitted openly that this time he fears
retribution from the Ministry if he gets involved and that his family's
welfare is his priority. "Bread for the family comes first, you know," he
confided. Since I want to terminate my position with the Ministry of
Health, he argued, I could afford to be more visible in relief work for
the Palestinians, which though not illegal is seen as highly objectionable
by the Israeli government. And we are speaking of sending drugs, food
and clothes, for God's sake!

What might be more effective is for our leadership to call on the
foreign diplomatic corps to take steps to prevent mass starvation
amounting to genocide in the Palestinian occupied territories. People
are being starved not only because they cannot go out to buy food,
but also because they do not have the money to buy it. They have been
prevented from working and earning an income for a long time now.

As chairman of the Galilee Society, I have also been called on by
colleagues to help in relation to the war with Iraq. Other NGOs have
asked that we establish an emergency psychological counseling center.
This would simply be copying what is already a standard service in
the Jewish sector, especially in the cities. Phone numbers have been
advertised nationally for one to call and get reassurance and advice
on what to do in case of family stress and if professional advice is
needed:

"The child is vomiting; could that be from poison gas?"

"I can't breathe through my mask when I put it on; could it be
defective?"

"I have asthma; what is the right type of mask for me?"

But, of course, the system does not care about Arabs. No such service
has been provided for Arabic speakers. There have been several failed
attempts by others in our community to provide such a service. The
format itself reeks of an Israeli army mentality, and I am reluctant to
allow myself and the Galilee Society to look like we are functioning
as part of that system. The counseling service is fashioned without us
in mind—or even with us as part of the problem. But my reluctance
was overruled by my colleagues on the board of the Galilee Society. I
acceded, especially when our administrator explained that, using the

excuse of setting up an emergency service, he was sure he could get a second phone line installed in our office, a major secondary gain for us.

My phone now rings. It is my friend Toufiq. Here is part of the one-sided conversation, as captured on my tape recorder:

"No, Abu-Morsi. No, I am not scared to come out. I agree with you, it is no fun staying locked indoors. But it is raining outside and, if I come out, it better be something worthwhile, worth braving the rain and the Scuds, not just for a cup of coffee ... Yes, planting a bed of radishes is worth the risk, but do you have seeds? ... I don't think you will find them in the village and I have no desire to travel to the city. You find the seeds and I'll risk coming over to help you plant them. Probably Abu-Tariq has them but he is in Ramallah and has not come home to Arrabeh since the start of the war ... And how is your wife doing? ... She is courageous, I have to admit. Yesterday I called to alert you guys when I heard the siren on the radio and she told me she was mopping the floor of the hallway and not going to abandon that and hide. All due respect, indeed! ... You know our friends in Rama, Abu-Nasim and his family, the people Rita, our senior volunteer, lives with? I caught Abu-Nasim off guard the night the sirens went off for the first time at about three in the morning. You guys called to wake us up, and I immediately called their home. I wanted to be sure they woke Rita up and took her with them into their sealed room. Abu-Nasim answered the phone on the first ring. I said, 'Good morning. Are you awake?' He shouted back at me very excitedly, 'No, doctor, no! I am not afraid, I am never afraid, NEVER!' I guess he misunderstood my question and responded with his true feelings."

Shortly afterwards, the phone rings again. This time it is my nephew Eyad to tell us that a distant relative, the father-in-law of his sister Afaf, passed away in the night. And now I can hear the announcement of the death on the mosque's loudspeaker. Actually, I have a tinge of guilt and shame related to this announcement. Last night Afaf called to tell me about her newborn baby showing signs of jaundice. I assured her, even without seeing the baby, that it was likely physiologic jaundice, considering that she is breastfeeding him. I asked about her sick father-in-law and she mentioned that the old man was quite uncomfortable, and that he had also lost control over his sphincters. Somehow, I sensed that the old man had taken a turn for the worse. I spoke to his son,

Afaf's husband, and he reassured me enough that I decided not to make a house call. After all, they live in another village, it was night already and missiles are usually launched in the evening, and a missile warning had been issued minutes earlier.

There is no ambulance service to the village in the best of times, much less now during the war. I thought of taking the old man to the hospital in my car. But the thought quickly evaporated and in the end I decided to wait till the morning before going and checking on him. In the meanwhile he beat me to it and probably saved himself the added pain and misery of dying attached to all the torture gadgetry that a modern emergency medical facility can throw at a dying old man. Or would anyone have bothered that much with an old man with his demographic coordinates—old, Arab, uninsured, dying of "natural causes"—and arriving at the regional central hospital during another Scud night?

18

In the Shin Bet's Sights

Addressing the UN annual meeting of the Working Group on Indigenous Populations on behalf of the Health for Minorities Working Group. Rita McGauhey, senior volunteer and advisor, on my left and my wife, Didi, in the back row, August 1992.

March 31, 1991

What began as a small initiative by the Galilee Society to help combat a measles epidemic in the Southern District of Israel, the Negev, has ended in a witch-hunt by the Ministry of Health against me and my organization.

Our involvement started unexpectedly with the spread of measles among the Negev's Bedouin population and, for obvious reasons, especially in the unrecognized villages there. We received a call for

215

help and sent down our mobile clinic and its team of two nurses to assist, gratis, in the emergency immunization campaign. Our team was assigned to the peripheral Bedouin communities that are particularly hard to reach, targeting all children under the age of eighteen. On the first day of the campaign we tracked down some seventy never-immunized kids, many of whom did not even have an ID, much less any proof of ever coming into contact with the preventive health services.

Oddly, however, at the end of the first day, our team was summoned to the office of Prof. Margolis, of the Beersheba Hospital Community Health Division, who was coordinating the campaign. He told the two nurses that the Ministry of Health's head office in Jerusalem had instructed him to dismiss the Galilee Society's team.

I spoke both to Prof. Margolis and to a colleague at the Ministry of Health, Dr. Bellmaker, the Negev's District Physician, who had formally invited us to the Negev and then formally dismissed us after one day of very efficient performance. With much apology, both told me that the fax banning us from participating in the immunization campaign had been signed by Elan Cohen, Deputy Director-General of the Ministry of Health.

This incident aroused my curiosity. Of late, this Elan Cohen has been on my case over several issues. Who is he?

Before joining the Ministry of Health, it appears, Cohen was a senior Shin Bet agent specializing in the Arab sector, first in the Galilee and later in the Triangle area. He won his political spurs in Menachem Begin's Likud government, when he was recruited as a special advisor by Ehud Olmert, then the Minister Without Portfolio in charge of Arab affairs, a position we sarcastically call "the Arabs' minister." (The Arab community also like to claim, jokingly, that they have their own "Jews' minister," a nickname given to the loudest and most openly nationalist Arab politician in Israel. Mohammad Mia'ari earned the name after it was reported that the Labor party and the non-Zionist Arab parties were in secret negotiations to form a coalition government. At the time, rightwingers tried to discredit any such talks by spreading improbable rumors that the Labor party was considering appointing Mia'ari to become the Minister in charge of Jewish affairs. Labor quickly denied that negotiations were taking place, affirming that they would never jeopardize the fate of the Jewish state by involving Arabs in its running. Mia'ari's nickname stuck nonetheless.)

Cohen and Olmert apparently got along so well that, when Olmert moved on to become Health Minister, he took former secret agent Elan Cohen along as part of his entourage. Eventually Cohen became Deputy Director-General in charge of personnel—and, given his background, he has taken a special interest in the few Arabs among the personnel. Certainly Cohen has not changed his spots since his Shin Bet days. To discredit me, he has accused me of being a PLO member—a very typical tactic used by the Israeli secret services.

The Ministry's determination to keep us out of the Negev has got me more interested in what precisely is going on there. I therefore went down to see the local health care delivery system for myself, meeting all the parties involved in the immunization campaign. All of them had been warned against dealing with the Galilee Society. Cohen had even come down from his Jerusalem office to deliver the warning in person, explaining in no uncertain terms that the Galilee Society is headed by a PLO functionary.

Our planned Health for Minorities 2000 conference has apparently also caused discomfort among the leadership of the Ministry of Health. The idea of linking our struggle for equality to that of such groups as Native Americans, Canadian Inuit, New Zealand Maoris, and Australia's Aborigines on one side, and to ethnic minorities such as blacks and Hispanics in the States and immigrant populations in Western Europe on the other, was too unpalatable. Bringing a constellation of such just causes together, with our own cause taking center stage as hosts and as the focal point of the debate, must have been the final straw for my bosses, who were already furious with me for orchestrating the first Arab Health Conference. In their eyes, I have added insult to injury. A decision was made at the highest level, involving the Health Minister, his Director-General, and the now outed secret agent Elan Cohen, to get rid of me—quietly.

The Ministry of Health issued a reminder to all employees of its existing regulations, especially highlighting the need to obtain permission from head office before joining the board of any NGO. "This obscure regulation has never before been enforced but it is still legally binding," the Association for Citizens' Rights in Israel (ACRI) told us in legal advice. As a result, three Arab employees of the Ministry have been forced to relinquish their positions on the board of the Galilee Society. We have accommodated the new reality by opening board meetings to all interested members.

Another board member, a doctor, has resigned from the organization altogether. He was told by his brother's business partner, another former secret service agent in our area, that if he wanted to advance in his medical career he ought to put some distance between himself and the Galilee Society. This board member revealed this information to me shortly before our problems began in the Negev.

As for me, forced by my superiors to choose between the Galilee Society and the Ministry of Health, I had no hesitation. My mind was already made up, despite the lure of promotion if I changed it. Finally after nearly two decades of vacillating, I have cut the umbilical cord that linked me to "legitimate" public health practice in Israel. Since then several things have happened to indicate that the attack on me will go beyond my dismissal. There is now ample evidence of attempts to discredit and disgrace me and the Galilee Society, and make me a pariah in Israeli health circles.

The PLO accusation has been given dubious "weight" by two senior Israeli journalists, Ze'ev Schiff and Ehud Ya'ari, in a recent book they published about the Intifada. Relying heavily on sources in the secret services, the pair allege that the Galilee Society received funds from the PLO, not directly but via an established funding organization called the Welfare Association. It is true that one of our financial backers was the Welfare Association; we took the entirely legitimate view that we should be able to rely on any funding organization that operates within the law, as the Welfare Association does. There was no reason why we should—even if we were able to—check on the financial resources or political support base of our benefactors.

But the PLO accusation is an effective tactic, of the kind used by secret services around the world when they want to disable activists. In the eyes of Israelis, being labeled a PLO operative is the equivalent for an American of being labeled a Communist in the McCarthy era. In Arab eyes, it is a two-edged sword: while glorifying me, it also warns anyone not secure in his position or source of livelihood to keep away from someone so clearly the object of Israel's wrath.

One of my former bosses, and I admit it feels good to have the adjective "former" in there, tells me that a recent decision to prevent me from testifying before the Knesset Subcommittee on Health came from the Director-General and the Minister of Health himself. I am not clear about this boss's motives but I want to believe they are pure; she constantly shares this kind of information with me. She marvels to me about the poisoned atmosphere and the grudge in the Ministry against me. "Why do they want you out? What do they have against you? How come when I say something it is called being leftwing or liberal, and when you say the same thing it becomes PLO propaganda?"

April 15, 1992

Rhoda has just called and I told her about our participation in the Land Day procession. I also let her know that her cousin Nihad was picked up by the police and kept in jail overnight till after the procession on the pretext that he had been writing Land Day slogans on village walls. As for the procession, it was very subdued this year, and Border Police were more in evidence than in previous years. In fact, they have been quite visible in our village for the last couple of weeks. This is in line with the recent aggressive show of force against Palestinians everywhere, including inside the Green Line, since the start of the Gulf War. The room for self-expression through peaceful demonstrations or processions is now much narrower. We, the Palestinian citizens of Israel, have responded by behaving meekly and submissively, befitting the pariah status to which all Palestinians have been relegated since their leadership embraced the side destined to lose in the Gulf War. Our local leaders seem to have been sapped not only of their energy but also of their pride. They seem to have nothing to say for themselves.

I am full-time at the Galilee Society and a very full time it has been indeed. We have several projects running simultaneously in the field while others are planned and fielded out to partners abroad. A clear central message runs through all of these: We exist and we suffer from discrimination and inequality. One day someone may want to sit down and compile all the documents that we produce in the process: project proposals, position papers, trip reports, annual and semiannual reports, and end of project reports. Here I want only to highlight the major institutional events that I have participated in, led, or even starred in.

Consigning them to these audio-memoirs cum confessionals should help me keep earthbound for a while.

The Health for Minorities 2000 Working Group met in August last year in Nazareth. The Galilee Society invited some three dozen foreign experts on the topic from eighteen countries across the globe. The event was covered well in the local Arabic press. It also involved us in intensive contacts with various embassies. Before the full-blown conference had to be downsized because of the Gulf War, we attempted to invite a prominent world figure with human rights credentials. Two of the obvious candidates, former US President Jimmy Carter and Archbishop Desmond Tutu of South Africa sent thoughtful letters of encouragement, which did much to add credibility to our efforts.

After a week of empowering exchanges of ideas and experiences, the working group formulated the Nazareth Declaration, setting forth a secretariat, hosted by the Galilee Society, to pursue a set of collective goals at the international level. The drafting of the document was a task stressful enough to make a young Aboriginal participant break into a run across the hilltops of Nazareth, barefoot and in swimming shorts. Apparently this is a traditional way of dealing with stress in the Australian outback. We are now working hard to keep the impetus of the declaration alive in the halls of the World Health Organization.

Of all the participants, the one that seemed to fathom the purpose of this group event best was Dr. Ghada Karmi, a Palestinian refugee living and working in London. Didi and I hosted her, her husband and her daughter at our house for the period. I took great pleasure from the fact that my invitation had permitted her, politically, emotionally and physically, to cross a barrier and revisit her childhood home in Jerusalem for the first time since she was forced out of it as a child in 1948.

Inadvertently Dr. Karmi returned the favor by curing Didi of her frequent panic attacks. Since the start of the Gulf War and the Scud missile scare, every so often, especially when driving in our new car, Didi would suffer episodes of palpitations in the chest and air hunger that would require her to pull to the side of the road and to step out into the open air to breathe freely. I would take her blood pressure, listen to her heart and lungs and reassure her that there was no physical basis for her shortness of breath. My reassurance would resolve the problem till the next episode. She refused sedatives. Then, while explaining to

Dr. Karmi and her family the experience of being locked up in the air-sealed room during the Scud attacks, she shouted with relief. "Now I know why my heart starts pounding; it's the smell of fresh rubber from putting that gas mask on. The smell, even the thought of it, gives me that claustrophobic feeling of panic." That was Didi's last attack.

In October the Galilee Society organized and hosted the second Arab Health Conference in Nazareth, with a wealth of scientific papers in addition to the declarative pronouncements of politicians and experts. True to form, the Ministry of Health boycotted the event and tried to ban its employees from attending. This was met with a collective decision from Arab professionals to break the ban, and in the end the District Physician found herself forced to send a lukewarm greeting on behalf of her office, lecturing us "natives" on our honor-bound duty to serve our country and improve ourselves.

And in February of this year the Galilee Society made a presentation at the second International Water Tribunal in Amsterdam, a public forum with no official standing or binding authority. One of the major functions of the Galilee Society is to agitate for the health and development rights of the Palestinian minority in Israel. Fiona McKay, a volunteer British human rights lawyer, assisted us in preparing the case for recognition of the basic human right to clean drinking water for the inhabitants of the unrecognized villages. The basis of the case was the death of a child in one village during an outbreak of hepatitis. Using epidemiological documents prepared by our mobile clinic team, we showed that the infection was spread through the polluted water the villagers were forced to draw from a nearby spring and to store in primitive conditions. For reasons known only to themselves, Israel chose to send its own officials to contest our case. They were so badly criticized by the international judges at the tribunal that, afterwards, the Arab lawyer who they had enlisted to defend them apologized to me personally, explaining that "as a lawyer I am occasionally forced to defend murderers, knowing in advance of the crimes they have committed."

We put on a convincing show, both because we had done our homework and also because, due to a technical error, our team was able to overhear through our headsets all the Hebrew conversations between members of the defense team: the Arab turncoat lawyer was fed his responses by a secret service man and officials from the

Agriculture and Interior Ministries. We had accompanying us, Jaa'far Farah, a handsome young Arab journalist who got along well with international media reps and wired back our success stories to the Israeli media. Erroneous headlines in Israel referred to our case being presented at the "International Court of Justice in The Hague"—a mistake we decided to let ride.

Two minor moments illustrate the atmosphere of international solidarity we enjoyed at the tribunal. When the Israeli defense team tried to question my integrity during my testimony, an old lady in the audience I had never met—the mother of one of the judges—was moved to declare: "That man is incorruptible!" Later in the day, the representative of a Catholic Dutch NGO, CEBEMO, that we had considered asking to finance some of our work, approached us with an offer of funding beyond our wildest dreams.

By going to the International Water Tribunal, we put our case on an equal footing on the international stage with such world-famous cases as the Seven Gorges Dam in China, the Narmada Dam in India, and the Quebec Dam in Canada. It brought the whole issue of the rights of the unrecognized villages to the consciousness of the public in Israel, if not in the whole world. A member of the panel of international judges, having heard our case, suggested changing the name of the villages from "unrecognized" to "de-recognized." Al-Hussainyeh and Kammaneh, the two villages of which we spoke, both predated the establishment of the state and were de-legitimized retroactively.

Shortly after my return to Israel, I was introduced to the Prime Minister's special advisor on Arab affairs, the man who keeps watch over agitators like me. Jokingly, I questioned his efficacy since he had not come to visit such an active body in his domain as the Galilee Society. He thought I was daring him. "You think I am afraid of you? You think you scare me with all your shenanigans in The Hague? I will come and visit you, you will see!" He never did.

My next plan for the Galilee Society is to approach funding partners to build a permanent headquarters for our organization. As well as providing an address for the entire Palestinian civil society in Israel, it would offer offices for nascent Arab organizations and a conference hall for gatherings boycotted by the government. Such a facility would be a first.

January 8, 1993

Last summer I came back from vacation to find that the Labor party was in power and that its leader, Yitzhak Rabin, had entered into a deal of sorts with the Arab Knesset members, including those of the Communist party. No Zionist party would ever consider a proper alliance with an Arab party, so the deal goes only as far as guaranteeing the votes of the Arab parties in support of the ruling coalition in exchange for promises that the government will look favorably at the long-neglected needs of the Arab population in Israel.

In line with this, Amir Peretz, a young Oriental Jew from a development town in the Negev who heads the Knesset Committee on Labor and Social Welfare, has been looking at what the Galilee Society is doing in the Negev. He was persuaded to take such a step by Tamar Gojansky, a Communist and active Member of Knesset (MK) on children's issues whom the Israeli media always casually lumps in with the "Arab MKs." The Negev's District Physician, Dr. Bellmaker, asked to be included in Peretz's tour of the facilities of the Galilee Society and those of the Ministry of Health. At the end, Peretz chided the two organizations for the obvious lack of cooperation between them, as if they were equals. Knowing the reality, I could only chuckle at the innocence of the guests. I am fully aware not only of the limited means of my own outfit but also of the ill-will of the other side, given the recent history of the attempt by the Ministry of Health to drive us out of the Negev.

I have reason to fear that I am being targeted in a wider effort by the Labor party and its liberal Zionist operatives to co-opt Arab activists by adopting our agenda and then watering it down to hollow slogans and election promises. The slippery Arab Labor MK Nawaf Masalha is courting me again, now in his capacity as the Deputy Health Minister. Last summer I came back from vacation to rumors Masalha had originated that I would be working for him. For a long time, while at the Ministry of Health and as coordinator of the Health Monitoring Committee, I have advocated the state drawing up a plan, with a timetable, for raising the health services in the Arab community to the same standards as the rest of the country. Masalha now wants me to head a committee that will draw up such a plan for him. Essentially, he wants to dump my proposal back in my lap.

April 22, 1993

The Galilee Society has launched a campaign to stop the establishment of a major industrial zone, named Tzipori, on the outskirts of Nazareth, on public lands that once belonged to three neighboring villages: Kafr Kana, or Kana of Galilee of Biblical water-to-wine miracle fame; Mashhad; and Reine. The state has claimed these extensive communal lands—*mashaa* under Turkish law—as its own. The area has now been attached administratively to the Jewish town of Upper Nazareth, even though geographically the planned industrial zone has no contiguity with the town. The decision does mean, however, that Upper Nazareth will reap all the tax and employment benefits from the industrial zone's establishment, while the three Arab villages will have to suffer its air, water, land and noise pollution. Needless to say the Tzipori industrial zone threatens the environment of the entire Lower Galilee.

The villagers first realized what was happening when they were served notice that their farmland was being confiscated to build an access road to a factory. An American company, Phoenicia Glass, is relocating to the new industrial zone after facing a wave of protests from local residents about the air pollution its existing factory causes in a suburb of Haifa. The large factory will be built on only 120 of the 1,400 dunams planned for the first stage of the industrial zone. So, the intention is to build tens, if not hundreds, of other factories. Phoenicia is likely to be so polluting and its management has taken so many liberties with the legal regulations that we expect to get a court order to halt its construction—despite the high-level contacts its chief executive, a former Israeli general, enjoys.

As well as raising public awareness and initiating a public struggle against the industrial zone, we are advising local authorities to object to the overall scheme and to the construction of individual factories. We object to the decision to turn this part of the rural Galilee into an industrial park instead of a tourism-related development, the natural option for this part of the country.

During our research in preparation for the court case we discovered the interesting background to the plans for the Tzipori industrial zone. It was originally initiated and approved a couple of years ago using emergency regulations granting exceptional powers to Ariel Sharon, then Housing Minister, to absorb the sudden influx of Russian immigrants following the collapse of the Soviet Union. Ten thousand housing units were supposed to be built in the area, with the industrial zone purportedly designed to provide employment for their Russian residents. As soon as the industrial zone was approved—a decision taken without the involvement of the Environment Ministry—the housing project was suddenly found to be unfeasible and scrapped. The industrial zone, however, has continued to evolve. This was apparently another of Sharon's tricks, designed to benefit a general friend of his while at the same time laying the groundwork for bringing to an end the chances of Nazareth and its surrounding villages becoming the center of Palestinian Arab culture in Israel. Certainly Sharon, an established war criminal, is crafty enough to play such games.

With this in mind, I plan to involve the Latin Church Patriarch Sabbah. He is a Nazarene and has the range of contacts and influence to aid in internationalizing the issue of saving his home town from the vagaries of industrialization for the benefit of others.

September 16, 1993

President François Mitterrand of France has awarded me the medal of "Ordre National du Merite" for my services to my people. At a Galilee Society fundraiser in Nazareth, I flaunted the award and several other international recognitions that have accrued to us. The French embassy's science attaché, whom I have known for a while, warned me, though, that a local journalist had tried his best to persuade the ambassador to rescind the award.

Lately, the same journalist has mounted a campaign of character assassination against me personally and against the Galilee Society as a whole. I have no factual evidence to support it, but my paranoid logic leads me to speculate that the Galilee Society's new environmental activism may well have raised the ire of former generals heading the project to bring polluting industries to the Galilee. Might they have paid the journalist to discredit me and the organization I head? Might they have tipped off their secret service agents? How long will it be before they turn vicious? Or have they turned vicious already? Is there a link between my direct confrontation with the Israeli military-industrial complex and my being detained by the immigration authorities at JFK airport in the United States for the first time in my life?

And that had to be on a very special occasion. Rhoda and her college mate, Seth, had their wedding in New York in early July. It was held in Central Park with a Brazilian band, a gondola ride and much singing, dancing and socializing.

Then we brought them back here, as planned, for the Arrabeh wedding with its four-night-long village-style celebrating in our backyard. We had busied ourselves with the planning and cleaning up of the garden for most of the year. Ty flew over from Hawaii with a girlfriend. His presence added greatly to our joy. And so did the presence of my brother Sharif and his wife Pat and their children, up from Ramallah. Seth's family—his father, sister, aunt and uncle—and a childhood friend all flew over from New York and had a great time.

January 2, 1994

For a while I have been involved in the task of trying to establish an umbrella organization for the Arab NGOs in Israel. The idea is to create a support structure to energize these NGOs, as well as establish a channel to develop the wider community. I and others are still grappling with defining the nature of the body we are hoping to create: the range of its membership and functions, who will run it, and how it will be funded.

In terms of funding possibilities, however, I have the feeling we are swimming against the current. The field officers of the Ford Foundation and NOVEB, a Dutch potential supporter for the project, would rather we work under the auspices of the New Israel Fund. The latter sees us as a competitor and unwelcome upstart. It all fits into a pattern of control that I personally reject. Although we at the Galilee Society welcome advice from the New Israel Fund, we refuse to receive funding from them and thus come under their control. Channeling funds in this way to Palestinian NGOs in Israel would constrain and even derail the real development strategies we need to pursue as a distinct national collective. Regardless of how "new" or liberal the image of this organization, our experience teaches us that they will always stay within the Zionist consensus: that this is a Jewish state and one must discourage all those struggling to promote their own independent interests.

Another possibility would be to seek US federal funding for this major undertaking. But here again we are stymied. The powerful pro-Israel lobby, AIPAC, on Capitol Hill is certain to deal a death blow to the prospects of any non-Zionist entity becoming established in Israel. It is mightier than any allies we might be able to recruit to our side. What is left is to turn to the old military axiom of attack as the best form of defense. We need to agitate for an equitable share for Arab citizens of the billions in aid allocated each year to Israel by America. I appreciate that there are very few American politicians willing to listen to such "nonsense." But raising the issue may at least give us a chance in a million to slip in some minor allocation of funding for our scheme in the foreign appropriations bill. Or, perhaps, it may bring about, in ways that I fail to fathom, my demise as a public figure and that of the Galilee Society as the lead civil society organization for the Palestinian minority in Israel.

For the necessary lobbying on Capitol Hill, and to stay ahead of the civil society game, I plan to take a one-year sabbatical, doing research on the topic at a university in the Washington DC area. At a minimum, this plan should satisfy my subliminal wish to escape for a while from Israel's oppressive atmosphere to somewhere where you are equally anonymous with all others in the formless gray crowd, and where life seems vaguely promising and the sky is the limit. In this vision, the Galilee Society would lead the effort of building on its local credentials while I would spend a year trying to open doors at the undisputed center of the New World Order, Washington DC. Our plan during that year would be to bring funding from the US federal government, American foundations, Gulf States and the European Union to build up an endowment, the income from which would be spent on collective NGO activities. The vision has me switching my commitment and efforts from the mother NGO, the Galilee Society, to the fruit of its most worthy conception, *Ittijah* (Direction in Arabic), as we have agreed to call our new umbrella organization.

On a different track, with the prodding of Dr. Sami Geraisy, I had joined an effort to establish a joint Jewish and Arab NGO called *Sikkuy*, Hebrew for "Opportunity." This organization, we hope, will tackle the difficult task of pressuring Israeli officials to own up to their responsibility for the injustices done to us in the past. Further, we will try to force them to act on such admission not only to redress the injustice but to rectify the structural faults in the system that led to it. Clearly, I am not in the lead here and this is a tall order. Still it will be my litmus test of this NGO, so far long on declarations and short on significant actions.

It has been a dry winter and Arrabeh's farmers are dismayed. Last Friday's sermon by Sheikh Kaid, broadcast live on the mosque's loudspeakers, admonished all of us, urging us to redouble our efforts at ending this terrible drought by sincerely repenting for our sins to the Almighty. His are not coordinated, I am sure, with the collective prayers of Kabbalistic Rabbis in Safad asking for the same favor. I listened to the blistering sermon while digging and watering my citrus trees. Most traditional homes have a single lemon tree in the front yard, always protected from the vagaries of the weather by the old folks doing their ablutions several times a day in its shade. Not only did the tree receive this year-round watering but it was also guaranteed the mystical benefit of the blessed water used by people as they purified themselves for their prayers.

Truly, the lemon tree in my family's yard was always green and fruitful, and so was the one in my uncle Salih's yard and in the yard of Sheikh Ibrahim, my aunt Nijmi's husband. The image of each of these venerable frail old men squatting down on his haunches in the shade of the lemon tree, balanced on one foot with the other stretched forward in midair to be washed by one hand with the thin stream of water from the spout of the ceramic jug held in the other, is both a beguiling childhood memory and an amazing yogic feat. And the old folks never lacked in vitamin C. This yogic art of the olden days has been lost with the advent of modern piped-in water. What a shame!

19
Reaping the Whirlwind

The recurring dream; on the pier at the house of grandmother (Popo) St. Morris (in shorts) on Kaneohe Bay, Oahu Island, Hawaii.

June 28, 1995

My big dreams are coming to a sudden end, collapsing under their own weight. I am on my way out of the Galilee Society, our new organization, Ittijah, and the Health for Minorities 2000 project. A group of young colleagues at the Galilee Society have banded together and, with behind-the-scene support from the field representative of ICCO, our Dutch main funder, demanded my resignation. The pretext is that, under my leadership, the expenses of the project to build a headquarters have eaten into funds for other activities. This is true only in a narrow technical sense reflecting the cash flow problem created by ICCO-imposed constraints.

From what I can understand, ICCO, the liberal Dutch Protestant Church charity that has been our major source of financial, organizational and even political support, has reached a decision, possibly at no higher level than its Middle East Department, to trim back our "exuberant overgrowth," to borrow a simile from my gardening. We must have set off alarms with them. Here we were, on the verge of taking up an international advocacy role and of establishing a permanent presence in Geneva on behalf of minorities in industrialized countries the world over, including in Holland itself. We are opening a new front against pollution dumping in our rural areas and are thinking of a permanent legal arm to take on adversaries from the very top of Israel's military-industrial complex. We have constructed the first ever home for a Palestinian NGO in Israel, a symbol of our independence and permanence. We envisioned a full-time international PR staff member. And we wanted to join hands with other Palestinian NGOs to form a national umbrella structure. And we have been doing it all with their money! Maybe we overstretched the limits of their tolerance in a partnership supposedly based on equality between donor and recipient. Maybe a decision was reached to downsize us to a more manageable level.

I had forgotten a cardinal rule of the NGO game; I failed to diversify the sources of support for my organization, putting myself and my group at the mercy of one "foreign master." As a result, I found myself caught in the jaws between the consortium of donors led by ICCO on one side and by the unbridled ambitions of a few of my young colleagues at home. I had little choice but to accept that my ambitious plan for the Galilee Society will be translated by others into a pale image of the original—it was that or risk the destruction of an organization I have spent a decade and a half building.

The reversal in the fortunes of the Galilee Society is even greater than in my own. By this time, in our quest for independent decision-making, we were preparing to shift to a five-year program cycle in which support from our "partners," as we came to call our funders, would be committed in advance for half a decade at a time and allocated to broad categories of action in the health field, with the decision on specifics left entirely in our own hands. My original negotiations on this empowering and progressive approach were conducted with my friend at ICCO, Sjord van Schoonefeld, a man with whom I had developed good rapport and mutual trust. Midway in the process, Sjord was replaced by another field officer. Also, my rebel colleagues, for their own reasons, saw fit to play along and go back to square one of project-by-project funding arrangement. It is a huge step backwards.

At the age of 58, I am far from ready to retire, however. I do collect a moderate pension from my period working for the Ministry of Health which, with Didi's salary, is sufficient to live on. But the thought of sitting back and relaxing gives me a chill. I lack the blissful gift of the ability to relax for extended periods. I do not even know how to work without a deadline, much less hang around with no specific assignment. I could teach, but where at? I hear the Palestinian University of Bir Zeit, near Ramallah, is opening a School of Public Health. But there are many candidates for the teaching posts and I am at the disadvantage of being a former Israeli government official. Teach at Haifa University? Fat chance! All Arab candidates are screened by the Shin Bet, and I know my standing with them. And in the Ministry of Health I am *persona non grata*. In fact I have not seen or heard from any of my former bosses there for the last thee years.

Private practice is a dead-end; Arrabeh has too many GPs and I am out of the loop. I could seek employment with one of the Sick Funds, a nine-to-five low-level job. From that distance perhaps I could even tie up all the loose ends regarding the termination of my duties with the Galilee Society, possibly resuming a normal relationship with the organization as a regular active member. But I would prefer not to serve again in an institution whose perimeters are set by a Zionist vision, even if I was able to work within Arrabeh. Public health and the public interest of my community are the only frames of reference I feel confident and comfortable basing my plans on. But public health is a field notorious for allowing its practitioners to starve their way to fame.

January 24, 1997

My attempts at finding myself through the United Nations service organizations, or at least fostering a significant involvement at UNICEF, have failed. UNICEF, like other UN bodies, turns out to be no more and no less attentive to human rights causes or attuned to the international "general good" than other organizations that I have dealt with before. My brief stint as a volunteer with UNICEF teaches that its basic approach is UNICEF first and then the children of whatever country you are dealing with second.

A special nursing course has finally opened for Bedouin girls in the Negev, a development I had contributed to under my various hats and with my constant haranguing of the system. I know that these girls will deal with tens of thousands of Bedouin mothers and children and save them much suffering and many unnecessary deaths. Still, my gut-level urge would be to get down to the Negev myself and deal with the deprived mothers and children there. When I look back, the greatest bursts of enthusiasm I ever experienced as a physician were in the early days when I would personally take a moribund child to the hospital using my car as an ambulance and my wife as the driver and persuade the hospital staff to admit it and worry about the payment later, thus assuming responsibility for its life and the expense involved in keeping it alive. The adrenaline rush came when the mother arrived at my clinic for a follow-up visit all smiles and gratitude.

That is no longer part of my rationale for returning to general practice. This time I am in it to assist my nephew to get professionally established in the village. I am on the verge of going back to work as a village-based family physician, associated but not employed by the General Sick Fund. I would like to initiate a new venture, the establishment of a private group practice. I keep telling myself that there is a lot of room for a major step such as the establishment of a regional hospital for the Battouf region with its some 50,000 residents. Such a hospital has been a community plan of mine, even if long dormant, ever since I returned from the United States. An imaginative but not so worldly-wise cousin of mine once approached a visiting bishop with an appeal on my behalf to fund the hospital so that "our pregnant women will not continue to need the services of those missionary infidels in Nazareth." So far, however, I have managed to attract only one physician, and even that is uncertain. It brings to mind the farmer who found a horseshoe and happily announced that he had only three more horseshoes and a horse to go before his transportation problems were solved.

I have rented a facility at a neighbor's house because of the ungodly traffic congestion around my own empty clinic. Every person in Arrabeh who needs a packet of cigarettes or a bottle of coke drives his car the 200 yards to the store. My original clinic is right in the center of the mayhem, next to the bank, post office and my brother's successful country store. On top of this pollution and the ubiquitous habit of smoking, the lack of physical exercise is part of this new lifestyle. Almost daily, young men in their cars fight over the right of way in the village cow paths now turned autostradas. A little over a month ago a minor incident of this nature escalated into a full-blown inter-clan conflagration with all of the "modern" village warfare weaponry. At least one government lackey used his gun in the incident.

I hope to get my nephew and namesake, the young Dr. Hatim Kanaaneh, youngest son of my brother Ahmad, on board as my partner and professional heir in the village. He is still training in general surgery. An American friend, when she was introduced to him, thought we must have been "cloned"—even though nephew Hatim is long-haired and much bigger than me. In Arabic, "al-kabir" means both senior and larger. Since he is larger while I am his senior by a few decades, our little nephews and nieces have struggled to find ways of identifying who they mean when they speak of "uncle Hatim al-kabir." The little ones have come up with "aunt Didi's Hatim" for me, and "uncle Hatim-on-call" for him, since that is what he does at the hospital most evenings.

In his literary rendition of a classic dirge-like Nazarene drinking song, Toufiq Zayyad, the poet mayor of Nazareth, summed up the experience common to me, my nephew and all other Palestinian foreign students in three words: "hanthalun aishu al-muhajir"—bitter as myrrh is the immigrant's life. My nephew is now back and doomed to the failure, frustration and humiliation that Arab foreign graduates, almost without exception, are routinely subjected to. Still, he is committed enough to his family and village to stick it out and aspires to follow in the steps of his respected uncle.

Palestine as an independent state seems on its way to happening, though not quite as Palestinians dreamt of it. The official story is that Palestinians are now mature enough for real politics; we are putting territorial greed and old hatreds aside and will deal with the reality of two states coexisting in peace. All of that says, perhaps, that we can expect relations with the Arab world to improve and the borders to open up. Or is that all just so much wishful thinking? For a while I have even dared to think of a health tourism venture based on the Galilee's geopolitical position in a peaceful and reconciled Middle East.

"Normalization and collaboration" are perfectly legitimate ways of doing business in the larger scheme of things, provided peace is given a chance. And Israel's economic ambitions in the region as envisioned by the Zionist megalomaniac Shimon Peres—a man who sees his nation, a Jewish Israel, dominating the Middle East marketplace, if not the entire world's—may just be strong enough to curb the country's political and military excesses as envisioned by another Zionist megalomaniac, Ariel Sharon—a man who through the view-finder of a cannon sees the actualization of Greater Israel, from the Nile to the Euphrates.

In fact, the international community is lapping up the Labor party and Peres's economic schemes. Locally, Peres argues that a peace deal, even a creaky one, will allow Israel to enter the Middle East economic arena and take advantage of its superior technical know-how. What I find insulting is that Israel's visionaries like Peres suffer not only from perhaps justifiable delusions of grandeur—in keeping with the Biblical injunction to be "a light unto the nations"—but also that they hold their neighbors in such contempt, regarding them as an amorphous mass of unending cheap labor and of undiscriminating consumers. I am not sure how much mutual growth and development potential can come from such a view. And we, the country's Palestinian citizens, are lumped together with this cheap mass of Arab labor.

Two days ago, Taha, a man from another clan, collapsed with a heart attack while puttering around in his garden. Someone pounded on my door and I ran over and tried to resuscitate him for over an hour with mouth-to-mouth breathing and pumping of his heart while surrounded by dozens of the neighborhood women and children. The emergency cardiac resuscitation team finally arrived from Karmiel, the neighboring Jewish city, but nothing helped and we had to let him go.

Taha was limited in terms of higher brain functions, his borderline handicap further compounded by his assignment at an early age, about the time he should have started school, to tending the family herd of goats in the surrounding hills. He learned to play the flute, the simple type fashioned out of a length of metal pipe with six holes on one side and a single one on the other. Whistling into it is the standard pastime of all goat herders in the Galilee, and goats learn not to stray far from its enchanting sound. Taha was not the best flute player, just barely passable for wedding parties in the neighborhood before stereo systems came into use for the purpose.

He had a male cousin with whom he entered into an "exchange marriage," where the men swap their sisters for wives. That cousin is a superb flute player—slim and tall, the right figure to bend down from the waist, parallel with the ground, swoop, twirl, and suddenly straighten up, shooting his musical arrows and shrill tunes at the heavens to the excitement and rapid-fire foot pounding and heel grinding of the circle of male *Dabkeh* dancers around him. He plays for women as well, but on such rare occasions he keeps an upright reserved posture.

Later Taha managed to get a job as a sanitation worker in the city, a feat of which he was proud. Occasionally I would give him a ride back to the village, during which he never failed to complain to me about all the other villagers who passed him without stopping; and he would finish every tirade with a barrage of curses directed at their ancestors and at the private parts of their mothers.

After more than a decade of marriage his cousin-wife was still not pregnant. The couple sought professional help at the best of modern medical centers, but to no avail. At the time fertility treatment was very expensive, as specialists were reluctant to offer it at facilities where they worked as employees, always finding an excuse to refer patients to their after-hours private clinics. Taha spent all of his regular income from the sanitation job in pursuit of the promise of a male heir. Then one day he took his wife to a traditional healer who found no fault with her and advised him to get circumcised. Circumcision is a festive occasion, usually for a child. Relatives and neighbors—in a village's geo-demographics, one and the same thing—came to wish the man well and brought presents of candy and toys. Lo and behold, soon afterwards his wife got pregnant and delivered a healthy male child and then another. A miracle, some claimed. Others say that all the traditional healer did was to explain to the virgin couple how exactly to do the act.

Taha's late father became very protective of his daughter-in-law cum niece. He would call me to her bedside at the slightest sign of a sniffle and pay the extra money I charged for unnecessary house calls. I recall one time when the old man woke me up at an ungodly hour because she had a sore throat or some other minor complaint. I asked why she could not have come over to see me, and he explained that she was pregnant and he did not want her exposed to the elements on a cold night. I pressed him further:

"Your other sons have cars. Why couldn't you wake one and have him drive her over?"

"The thing I hate to do most is to wake a child of mine from a deep sleep on a night like this," he said magnanimously.

Too bad I was only his distant relative.

Earlier in the week Didi, I and two friends went to the premiere of a play, *Suhmata*, performed in the bosom of nature. I, for one, battled with tears in my eyes for over half the performance. The play was very reminiscent of things I saw and heard in my childhood. It concerns an old refugee man introducing the ruins of his destroyed village, Suhmata, to his Israeli-educated grandson, who is about to marry a Jewish woman and to enlist in the Israeli armed forces. The grandson's impending marriage has little to do with the story, except to emphasize the emotional and cultural distance between him and his grandfather and to highlight the vast difference between the two realities of their separate existences. The old man relives moments from his youth and from the Nakba in 1948. The play was emotionally very affecting, particularly because of the setting itself. It was performed in a clearing by the remains of the church in the ruins of Suhmata itself, with cactus and fig trees and the stones and half walls of demolished homes for a backdrop and the setting sun for lighting, a most befitting stage.

The producer and co-author is a young man from the nearby village of Buquia'a who studied theater in the United States and became the director of a theater company in the city of Seattle. He collected stories from his village neighbor, an old refugee from Suhmata, and jointly wrote and produced an English-language version in the US with a professional playwright. A local theater group produced it in Arabic and decided to stage it on the actual ruins of Suhmata. The two authors, the old man whose story the play tells and his family, and the rest of the audience attended the premiere under the watchful eyes of a contingent of police. The police had originally given notice that the play's performance in Suhmata was illegal, but Adalah, a new legal center for Arab minority rights jointly established by the Galilee Society and the Arab Association for Human Rights, challenged the police decision, which was overturned.

And that is what I actually wanted to say to Runa MacKay in the letter I wrote her: "In 1980 you were party to a small step; you shared in realizing a dream. That small step, the founding of the Galilee Society, indirectly and unbeknownst to you, made it possible for refugees from Suhmata to 'celebrate' their loss and dispersion in the ruins of their church. Is that what you dedicated your life to a medical charity to achieve, I wonder?"

March 10, 1999

I am embarking on a new project: the establishment of a center for child rehabilitation, the first for Arabic-speaking children in rural Galilee. A young neuro-psychologist from the village suggested the idea to me as an alternative pastime to gardening. He saw the rising number of health professionals in our villages and the limited opportunities for them to use their knowledge and skills locally. Our young professionals continue to work as solo practitioners in their respective fields. He, for example, works in a General Sick Fund medical center outside Tel Aviv, making the three- or four-hour return trip twice a week, often just to see his next-door neighbor. The Sick Fund serves mainly as a formal address and collects the fees. The self-evident solution is to create the same framework locally in which the rural Arab patient and medic can meet. With a self-congratulatory sense of heroism, we are calling it Elrazi Center, after the tenth-century Arab physician, the first ever pediatrician.

Am I not trying too hard? Is it not time I yielded to the recurring dream of returning to Hawaii that keeps disturbing my sleep?

20
Déjà Vu

With the South African Minister of Justice, Dulla Omar, and an assistant at the house of Mohammad Abu-al-Haija in the unrecognized village of Ein Hawd.

January 20, 2001

It is virtually impossible to force a functioning state to face up to the issue of its own accountability. In an ultimate sense, a state that holds itself accountable for an action is also a state committed to correcting it, or guaranteeing that it will never happen again. That is a much more serious matter than agreeing to monetary or even moral compensation for the harm done. But it is that kind of accountability I see as the debt the state of Israel, "my state," owes me and my community for the historical injustice committed against us for the past half a century, since we became citizens through no choice of our own. During that period, we have faced inequality, institutional and judicial discrimination, systematic collective marginalization and the near-denial of our humanity, even as our state has denied it treats us in such ways.

In the early 1990s, starting with the premiership of Yitzhak Rabin, a new era began: Israel recognized that discrimination had taken place against the Palestinian Arab community inside Israel. But so far it has been the mere recognition of a fact, seen and related to by the Israeli government as if it were a natural phenomenon of the sort that obliges no one to act differently from the way they have done in the past. It is barely an admission of responsibility, let alone of accountability.

Then, a few months ago, the Palestinians in the occupied territories mounted another Intifada to remind the world of the injustice of Israel's continuing occupation and of its insistence on dehumanizing them, erasing their culture, and denying them hope. Our youth, here in Israel proper, were enraged too by Ariel Sharon's desecration of the al-Aqsa Mosque. They demonstrated both in protest at the injustices they themselves have suffered and in support of their brothers and sisters across the Green Line. Israel's finest liberals, who were in charge of the country, decided to teach us a new lesson. After all, it has been two dozen years since the last one, when our youth tested the mettle of the system by striking for a day, on Land Day of 1976. Then the "liberal" pair of Yitzhak Rabin and Shimon Peres taught them a lesson by sending the security forces to break the strike, killing six and injuring hundreds more. Now 24 years later the heirs to that "liberal" legacy, Ehud Barak and Shlomo Ben-Ami, took aim—through their police force—and picked off thirteen innocent Palestinian youths, Arab citizens of Israel. The Israeli media and public are quick to point the finger of blame at us. We have become the enemy within, our towns and villages cordoned off and boycotted by phone repairmen and food distributors alike. The electricity technician will enter Arrabeh for emergency repairs only under the protection of an armed convoy; the police venture in only in bulletproof vehicles. And why should anyone investigate those thirteen deaths? We are the aggressors by definition.*

* See Foreword.

October 20, 2001

In Arabic, we say: "*Sharru al-baleyyati ma yudhik*—The worst calamity is one that makes you laugh." The whole world has gone crazy and I feel like laughing aloud, idiot-like, at what I see and hear.

I am an Arab, a Palestinian and a Muslim; I also have family in Lower Manhattan. I am very proud of each of these facts and should not need to explain or apologize for any of them. I do not owe my humanity—all I need to understand others and be understood by them—to any of these attributes. Yet my mother-in-law is worried enough to call and beg me not to visit the US in the near future. She is Chinese and is reminded of what life was like for Orientals in Hawaii in the days and months that followed Pearl Harbor. I call my son, who lives in California with his ethnically Japanese wife, to advise him to keep a low profile. After all, he identifies himself as a Palestinian Arab and is the contentious type. I am afraid he may become defensive about who he is or about Islam, the stronger half of his two faiths. In our family we have always fallen back on the common ground of our humanity and love, and that has sufficed. It is a rare occasion that requires us to declare openly for agnosticism. We celebrate Christmas and Easter in the Muslim setting of our village in the Galilee, and we have always remembered to celebrate Ramadan, *Eid al-Fitr* and *Eid al-Adha* when in Honolulu. It always pleased our children to be unique, exotic and better informed than their peers. Now I am worried what my son's uniqueness, and his wider horizons, may bring in adulthood. He reassures me that his circle of friends and contacts are well-informed and would not think of harming others for being different. To me, that implies such behavior is not the norm elsewhere in America.

Two days ago I had a long chat with my 101-year-old neighbor and patient. I have been slowly coaxing an ingrown toenail out of the flesh of his left big toe. A devout Muslim, he drops in at the clinic every Friday on his way to the mosque for the noon prayer. For his age group, he is considered to be well-learned and is known by the very honorable nickname of *al-Qadi*, the Judge. Our chat is mostly one-way, as he does not like to use the hearing aid I have prescribed for him. So, I wind up nodding my head while he speaks. I shouted one question to him, about who runs errands for him at home. His response embodied the generational gap doubled and redoubled. He was loud, as is usual for the hearing impaired, and lengthy, as is usual for the lonely elderly. Finally he got to the point: "My two boys [both over sixty] avoid me; their children turn away and pretend that they do not hear me when I call them; and the children of those are even worse. Each generation is worse than the preceding one. The very young are the devil himself. I swear to you, they are Osama Bin-Ladens, every one of them!" And I thought he was a devout Muslim! The world is simply too complicated. In the currently imposed duality of the world, where am I to place al-Qadi? Is he with George W. or with Osama?

He is not the only one who seems at a loss where to turn next. The other day as I left for Nazareth to service my car I picked up a neighbor who runs a furniture store. He told me how badly his business is doing. "People are not buying furniture; they are sitting on their savings," he deadpanned unintentionally. He worried about not being able to meet the monthly payments for his son Ashraf's college education in Germany. "How is it Ashraf's fault? Why should he be forced to abandon his studies in Germany when some crazy Saudi takes his anger out at the Americans?" he concluded, obviously failing to grasp the irony of his statement denying any connection between young Arab students in Germany and what has happened in America. "What shall we all do now? Just sit home and wait for the bombs to start falling?"

So, what reason, in principle, do I have to quarrel with Osama? If only he was smart enough to restrict his damage to property and not to include people. Osama, some say, merely delivers the sermons and outlines the principles; he leaves his followers to figure out how to interpret and implement the practicalities of making life "as bitter for Americans as it is for Palestinians," as he promised to do. He does not realize that, in making my daughter's life in New York as bitter as my brother's in Ramallah, he puts an unfair strain on me. If somebody would tell me the coordinates of his cave in Bora Bora, I would let him know and see whether it had any effect on his strategy. Which reminds me of the response Saddam Hussein once gave when told by journalists that, in targeting Israel with his Scud missiles, he might hit one of the Palestinian towns there. His response was poetic: "I am not sifting lentils for soup. So what if the soup has a few stones in it?" So, are we destined to boil in the soup this time around or not?

As Abu-Ashraf, the furniture man, said, all we can do is to sit at home and wait for the bombs to start falling. That might be a rhetorical figure of speech for me but for my brother in Ramallah it is real. As it would also be for my daughter in Lower Manhattan—figuring out with which breath she might inhale anthrax spores—had she and her family not moved to Italy for a year, a decision they had implemented shortly before all hell broke loose in their neighborhood.

But I digress. How does the common man here feel about the surreal images of terror from the US? Well, most people, apart from the odd car salesman, do not give a damn about how well the American economy fares. They have been struck by an immediate sense of horror, which might be followed by a sense of remorse for sharing more genes with the handsome devil who is presumably behind it all. But then again we share more than 99 percent of our genes with chimps. So, genetically speaking, we are splitting hairs and our bickering is about that remaining 1 percent.

Being held ultimately responsible by six billion 99-per-cent-chimp-people for all of their failures, and for being the barrier to the realization of their dreams, is not an enviable position in which to find oneself. And that, Mr. President, the leader of the only superpower and the one dominant super-culture, is the position in which you have put yourself. We all, the entire six billion 99-per-cent-chimps, want to enjoy the material benefits of American culture. More than half of us, the younger ones without the turbans, want to move to America tomorrow. If you cannot cope with that, then at least spare some effort to make our lives less miserable. Stop begrudging us the benefits of our own natural resources. Stop aiding and abetting those who oppress us, your dictator friends and military occupiers. Stop invading us with your naked-girls-and-violent-men culture. Stop exporting your weapons to our warlords. In short, stop being so American!

I have no personal quarrel with America, since I had the fortune to enjoy its many benefits. I made my own free decision to escape from it for the safety and rewards of living in a backward Palestinian village in Israel. But I can hardly admit to my neighbors that I lived the American dream, even if only for a while. That is how alienated most of the six billion of us are from what you take to be your God-given right.

I'd better stop before I offend somebody. Yet the silence grows deeper by the day in the West about the aggressive policies being pursued by the mighty in my Middle East neighborhood, the unbridled violence unleashed by your bully on our block, Israel. The reluctance of the Western publics to criticize their governments, not to mention to stand up to Israel's aggression, is matched only by the blind acceptance by so many Muslims in Third World countries of the legitimacy and leadership of the hard-liners among them. This is a fine topic for debate when one is at a safe distance from it all, but here in Palestine and Israel we have been living for some time at the mouth of an evil volcano of violence. Even without assigning blame for who started it, there is no denying that the very world leaders who now categorize all of us as either "with us or against us" are those who bear ultimate responsibility for not quelling the Middle East's violence, if not for fanning the flames.

I am not sure that I have the means to articulate the imminent disaster I sense. It is not limited to Palestine and Israel, or even to this region. Maybe my sense of impending universal evil derives from the fact that I have family and friends all across the world. But that is the case with many people I know in the present age of the global village, and yet I find such acquaintances keeping their sanity and going about their daily lives as if nothing much has happened. Sure enough, they decry the current state of world affairs and most are ready to take sides, sounding off about the wrongs and rights of actions taken by one side or the other as if this was a theoretical debate about a hypothetical situation. Then, they move on to deal with their daily tasks.

That is where I feel inadequate, bothered, and distracted. I want to do something beyond just taking the side of one or other of the contestants in the many violent conflicts around the world: the US versus the Taliban, Israel versus Palestine, Russia versus Chechnia, Algeria versus Algeria, to name only a few. Some say you have to stand with justice. I am willing for the time being even to leave that alone, not only because justice has become relative but because I sense that we are facing a human crisis. And in cases of emergency, we doctors give priority to saving lives—only after that do we address the issue of justice.

June 7, 2002

How does one relate an incident so it feels in writing as it was in reality? What happened last week on a visit to Jenin Refugee Camp

was out of character for me. I exposed my feelings so openly that
Zainab, my first nurse and the wife of my closest friend, thought I
had lost it. She has not seen me weep before in the 32 years of our
professional camaraderie.

We visited the camp as part of a medical aid mission from the
Palestinian community in Israel, to offer help to the camp's inhabitants
after the horrifying rampage by the Israeli army in April.* We worked
in the dilapidated UNRWA facility for four hours, during which time
I cared for over twenty sick children. As we were leaving, we decided
to walk through the rubble of the section of the camp flattened by the
Israeli war machine more than a month earlier. I have walked through
ruins before and sensed the air of total loss that engulfs the whole space.
This time I looked at details: the remnants of a family living room with
some of the furniture still in place under the caved-in walls; a plastic
flower basket hanging between the iron bars protruding from the half-
ceiling; a wheelchair hanging from a fallen balcony (we were told the
paraplegic survived his fall); pieces of broken toys, the remnants of a
musical string instrument, flattened pots and pans. Here and there a
few families sheltered under a blanket strung across four sticks over
what used to be their camp home, their supposed refuge away from
their original home within Israel.

Halfway through our walk I noticed a middle-aged man, thin,
unshaven and covered with dust, kneeling inside a shallow ditch he
had cleared in the middle of the rubble. The ditch was about two
meters long by one wide, and about one meter deep, about the size
of a freshly dug grave. The bottom was well-packed solid ground,
obviously a part of the original camp ground, and the two sides were
the base of concrete walls, one with faded blue paint. I walked closer
to him, but he did not notice me. Instead he continued clearing the
rubble with his bare hands, totally absorbed by his work and with a
very determined look on his face. I greeted him with the traditional

* _Jenin massacre:_ In April 2002, Israel mounted an alleged reprisal attack against
the Palestinian Jenin Refugee Camp resulting in the deaths of scores of fighters and
civilians and the razing of a large area of the camp. Despite much debate, mostly
academic in the extreme, both the UN and Human Rights Watch deemed Israel's
actions to be war crimes. Mohammad Bakri's documentary film, _Jenin Jenin_, gives
a Palestinian perspective on the massacre. It is ironic that the architects who later
planned the razed section's renovation reportedly designed its alleys to accommodate
Israeli tanks.

"May God give you health," to which he responded absentmindedly, almost mechanically. He continued shoveling out the dirt, only this time throwing the handfuls in the other direction. He was obviously preoccupied but not distraught. I persisted and inquired about what he was looking for. He turned to me and said sarcastically, "Gold, what else?" Again, I persisted with my question. Then he sighed and looked away with a certain sense of shame. "This is the alley on which my house opened. You are standing where it used to be. This is my neighbor's home. I just wanted to clean in front of my house."

That did it. I could not hold the grief and sadness anymore. It hit like a bolt and I started sobbing. I crouched down, took my glasses off and tried to dry my eyes. But it would not stop. I kept sobbing and my silent gulping for air became louder. Then I just let go and sobbed loudly, momentarily lapsing into the dark abysmal loneliness I felt when as a teenager I came home to find my mother dead and already buried. I regained control only when two men held me around the shoulders and tried to comfort me. One was the same man digging for gold; the second man, I found out later, was a young man nicknamed Michael Jackson, the now-unemployed leader of the camp's renowned folkdance troop. They both kept repeating to me one reassuring statement: "We are strong. We will outlive this and overcome the destruction."

As I walked away, I was ashamed of the scene I had made. I noticed a group of foreigners being shown around, a group I discovered that were from Iceland and being guided around by Peter Hansen, the director-general of UNRWA. I introduced myself to him and demanded that the capabilities and unique position of the Arab community inside Israel be factored into any plans for the rehabilitation of this and other camps. He acquiesced, agreeing to focus on the psychological health of the camp's children, and we set a time for a meeting.

On my way home, my newly found unabashedness continued. As I got in my car, which I had left safely in a village outside of Jenin, I saw a housewife baking wheat bread in an outside oven in front of her house. I was hungry and the smell of fresh bread was irresistible. I remembered my mother's freshly baked bread. A child came out of the house. I offered to give him five shekels for a loaf. He ran to his mother and brought two. As he brought the bread the father showed up and told the child not to accept the money. When I insisted that I had to honor the deal I made with the boy the father got a little upset and half-jokingly threatened to break up my car if I insult him and his child any further. He wanted me to come into the house. I apologized for being in a hurry. I was on my way to my nephew's engagement party. He went in and brought back a plastic bag with a special homemade delicacy—freshly baked paper-thin bread rolled in ghee and sugar. It was delicious. I ate it as I sped off to the party, getting it all over the white clothes I always wear when on a medical relief mission. People at the engagement party had to excuse my looks. They realized I'd had a rough day at the Jenin Refugee Camp.

June 1, 2005

I am at the tail end of my planned three-stop pleasure tour of the United States. The pleasure was fouled up early on, at Newark Airport, my port of entry into the country. This was the third time in a row that the immigration authorities have delayed me for questioning as I have flown into the US. Last time they made me and Didi miss our flight from Vancouver to Honolulu. At least on that occasion I was able to track down a long-lost high school friend in Vancouver and we spent a very pleasant evening in his company.

The current encounter, however, had no saving grace, except, perhaps, the discovery of the source of my troubles with the FBI. Their special agent at the airport made it clear, after four hours of interrogation, that the Israeli authorities have placed my name on some sort of list of potential or actual terrorists that the US should watch out for. That explains why I was paged over the public address system as I was boarding my flight at Frankfurt and requested to go through security a second time, a request that had come "from the Americans," as the apologetic German steward explained to me. His boss was so infuriated by their lack of confidence in his inspection system that he used foul language to express his opinion of "the Americans" and argued vigorously with the steward who accompanied me. He was about to refuse the request, when I expressed my readiness to be frisked by as many agents as anybody wanted.

Over the years, and after dozens upon dozens of trips in and out of Israel, I have grown tolerant of manhandling by security agents. I still recall the time a young Israeli officer got flustered by my bulging bunion. He had me take my shoes off, then my socks, and still had to squeeze it several times before letting go of my foot. You have to give it to the Israelis when it comes to thorough searches. Or, perhaps, the young man had a fetish of some sort! I also recall my embarrassment, and the alarm of the security officer, the time Didi and I accidentally switched our identical carry-on bags; I failed to identify a suspiciously shaped item neither he nor I were familiar with. It was a pack of tampons.

The one time I really lost my cool was in March 2000 on the return leg of an El-Al flight from New York. We had spent a few exciting weeks with our daughter elated with the arrival of Malaika, our first grandchild and that was what I casually informed the security agent who picked us out of the line of passengers at the airport.

"You must have taken many photos of your new grandchild," she said.

"Yes, of course!" my wife piped up excitedly. "A dozen films at least."

"I want to see them all. Take your luggage to the side and find the photos for me," the young woman said with a big smile.

The trouble was that we had a total of six pieces of luggage that we had packed over the period of our stay in New York and the pictures were spread randomly among all the clothing items, the presents and souvenirs that we had gathered over the entire period. I simply couldn't fathom the rationale for that request, but apparently, like God, El-Al security agents work in mysterious ways. We both tried to explain, implore and protest—but to no avail. I finally raised my voice and demanded to speak to her superior but had to tone down my voice when I was threatened with spending the night at the airport. All through the flight I worked on a letter of complaint which I lodged with El-Al offices upon arrival in Israel. A few weeks later I received a response from the airline's PR office explaining to me that all that happened was within the realm of the expected and was for my own security as a passenger. The lady then went on to explain that she is sending me a consolation present that she hoped would help me get over my upset. It turned out to be a hand puzzle, presumably for me to use when I feel fidgety. I learned my lesson and informed my travel agent never to fly me on El-Al again, despite the airline's cheap prices to New York.

At Newark, the special agent's questions were all designed to discover whether I have, or have had, any links with the PLO or made any donations, even if indirectly or unwittingly, to any terrorist organization. He claimed that he "went to bat" for me on the phone with "the guys in Washington" who would otherwise have barred me from entering the country. He kept asking, "What reason do you think we have to bar you from entering the United States?" It reminded me of the style of prying my superiors in the Ministry of Health used with me when the then Health Minister, Ehud Olmert, and his former Shin Bet agent, Elan Cohen, were trying to get me dismissed. "Why do you think Olmert and Cohen want you out?" they would ask.

Maybe this agent at Newark was simply playing the role of good cop. His final advice to me was to clarify the issue with the visa section of the American embassy back in Israel and ask them to amend the database they have on me. Fat chance! Most of the staff there are Israeli citizens, who are unlikely to be much impressed by my protestations of innocence. After all, I know that the Israeli secret services hold me in suspicion because of my activism for equality in health care for the Palestinian minority in Israel. Even the use of the term "Palestinian" to refer to myself is cause enough to upset their sensitivities, possibly enough for them to want to make life difficult for me in every possible way. And what is simpler in the current atmosphere of paranoia and anti-terror mania than to put my name on a list supplied to fellow secret agents in the US, who are light years away from the petty vengeances of the little informers in my hometown or in my office, those who originally smeared me, perhaps for taking myself seriously or for openly refusing to cooperate with them. To quote an analogy from Arrabeh folklore: "It is like a whore's life story; you know how it starts but never how it ends."

Whether through the graces of the Newark airport agent or by virtue of the constraints imposed by American law on his powers, I was finally admitted to the US and took the shuttle to my daughter's apartment where I was wined and dined for four days and where the unending marvels of Malaika, my granddaughter, could captivate me forever.

My next stop, a few days later, was Mount Vernon, Iowa, where I had a wedding to officiate at. Getting there was another experience so ridiculous that I can only laugh about it. The moment the airline agents looked at my name on the screen, their expressions changed. I could see their jaws drop and the red lights flash inside their heads. They had a lengthy consultation by phone with headquarters, asked me questions about the contents of my bags, gave me my boarding card and referred me for a thorough luggage inspection. As I handed the boarding card to the woman directing the passengers prior to inspection at the gate, she highlighted the four Ss at the card's corner, indicating my excessive danger level, to the security agent. That made him come to full alert and shout loudly "QUAD S" down the corridor, provoking two agents to rush over to take me aside for an especially thorough frisking. Under normal circumstances it would be grounds for bringing charges against those guys for sexual molestation, because the touching was quite uninhibited and the stroking extensive and repetitive.

Arriving at Des Moines airport in Iowa I was met by my friends Jagy and Marquita. My entire trip revolved around my role at their son Jai's wedding to the beautiful Brandi Logan. Earlier this year, I received the strangest request ever made to me by a sane person. Brandi and Jai wanted me to officiate at their campus wedding. They couched their request with such compliments about my family life and my foolish loyalty to one woman, though my religion allows me four, that I felt obliged to accept. I am no cleric and I protested my innocence of all things sacerdotal, but the couple guided me through the process of on-line ordination with the Universal Ministries. The website repeatedly affirms the church's seriousness of purpose and beseeches applicants not to register their pets. I did not, and within a couple of days I had my formal certification as the Reverend Hatim Kanaaneh.

September 5, 2005

Mohammad Abu-al-Haija, the founder and head of the Association of Forty, is still campaigning on behalf of his own and the other unrecognized villages. I had not seen him for nearly a decade when two months ago we met at a public function. I asked for his current mobile phone number and he handed me a business card. He had opened a restaurant, offering food in his own home in the now partly recognized Arab village of Ein Hawd in the middle of the Carmel National Forest, a short distance from Haifa.

Yesterday Didi and I arrived an hour before sunset with our friends, Toufiq and Zainab, all of us now retired and available for impromptu socializing. They had reserved for us the best table in the house, the one with a full view from the second story of the sun setting over in the

Mediterranean. The restaurant is perched high above the pine forest, planted by the Jewish National Fund, that has long replaced the family's olive orchards. Mohammad interrupted an emergency meeting of his local committee to come over with his wife and children to greet us. We hugged and kissed affectionately.

"*Mabrouk!*—Congratulations! And more power to you," I said. "This is fantastic. Is the building licensed?"

"Of course not!" he replied. "These things take time, you know. Like all our houses here, it has a demolition order. The business started almost by accident, when my wife added a couple of extra plates to our dinner table for guests who made an appointment. But eventually we could not handle the demand anymore. On Saturdays I have the whole extended family waiting on guests and washing dishes. Finally, I gathered the courage and built the restaurant in the space of five weeks. We were so fast that the authorities did not even have time to come back and check on the construction stoppage order they had issued. And I am in good standing with the Regional Planning Committee!

"It took us thirty years to get Ein Hawd recognized and it will take us another thirty to get licenses for our homes. In the meantime my guests here at weekends include all of my enemies, from local politicians to Supreme Court judges. They have no shame. They come and eat at my table and still want my home demolished and me and my family out of here.

"But even the worst of them are talking to us now. You noticed the fresh repairs to the road on your way here. The regional council decided to cover the costs of the work up to 25,000 shekels. I kept coaxing the work crew and stretching out the work contract till it reached four times that much. They will find a way to cover the money. Tonight I am meeting with my village committee to decide on our best negotiating strategy tomorrow as regards the Israel Lands Authority, which is offering to lease us the land on which the village stands, originally our olive groves. I have indicated that we may be willing to pay a nominal price of one shekel per dunam. That offer should satisfy them since it would mean that I recognize the state's ownership of my land, something we have never done before."

Did I sense a tone of resignation in his voice? Are members of the Abu-al-Haija clan finally reconciled to the decision to relinquish their claim to their land? Or does he have another trick up his sleeve?

He went back to his committee meeting, and the waiters and cooks, his entire family, proceeded to host us with no end of delicious home-cooked Palestinian dishes. There is no menu; you eat what they have cooked for the day. Eventually, his wife and children joined us at the table for coffee and sweets and to reminisce and renew the old social ties between us. I knew all of the children as toddlers. Now they are still small but they are college graduates and high school students. I wonder if their stunted size is not a reflection of the hard times they went through when Mohammad struggled to provide for his large family while hosting at his own expense and in the best of rural Arab traditions all the well-wishers that blew across Ein Hawd. Certainly the youngest is tall enough—perhaps a sign of recent better days, at least financially. Or am I reading too much into some genetic freak occurrence?

The youngsters seem well-adjusted and as well-educated as any group of young adults in the country, though in their youth the long dirt road to the closest bus stop on their way to school and back "ate many layers of skin off of their heels," as we say in local parlance. Now the oldest has a degree in computer science, the second in interior design and the third in fashion design. We chatted at length about the old days and the hard-earned advances they have made for their village. The mother kept repeating very proudly: "The authorities now collect *arnona* [the municipal land tax that qualifies one for municipal services] from us. The school bus comes all the way up here for the older children. We have a regular school up to grade six with teachers who compete for the principal's position." I can still remember the heroic struggle they made to establish a kindergarten in the village and to force the Ministry of Education to cover the teacher's salary.

It all brought back fond memories of the many visits I had made to this village in support of Mohammad's struggle for recognition. The last time I had eaten in their home was eight years ago when I took Dulla Omar, the late Justice Minister of South Africa, on a private tour of the unrecognized villages. Then, the house was crowded; now they have a huge space with dozens of dining tables, each with the pictures and visiting cards of patrons scattered under the glass covers. It makes for a random listing of who's who in Israeli society, from leftist activists and artists who occupy the original homes of the Abu-al-Haija clan a short distance away in the now exclusively Jewish old Ein Hod, to the army chief of staff and mighty industrialists.

Under the glass cover of our table, I noticed a picture of Mohammad shaking hands with a man in uniform. I found a way of addressing my suspicions without offending:

"This man looks exactly like President Clinton. Is that really him?"

"No, uncle! This is the chief of the fire brigade in the area. He helped us extinguish the forest fire around the village with his own bare hands. The fire trucks arrived without water and here, of course, we have no water supply. He got so angry and frustrated that my father had to calm him down."

Things do change in this country, but not always for the better. By now, "transfer" in its various forms—whether "population exchange," "demographic security," or even "development of the Galilee and the Negev"—is an accepted part of the political discourse of all the Zionist parties and their leaders. It is part of the current political consensus, neither denounced by civilized people nor denied a central place in "normal" news by the Israeli media. Recently a Palestinian child was shot dead by the occupying Israeli forces. His parents donated his organs to five different patients, including a religious Israeli Jew who declared that, had he known in advance, he would not have accepted an Arab heart in his body. The media presented the item as mildly humorous news, with barely a word of condemnation. A country that has elected Sharon, a veritable war criminal, as its leader and promoted him to the point where the most powerful man on earth, George W. Bush, pronounces him "a man of peace," does not have to shy away from policies that are crimes against human rights. Spin doctoring—known locally as *hasbara*—is a highly developed art in this country, especially when dealing with Palestinians or when reporting to "our American allies."

At the airport, leaving Israel on our frequent trips, Didi and I still receive the standard VIP treatment reserved for Palestinians. Nothing has changed except that, at our age, we find the harassment more insulting. This summer we witnessed how well our son, Ty, handled it as he left from a visit. A security official tagged him red and he was put through two and a half hours of inspection and body searches, with the agents spending much of their time swiping every last item in his possession with their chemical detectors. Here was this strapping young man with full credentials as a manager in a major US firm who is proud to identify himself as Palestinian Arab. By all accepted Israeli standards, Arabs are "not to rise above the level of our pubes," as the Hebrew slang puts it—and as a journalist once sarcastically entitled her interview with me. In this sense, Ty must seem very threatening indeed to the security agent who first identified him as an Arab in the line of travelers. So Ty got what he deserved. I was proud of the way he conducted himself, taking it all in his stride, maintaining an indignant but dignified demeanor, answering their questions with the minimum of words while his body language clearly said "Fuck you! I am above your silly tricks." We had planned on having breakfast together after the check-in, but he was escorted to the plane by two security officials and we had time only for the briefest of goodbyes, a hug and a kiss, under intense scrutiny.

In the Department of Arab Education, the cat is finally out of the sack. At the start of the last school year, the Director-General of the Education Ministry let down her guard in an interview and admitted the well-established practice of consulting the General Security Services, the Shin Bet, before appointing Arab teachers. This created uproar in the media and several "liberal" former ministers of education piped up with recollections of attempting unsuccessfully to cancel the regulation. I recall that the existence of this practice was disclosed two and a half decades ago, in the final report of a government-appointed committee on the future of Arab youth, in which I participated and which was headed by the late Dr. Sami Geraisy. Our revelation was recognized at the time as a major provocation and was later assumed to be one of the reasons why the report was shelved and never acknowledged officially. Instead, we leaked the report to the press. It quickly gained the status of a reference source, being the first publicly available well-researched document on the status of the Palestinian Arab citizens in Israel. Not long afterwards, a team of academics at Haifa University, following in our footsteps, repeated the same feat with the appropriate academic referencing and documentation, supported by a substantial grant from the Ford Foundation.

After the interview's publication, the Education Minister, Limor Livnat, stood by her Director-General, thus turning the previously secret practice into fully sanctioned government policy based on "security considerations." Now it is official.

Only recently I learnt of another layer of subterfuge on this matter. I had brief dealings with a senior Arab official at the Department of Arab Education, a simple and transparent lackey. I took it upon myself to introduce him to the basic concepts of education for people with learning disabilities, a novel field for the Arab department. I even had to persuade him that a department for learning disabilities could be found in the main Education Ministry and personally introduced him to its head. At the end of each meeting, the man would tell me: "Just make sure to copy your letter to my deputy, Moshe, at the same address." I began to doubt if he ever read his own copy since his deputy was always the one to handle the matter directly with their joint secretary. Eventually, I realized that his Jewish "assistant" or "deputy" was a codename for the undercover Shin Bet operator who shadows all such high-ranking Arab officials, the one who actually makes the decisions in their name.

This reminds me of my nephew and two fellow high school teachers in Arrabeh who lost their jobs because the Shin Bet objected to their employment. An Arabic saying tells of a person who threatens another with striking him so hard he will land in Mecca. The threatened person's response is: "Fine, you will make a pilgrim out of me." The three dismissed teachers went on to become very successful "activists": one studied pharmacy and now heads an NGO dedicated to child education and puts out an Arabic-language children's magazine; another has become Secretary General to a major Arab political party, Tajamu; and my nephew, who received his doctorate in anthropology from Bergen University in Norway, has established and still heads an NGO that provides aid to Palestinians in the occupied territories. Currently he teaches at Bir Zeit University and has an informative website dedicated to Arrabeh and the Galilee, www.jalili48.com.

The saga of the interminable struggle to establish an Arab university in the Galilee apparently came to a halt a few months ago when Shimon Peres, the wily old fox of peace and nuclear arms fame, dealt it a death blow. In the most recent of his political incarnations, as the Minister of Development for the Galilee and the Negev, he responded to the undiminishing clamor from Arab civic and political groups for their own university by allotting millions of shekels for the establishment of an "Arab" university in Karmiel, a Jewish city in the Central Galilee and the throbbing heart of the Zionist scheme for Judaizing the Galilee. Israeli labor laws guarantee priority in all the key staff positions in such an "Arab" institute to Karmiel's exclusively Jewish residents. In a not unrelated issue, it was revealed this week that the administration at Haifa University has been warning its foreign students against visiting Arab communities in Israel for years.

I was recently recruited by a new acquaintance, the chair of the board of the Jewish-Arab Center at Haifa University, to join his board. On the first written communication I received from that supposed forum for coexistence, I saw my name next to that of Arnon Sofer, a professor of geopolitics at Haifa University and the architect of the demographic "time-bomb" theory regarding the Palestinian citizens of Israel.* Sofer, the scientific father of transfer policies in Israel, has been advising successive governments. I resigned in disgust and terminated my "friendship" with the chairman, who defended his decision on the basis of the need for democratic pluralism in his institution. This came on the heels of my resignation from Sikkuy, where I had recently assumed co-chairmanship of the organization. I discovered that Aluf Hareven, a former Israeli intelligence official, has been the backseat driver of the organization all along. His most recent project, launched under my nose, was to preach decency and proper manners to the soldiers at checkpoints in the occupied Palestinian territories. The profane audacity of the project in its aspiration to ascribe civility and even compassion to soldiers enforcing a cruel and bloody occupation is matched only by the Israeli army's supreme spin-doctoring in its claims of "purity of arms."

In both of these misadventures, I find myself needing to shake myself violently to snap out of the hypnotic trance I have been lulled into by all the sweet talk of coexistence—our coexistence as the lesser partner in the "Jewish first," meaning "Jewish only," democratic state.

* On the demographic "threat," see Foreword.

Déjà vu! Rhoda, my anthropologist daughter, is conducting research on the few Arab youths who volunteer to serve in the Israeli security establishment. I assist her in recruiting interviewees. Only two brothers, hardened social outcasts in Arrabeh, refuse to meet Rhoda. They live on the outskirts of the village, across the road from the gas station where, decades ago, the late Hajj Yousif was dumped out of a taxi, unconscious, to die from his head injuries. The Israel Lands Authority has since claimed his land there and awarded it to these two "loyal" brothers.

One spring afternoon, on an impulse, I take my granddaughter, Malaika, and half a dozen of her age-mates from among my many grandnephews on an outing to a nearby national park. We fight our way through the mayhem of traffic in the main street of Arrabeh, newly topped and with dry sidewalks. There is no sewage overflow nowadays. Like some forty other Arab towns and villages, Arrabeh has benefited from the Galilee Society's Revolving Loan Fund to plan a central sewage network, and has managed to connect most of the village's homes to a collection system. Like most Israeli rural communities, Arab and Jewish, its sewage flows into the next valley. Wadi al-Majnoun (Crazy Valley) in Military Area Nine was once a favorite site for our weekend excursion in the pristine Galilee wilderness. It now flows with the collected sewage effluent of Karmiel, Sakhnin, Arrabeh, Dier Hanna and several other smaller communities. The weather is perfect for a hike with my granddaughter but Wadi al-Majnoun is off our list.

The national park we visit this time is on the grounds of what once was prosperous Lubyeh, near a new landmark: the only McDonald's restaurant in the area. I take the children there for a treat. We all get a whiff of the polluted westerly breeze blowing to us across the thriving Tzipori industrial zone by Kafr Kana. The Galilee Society and half a dozen environmental protection groups continue to battle against the pollution from this and other major offenders. Very early on, we forced the Phoenicia glass factory to spend several million dollars to clean up its gas emissions. But pollution is part of development and we continue to "develop" the Galilee, or so our decision-makers want us to believe.

The McDonald's is next to a military monument and museum at a road intersection better known as the *Golani* Junction, in celebration of the IDF crack troops of the same name. In my youth we knew the location as *Meskana*, the last encampment site and watering hole for the

Crusader armies before they succumbed to thirst and Saladin's swords. Meskana was on the outskirts of Nimreen, the home village of Zakiyeh, Hajj Yousif's old flame. None of the children and few of their parents, questioned when we came home, recognized any of the old names I blabber about. They do not even know the *Horn of Hittin*.

Somehow, it all ties in; it all adds up! And it saddens me and leaves a vague bitter taste of defeat and guilt.

21
A Little Piece of Palestine

Tending my ancient olive tree, with granddaughter Malaika.

April 30, 2006

My central gardening achievement this spring has been the realization of my long-held dream of transplanting an ancient olive tree to grace the entrance to our yard. Friends and relatives have not stopped coming to view it. To guard against the evil eye of so many potential jealous admirers, my sister Jamileh has adorned its gnarled two-meter wide trunk with a huge blue bead and an amulet purchased on her pilgrimage to Mecca. Since the tree's arrival I have reshaped the western side of the yard to measure up to its imposing stature and majestic look. I have refashioned the iron gate, the "mosaic" entryway, and the metal fence around the entire property. I find myself obsessed with daily tending to the tree's welfare: watering its roots, manicuring its bark, and checking for signs of new growth sprouting from its branches, stripped clean during the transplanting process.

In Palestine, and probably in the wider Middle East, olive trees are described in terminology used to specify their relative age. *"Rumi"* olives are those whose age is counted in millennia, their origin attributed to the golden era of the Roman Empire when the planting of olives was popularized throughout its domain—though at one point a local ruler was apparently enraged enough to decree the destruction of all olive trees in Jerusalem. A local tour guidebook identifies as a "must-see landmark" an olive tree on the Wadi Salameh hiking trail that winds among neighboring hills—the location from which I moved my own tree. The guidebook estimates the age of that landmark tree to be over 6,000 years. That is sacrilegious, of course, if you are a strict follower of the Jewish faith. According to that calendar, we are now in the year 5777 after creation. Obviously, that puts my tree at about the same age as God himself. Such an assertion is not so blasphemous to Galilean ears accustomed to hearing local bards declaim their lovesick song: *"Tathal ahibbick ta-yikhatier rabbina*—I will still love you when God turns old and feeble."

The second age category is that of *Amari* olive trees, generally assumed to be from the era of Arab rule in the area. The age of Amari trees is estimated in centuries. A Rumi or an Amari olive tree is also known as *a'amoud*—a pillar, in recognition of its stability, permanence and stature, physically, figuratively, and economically. This is in contradistinction to a *nasbeh*, Arabic for a monument or a memorial structure. A nasbeh is valued far in excess of its actual economic worth. To me as a villager, the term has romantic connotations evoking youthfulness, vigor, and the promise of future material wealth.

Ancient cultures had a mystical fascination with the olive. Adam was buried with an olive seed in his mouth, Noah eased his ark on land after the dove brought back an olive leaf as a sign of the return of tranquility, and the olive branch is the universal sign of peace and reconciliation. The Greeks received only two special gifts from their Gods: the olive and wisdom. Athena herself bequeathed the olive to her city, Athens, as an inviolable symbol; anyone desiring to harvest its sacred fruit had to take a vow of chastity. Olympic victors were crowned with olive wreaths and rewarded with huge amounts of olive oil, up to four tons. Hippocrates recognized the salutary health benefits of olive oil, while the ancient Egyptians used it for mummification and stocked their Pharaohs' tombs with cured olives. The aphrodisiac powers of the olive fruit are legend the world over. The olive tree inspires and amazes: its majestic solitude in the stony Mediterranean terrain and magnanimous silence in the face of droughts and downpours have echoes of immortality.

In this, our holy land, the arrival and eventual hegemony of monotheism did little to contain the olive's godly pretensions or to dislodge it from the inhabitants' hearts. Jews incorporated the wood of the olive into their Holy of Holies on the Temple Mount, and their most glorious revolt against the Romans was energized by the miraculous performance of its oil. The entire Christian church is referred to as an "Olive Tree" and its prophets were anointed with olive oil. What Christian does not know about the Mount of Olives! In our local churches, till the present day, no baptism is complete without the priest marking the forehead of the baby with the cross, his forefinger dipped in holy olive oil.

Mention olives in any rural social setting here and an air of seriousness and veneration bordering on awe materializes instantaneously, even in the most secular of circles. People start mumbling the name of Allah and his blessed prophet, or the Blessed Virgin Mary, in due respect. Of all fruit-bearing trees only the fig, perhaps the first plant to be domesticated by humans anywhere on the face of the earth, has an equal moral stature, weighty enough for Allah to adorn with it the opening passage of a chapter in his holy book, the Koran. In another setting Allah, the creator and light of the universe, compares his own luminescence to that of a star-bright crystal lamp in a niche, the lamp fed oil from a blessed olive tree, the tree existing in a mystical location "neither easterly nor westerly." Could that be my tree, I wonder?

An olive tree produces more oil and of a higher quality as it ages. Like wine, the older the more rewarding and intriguing. Yet, a local turn of phrase in our region attests to the special emotional investment traditional farmers have in their olive seedlings. When someone commits a particularly heinous crime or speaks utter nonsense violating other people's sensitivities, villagers commonly condemn the act as a deed deserving retribution by doing damage to the aggressor's olives. "*Haki bitqashshar aleh nasib*," they would opine, "talk deserving of stripping the bark off of young olive trees," the harshest of all possible punishments short of physical elimination of the person himself.

In our fourth grade reader, a collection of Arabic literary gems selected by the venerable Palestinian educator Khalil Sakakini, we read a story about Khisru, the wise Persian king. Seeing on one of his royal outings an old Arab farmer planting olive seedlings, the king questioned the man about the meaning of his labor. He must realize, Khisru reasoned, that the trees would never come to fruition in his lifetime. "They planted, we eat; we plant, they will eat," the old man responded, enigmatically summing up the multigenerational interdependence of olive farming. The king was struck by the simplicity and astuteness of the explanation. "*Zih!*" he shouted to his servants, using the Persian royal codeword for ordering a monetary gift for a subject.

"You see, your majesty, my olive seedlings have already yielded their first crop," said the farmer pocketing his prize money.

"*Zih!*" the king shouted again, "and let us get away from this Arab before he robs us of all of our imperial reserves."

For the past five years I have had an urge—no, more, an infatuation—to add an ancient olive tree to my garden. It started when I found the remains of an ancient Rumi olive tree lying on the edge of a field belonging to a fellow villager. I was taken aback by the crime of allowing such a living record of farming life in these parts to be chopped for wood. My attempt at resuscitating it apparently came too late, the tree trunk having been out of the ground for a couple of weeks before I saw it. Still, as I did my utmost to bring it back to life, it responded to the attention by sending a new shoot out of the ground. The trunk itself was never revived, and now I use it as another stand for displaying my fossil finds from Mount Carmel.

As my failure fully to revive that wisp of ancient history sank in, I developed an obsession with Rumi olive trees, so firmly rooted, generously predisposed and wisely accepting of history's perturbing turns and twists. Something about those trees evokes in my heart fond

memories of my early childhood, days when we lived and labored in
our olive orchards. I had to have one in my front yard. Every hike I
took in the Galilee wound up being a hunt for the perfect Rumi tree. I
saw thousands but each had something missing: some were not majestic
enough in shape, squatty or too tall; the trunk of others was hollowed
out to a mere thin shell that would not stand the physical injury of
the transplanting process; and still others were not old enough. Last
year, when a neighbor decided to pull out half a dozen old olive trees
to empty the land for construction, I accepted his offer of one tree as
a present. It was not exactly what I wanted but, then again, it was free
of charge and I would be saving another venerable eyewitness to the
history of our village. Even if its trunk was not carved that beautifully
by the exigencies of history and natural phenomena, it still was of
an age and height that compared favorably, for example, with those
venerated olives in the Garden of Gethsemane. But alas, in the process
of moving it, the trunk was damaged and I was left dreaming of my
perfect olive tree again.

Then one weekend I accepted the offer of a friend to drive to his own
olive grove in Wadi Salameh. He owed me a favor and had heard of my
Rumi olive prospecting. We saw several worthy a'amouds that he or
one of his relatives owned, but none fit the picture I had in my mind,
my imagined tree occupying the space in my redesigned garden, a tree
whose mere sight would inspire visitors and passers-by to reconnect
instantaneously to our ancient roots in this historic land.

But leaving the site, my eye was caught by a beauty of an olive
tree, a Rumi a'amoud of imperial stature, imposing configuration and
monumental proportions. It stopped me in my tracks. I knew I belonged
to that tree. It was the long-lost mother I had been searching for. It took
total possession of my senses. The struggle of proving our relationship,
our belonging to each other, to the rest of the world started right then
and there. I had to find the person who had formal title to "my" tree.
That took the better part of a year. No one seemed to know to whom
the well-tended piece of land around it belonged. A search of land
records in the surrounding villages yielded the promising result that
the land belonged to the Nassar family in Arrabeh, my village. I started
inviting friends and distant acquaintances from that clan for rides in my
new Subaru Outback. The rides invariably took us past that a'amoud.
I had to be careful not to divulge my love story with the tree for fear

of driving its price beyond my financial means. Eventually the trail led to the land's owner, a school friend from my childhood days.

It was then that I discovered a historical curiosity about olive trees that is common knowledge to most farmers in the Galilee. Although the old school friend owned the land, he did not own the tree itself. That honor belonged to another former classmate of mine, one from Dier Hanna.

In the shadows of the Ottoman Empire, subsistence farming and heavy land taxes had yielded a real estate system that valued the productive olive tree more than the land on which it stood, thus allowing one to own a tree independently of the land. Once I uncovered this strange system, everyone in the village with whom I discussed it quoted an example of conflict and intrigue between neighbors or relatives prompted by this separation between ownership of the tree and ownership of the land on which it stood. Apparently, such circumstances obtain only in the case of ancient olive trees; no other tree has the permanence, status and traditional value as a source of livelihood to rate a special custom or even an Ottoman law recognizing its sanctity.

Though the owner of the tree does not own the land, he or she has at their disposal, for as long as the tree lives, 64 square meters of land around it, an area traditionally recognized as the olive tree's *mihrath* or cultivation space. In other words, the olive tree "owns" the land around it. In fact, that is the wording of a local axiom: "*Ezzatoun bumluk*"—Olives own, it states simply. At least in my case, that depicts the true relationship between me and my tree: it possesses me more than I it. And in the constricted perspective of rural life, that meant forever: the ownership of such an a'amoud devolved down the generations in patrilineal inheritance, just as the land did in a parallel, separate fashion. When the male descendants divided an inherited field between themselves, such a division took the number and known productive potential of the olive trees into consideration and not the area of the land.

No self-respecting villager would ever think of messing around with these sacred inheritance traditions, even when everyone knows that the rules of tree ownership would never stand the test of modern reality in an Israeli court of law. Both sides to such a conflict would probably end up losing out, somehow, to the superior interest of the Israel Lands Authority. So, everyone keeps away from the courts and settles land claims internally, in the traditional manner of consensus-seeking among honorable neighbors. Only in one known case in Arrabeh did a farmer violate the honor code of conduct and set fire to an a'amoud on his land belonging to a distant relative. With the death of the tree, no further claim could be made to its mihrath. End of conflict. Shortly, though, he lost a son and one of his work oxen broke a leg.

The wife of the landowner from Arrabeh on whose field my Rumi a'amoud stood was effusive in welcoming my proposal. It would free their land of the intrusive presence of another family's tree. She went as far as equating this intended good deed of mine with the time I cared for her little son, now himself a physician, when he came down with polio. I graciously accepted her thanks, black coffee and dish of home-made sweets.

Then I made a second visit, this time to my former classmate from Dier Hanna. He is a huge man and he gave me a long and sincere bear-hug leaving me momentarily breathless. After coffee and fruits, I broached the subject of the tree. He turned pale, twirled the tip of his mustache with his fingers, coughed nervously, while his breathing became noticeably labored. He seemed to be in a real bind. Apparently he found it difficult to deny me my first ever request for a favor from him, especially after the welcoming hug, but found it equally difficult to commit such a treasonous act as selling an olive tree that has been in the family for who knows how many centuries. He excused himself and left the room to consult with a brother. A short time later he returned beaming. Eureka! "The last wish of our late father when we gathered around his death bed in this room was that we guard our land, our olives and our womenfolk; in short, our honor. But you took good care of him in his old age; he was always pleased with the way you treated him when he fell ill and came to your clinic. We know he would have given you that tree if you had asked him for it. It is yours on two conditions: No money will be involved and you will put a sign identifying the tree as a present from the Khalaileh clan." The deal was done and I tried to thank Ahmad with a failed bear hug of my own.

Last spring, when I first saw my tree, I started digging a hole in my garden where I planned for it to stand. In the cool afternoons I would be joined by Bashar, one of my many solicitous teenage grandnephews.

We would take turns digging and shoveling the earth out. By the time the rains started in late autumn, we thought we had accomplished the task; we had dug a circular hole, two meters across and one and a quarter meters deep.

On Thursday, two days before I was due to bring my "bride" home, I consulted with a friend, a civil engineer. We visited the tree together and he took exact measurements. Bashar's and my labors had not been totally in vain. The depth of the hole was adequate but we needed to double its area. Bringing in any mechanical equipment was out of the question; it would mess up my garden. I contacted Camal, a good manual ditch digger, and he estimated the assignment would require a minimum of two days' labor. He wanted to start on Saturday, the day the tree was due to arrive, as Friday was set aside for praying at the mosque. I pressed him and finally he agreed to do the work in a day, provided I pay him for the two days' work. I did not quibble; I wanted to get the job done before somebody changed their mind about my tree.

On Friday morning, Camal showed up early. By noon he was finished, making it to the mosque just in time for the noon prayer. He even had enough time to do his ablutions in the hole he dug, an auspicious sign for the success of the transplanting operation. The water used in washing the head, face, hands and feet of a good Muslim in preparation for entering the mosque and standing before Allah has near-magic powers, almost sacred in its value. After he collected his money, he picked a bunch of grape leaves and a pocketful of green almonds from my orchard for his wife to satisfy her cravings in early pregnancy. She was carrying a boy this time, after four girls, so Camal was catering to her every wish. Camal is a borderline mentally handicapped young man, mainly due to cultural and environmental deprivation. But, boy, does he dig ditches! At this stage in my biological life, and with my current range of interests, I think I would opt for his muscle power if it were on offer for exchange with other bodily systems of mine.

Then came the mechanical part: the heavy equipment to dig my tree out; the lift with a minimum capacity of ten tons to raise it out of the ground and then lower it again into the welcoming womb Bashar, Camal and I had prepared for it; the wide platform truck to carry it the ten-mile distance between the two locations. Finally, Camal would return to cover its roots with a few tons of fertile soil.

Fortunately, the operation took place on Saturday, the Sabbath day when Jewish agricultural and forestry inspectors rest. An Ottoman law, still on the books in Israel, prohibits endangering the life of an olive tree. To enforce it, a permit has to be obtained before an olive can be moved from one location to another. I learned of the requirement, however, only after we had finished digging around my tree. I could not leave its damaged roots exposed and jinx the whole project. But equally the contractor I had commissioned to do the task was afraid for his livelihood; if caught, he would be heavily fined and his equipment impounded for a month. It makes one wonder how Israeli contractors and military commanders have been arranging so easily the "transfer" of so many ancient Palestinian olive trees from the occupied West Bank. According to reports in the Israeli media, this is big business, with the stolen trees sold for tens of thousands of dollars to the wealthier residents of Israeli suburbs.

To allay the contractor's fear, I personally guided the truck over a rocky unpaved back road so as not to be seen with our illegal heist on the open road. The scariest part, though, was negotiating the roads through Arrabeh. Not only did we have to move through some particularly narrow alleys but also the height of my tree on top of the moving platform exceeded that of the electricity, phone and cable TV lines strung haphazardly across the village skies. The contractor wanted me to sit atop the tree and manually lift or cut obstructive wires. The thought of parading through the village in such fashion did not appeal to me. I paid him an extra amount and he enlisted the help of a friend for the task. I prayed for Allah's protective graces all the way home. Mercifully the clandestine operation was completed, but not without the typical rural communal fanfare and curiosity-engendered assistance and interference from a dozen curious neighbors and twice as many children.

I do not feel any inkling of remorse about having broken the law. After all, the wise Ottomans wanted to protect olive trees, and mine shows every sign of being alive and vigorous. Had I been a Hellenic subject, however, I might not have taken the risk. In those days endangering the life of an olive tree was punishable by death, and I certainly want to be around to tend and enjoy the new addition to my garden.

The horrific sense of history inspired by this continuous biological link between me and my land is simply awesome. Are the Palestinians not the historical descendants of the Minoans of Crete? Were the Minoans not the first olive farmers in recorded history? Did Minoan culture not revolve around the trade in olive oil? Was the trade by way of Phoenicia? Could the Phoenicians, Canaanites, Israelites, Egyptians, Hyxos, Romans, Greeks, Persians, Arabs, Moguls, Crusaders and Turks have played a role in influencing the life and physique of my own tree? Yes, indeed, they may have. Any or all of them may have enjoyed the afternoon Mediterranean breeze in its cool shade. Any or all of them may have tied their trusted mounts to its sturdy trunk and cut a fresh shoot from its base to hurry the steed along—the reason, most likely, for all the beautiful, football-size knots on its trunk. Any or all of them may have seduced, or raped, one of my maiden progenitors, leaving his telltale imprint on my amalgam of genes. And any or all of them may have dictated their rules and regulations to my ancestors, who submissively incorporated them as "ours."

But at bottom, it was those Minoan olive oil traders and their Palestinian descendants, clinging to their land and subsisting in the shadow of their olive groves, that morphed into an ambitious nation laying claim to Arab culture, the last dominant culture of significant impact. My tree knows and attests to all of that; that is how it all started. This gnarled behemoth, with its two-meter wide, beautifully sculpted trunk and over ten square meters of exposed root system saw it all. I can prove my belonging to this piece of the earth's crust through it; its roots are my surrogate roots. And they are taking hold in my land that I inherited from my father, who inherited it from his father, who ...

Index